GUIDE TO KULCHUR

This wafer of wax is caught, as was the custom, between two surfaces of paper in a letter from the young Salustio Malatesta. The Pisanello medals are known, the seals are unknown or less known. I give the reproduction of this one to indicate the thoroughness of Rimini's civilization in 1460. If you consider the Malatesta and Sigismundo in particular, a failure, he was at all events a failure worth all the successes of his age. He had in Rimini, Pisanello, Pier della Francesca. Rimini still has "the best Bellini in Italy". If the Tempio is a jumble and junk shop, it nevertheless registers a concept. There is no other single man's effort equally registered. Sigismundo brought back Gemisto's coffin, and I leave the reader to decide whether without that incitement to curiosity even Herr Schulze wd. have dug up the illegible ms. in the Laurenziana or anyone noticed the latin pages bound in at the end of an almost unfindable edtn. of Xenophon. 1460, 140 years after Dante.

EZRA POUND

GUIDE
TO
KULCHUR

. . . .

A NEW DIRECTIONS BOOK

Manufactured in the United States of America
New Directions books are printed on acid-free paper
Published in Canada by Penguin Books Canada Limited
New Directions Books are published for James Laughlin
by New Directions Publishing Corporation
80 Eighth Avenue, New York 10011

TENTH PRINTING

To
LOUIS ZUKOFSKY
and
BASIL BUNTING
strugglers
in the
desert

This book is not written for the over-fed. It is written for men who have not been able to afford an university education or for young men, whether or not threatened with universities, who want to know more at the age of fifty than I know today, and whom I might conceivably aid to that object.

I am fully aware of the dangers inherent in attempting such utility to them.

PREFACE

In attacking a doctrine, a doxy, or a form of stupidity, it might be remembered that one isn't of necessity attacking the man, or say "founder", to whom the doctrine is attributed or on whom it is blamed. One may quite well be fighting the same idiocy that he fought and whereinto his followers have reslumped from laziness, from idiocy, or simply because they (and/or he) may have been focussing their main attention on some other goal, some disease, for example, of the time needing immediate remedy.

The man who builds dykes is not of necessity an anti-irrigationist.

It is my intention in this booklet to COMMIT myself on as many points as possible, that means that I shall make a number of statements which very few men can AFFORD to make, for the simple reason that such taking sides might jeopard their incomes (directly) or their prestige or "position" in one or other of the professional "worlds". Given my freedom, I may be a fool to use it, but I wd. be a cad not to.

Guide to Kulchur: a mousing round for a word, for a shape, for an order, for a meaning, and last of all for a philosophy. The turn came with Bunting's line:

> "Man is not an end-product,
> Maggot asserts."

The struggle was, and still might be, to preserve some of the values that make life worth living.

And they are still mousing around for a significance in the chaos.

E.P.

20 June 1970

This edition is for my valued friend and publisher, James Laughlin.

CONTENTS

9

CONTENTS

CONTENTS

CONTENTS

PART I

Section I

I. DIGEST OF THE ANALECTS
that is, of the Philosophic Conversations

Said the Philosopher: You think that I have learned a great deal, and kept the whole of it in my memory? Sse replied with respect: Of course. Isn't that so? It is not so. I have reduced it all to one principle.

COMMENT: This passage from the XV chapter of Analects, that is of the Philosophic Conversations, gives me my warrant for making a digest. Rapacity is the main force in our time in the occident. In measure as a book contains wisdom it is nearly impossible to force any printer to issue it. My usual publishers refused the *Ta Hio.* What hope have I with a translation of the whole Analects?

Fan Tchai asked Kung the master (viz Confucius) for instruction in farming. Said the Master: I know less than any old peasant. He made the same reply about gardening: An old gardener knows more than I do.

Tseu-Lou asked: If the Prince of Mei appointed you head of the government, to what wd. you first set your mind?

KUNG: *To call people and things by their names, that is by the correct denominations, to see that the terminology was exact.*

正名

"You mean that is the first?" Said Tseu-leu. "Aren't you dodging the question? What's the use of that?"

KUNG: *You are a blank. An intelligent man hesitates to talk of what he don't understand, he feels embarrassment.*

If the terminology be not exact, if it fit not the thing, the governmental instructions will not be explicit, if the instructions aren't clear and the names don't fit, you can not conduct business properly.

If business is not properly run the rites and music will not be honoured, if the rites and music be not honoured, penalties and punishments will not achieve their intended effects, if penalties and punishments do not produce equity and justice, the people won't know where to put their feet or what to lay hold of or to whom they shd. stretch out their hands.

That is why an intelligent man cares for his terminology and gives instructions that fit. When his orders are clear and explicit they can be put into effect. An intelligent man is neither inconsiderate of others nor futile in his commanding.

KUNG on the MAKE MORE WORK FALLACY

Analects XI

The inhabitants of Lou wished to put up a new public granary. Min-tseu-kian said: Isn't the old one still good enough?

Is there any need of a new one which will cost much sweat to the people?

Said Kung the Philosopher: If that man opens his mouth, he speaks to some purpose.

COMMENT: The old granary was still suited to its purpose. Kung is against superfluous labour that does not serve a purpose.

Said Szetsun, or rather so says his translator: "The sayings of the great sages are ordinary." This I take to mean that there is nothing superfluous or excessive in them. When one knows enough one can find wisdom in the Four Classics. When one does not know enough one's eye passes over the page without seeing it.

"*Sse goes beyond the mark, Chang does not attain it.*"

"*Meaning that Sse is superior?*"

"*NO,*" said the Philosopher.   XI.15

May we not suppose that XII, 9 of the Analects teaches the folly of taxation?

May we not suppose that the last phrase of this paragraph denounces the futility of great stores without orderly distribution?

May we not suppose that the answers in XIV, 10 of the Analects have been treasured as examples that Kung employed the right word neither in excess nor less than his meaning?

Humanity? is to love men.

Knowledge, to know men.

It is written: Fan-tchi did not understand what Kung meant by these answers.

It is difficult to be poor and feel no resentment. It is by comparison easy to be rich and not be puffed up.

Said Kung the Master: I have passed whole days without food, entire nights without sleep for the sake of my meditation, and in this there was no real use. It wd. have been better to have studied something in particular.

XVI. I. I have heard ever that possessors of kingdoms and the chiefs of great families do not complain of small population, nor of exiguous territory, nor even of the poverty of their peoples, but of the discord between people and ruler. For if each has his part that is due him, there is no pauper, there is harmony, there is no want among the inhabitants.

In the first book of the Lun Yu it is written the lord of a feudal kingdom shd. not demand work of his people save at convenient and/or suitable time.   I.5

Duty in the home, deference among all men. Affection among all men and attachment in particular to persons of virtu (or virtue).

Seek friends among equals.

I am pro-Tcheou (in politics) said Koung fu Tseu.

They examined their predecessors.

DIGEST OF THE ANALECTS

(The full text being: they examined the civilization
and history of the Dynasties which preceded them.)

● ● ● ●

There is one chapter in the anonymous translation
that I have tried in vain to improve, that is to say I can
not find a more balanced translation:

You have heard the six words, and the six becloudings?

*There is the love of being benevolent, without the love of
learning, the beclouding here leads to foolish simplicity.
The love of knowing without love of learning, whereof the
beclouding brings dissipation of mind. Of being sincere
without the love of learning, here the beclouding causes dis-
regard of the consequence. Of straightforwardness without
the love of learning, whereof the beclouding leadeth to rude-
ness. Of boldness without the love of learning, whereof the
beclouding brings insubordination. The love of firmness
without the love of learning, whereof the beclouding con-
duces to extravagant conduct.*

Here in the ideogram called "beclouding" we find
confusion, an overgrowing with vegetation. Yet there is
no better word for this in english than beclouding. "Ex-
travagant conduct" is shown in a dog pawing a king or
trying to lick the king's ear, which is said to mean a dog

wanting to rule. In the other ideograms there is nothing to give better meaning than the words used by my predecessor.

In the "ONE PRINCIPLE" text we have four common signs: *one, by, passing through, emerging.* And Pauthier is deeper than the translator who has chosen to interpret this "pervading".

The second sign is said to be the reverse of fixed, or stopped, in the third sign we have the string passing through the holes in the coins, in the fourth we have the earth, the stem and the leaf.

The *ch'ing ming* text can mean also that functionaries shd. be called by their proper titles, that is to say a man should not be called controller of currency unless he really controls it. The ch'ing is used continually against ambiguity.

The dominant element in the sign for learning in the love of learning chapter is a mortar. That is, the knowledge must be ground into fine powder.

Il maestro ha detto che ora dobbiamo
comperare un altro libro cioè il
susidiario di quinta . . . . li ci sono
dentro le cose principali cioè tutto,
religione, storia geografia conti
scienze e la vita del uomo. . . .

M.R.

2. THE NEW LEARNING
PART ONE

(a bit dry at the start, brother, but bear up, I will come to something about page somewhere or other)

Despite appearances I am not trying to condense the encyclopedia into 200 pages. I am at best trying to provide the average reader with a few tools for dealing with the heteroclite mass of undigested information hurled at him daily and monthly and set to entangle his feet in volumes of reference.

Certain ground we have gained and lost since Rabelais's time or since Montaigne browsed over "all human knowledge". Certain kinds of awareness mark the live books in our time, in the decade 1930 to 40. Lack of these awarenesses shows in the mass of dead matter printed.

No living man knows enough to write:

Part I. Method.

Part II. Philosophy, the history of thought.

Part III. History, that is of action.

Part IV. The arts and civilization.

Even though what I am about to say might be sorted out under such headings.

Kung (Confucius) we receive as wisdom. The greek philosophers have been served up as highbrows. We know them as ideas, each handed us as a maxim. Epicurus as an allusion to hedonism, Pythagoras perhaps an exception.

If a man have sufficient curiosity to look for a basis in fact, in the surviving fragments authentic or attributed to these antient worthies, he will probably find that Epicurus wrote "Pi-jaw".

The distinction I am trying to make is this. Rightly or wrongly we feel that Confucius offers a way of life, an Anschauung or disposition toward nature and man and a system for dealing with both.

The occident as a result of 1900 years of fact and process feels this way toward Christianity, but not toward any brand of philosophy. Philosophy as the word is currently used means a highbrow study, something cut off both from life and from wisdom.

I am not saying that this is what should be. I am observing a situation. If you consider the occident, or all European or Mediterranean life for 2500 years, as something to be watched in a test-tube, you might make the following clinical observations on successive phases of process. As against China or as much as France knew of China in 1837 when Pauthier and Bazin pooled the results of their research.

The shored relics of a very human and high state of culture as immortalized in the *Iliad* and the *Odyssey* (roughly dated 9th or 10th century B.C.).

Let us say roughly that Kung lived on into the time of Pythagoras and of Aeschylus, 469 B.C. to 399, 427 to 347, 384 to 322, carry on from the birth of Socrates to

Aristotle's death, Plato between them. A job lot of ergo-
teurs follow them. And by 200 B.C. the scope of Western
thought has been more or less outlined.

It cd. be argued that the "main ideas" were all pres-
ent in greek philosophy, that they had all been threshed
out and are more clearly presented even in the remains of
greek philosophy than they can be from a study of what
is called "Christian philosophy". Certainly this is the
general view one wd. get from so excellent an expositor
as Francesco Fiorentino.[1]

Yet in a sense the philosophers gave way to Christian-
ity (however much a few of them coloured it or even
shaped and directed it).

Can I direct the reader's curiosity by prodding him
with the probability that 50,000 people can define a
stoic for every one who knows or has heard that Zeno
was the father of stoic philosophy.

Measuring these greek teachings by their impact on
modern life, the terms stoic, cynic and epicurean still
have vulgar significance, though the last term has a
meaning which Epicurus wd. have disliked. "Cynic" is
hardly used as a mark of contempt, and "stoic" still has
pretty much its hard incomplete narrow sense, a hard-
boiled partial disposition insensitive to a great part of the
spectrum both intellectual and emotional.

The student knows, or can ferret out the evidence, that
Zeno, Epicurus, Pythagoras did teach a modus vivendi,
did advocate modes of life, and did not merely argue
about certain abstractions.

---

[1] *Storia della Filosofia.*

THE NEW LEARNING

The point for my purposes is that the man in the street in England and the U.S.A. 1938 lumps 'em all in with the highbrows ... I mean as distinct from roast beef and the facts of life, as distinct from the things that come natural, ideas that he drinks in with his "mother's milk" or from the synthetic feeding bottle of the occident as we know it.

Christianity and/or religion in the anglo-saxon world of our time has been something optional. Some of us went to church in our childhood and some didn't.

George Washington refused to be cornered on belief and confined his statesmanlike utterance to appreciation of "the benign influence of" the Christian religion.

"Belief" as the pious once used the term is alien to our age. We may have a respect for the unknown. We may have a pious disposition. We may have a wide sense of possibility.

The child of the age—say that age was the last half of the "age of usury" (XIXth century) or the first third of this one (the XXth)—is so accustomed to the loose waftiness of demoliberal ideology that it takes sharp speech to open his mind to the thousand and more years of Europe, during which the intellectual hard work of the West occurred INSIDE the Church Catholic.

And here we shd. set out two axes of reference.

I. There flourished during the best age of "scholastic thought" a very great and high verbal culture. Having almost nothing but words to deal with, the ecclesiastical doctors cared for (that is took care of) their terminology. A method of using words, a method of definition arose, or was kept, tended, developed, and we, today, lose a great deal by not knowing it, I mean by not knowing it as deeply and finely as they did.

II. The Church declined, as a force social, as a force intellectual, when its hierarchy ceased to believe their own dogmas.

Free, gratis, and as if it were thrown here from another section of these notes I set down another axis, which will to most readers seem wholly irrelevant and fortuitous.

I suggest that finer and future critics of art will be able to tell from the quality of a painting the degree of tolerance or intolerance of usury extant in the age and milieu that produced it.

That perhaps is the first clue the reader has had that these are notes for a totalitarian treatise and that I am in fact considering the New Learning or the New Paideuma . . . not simply abridging extant encyclopedias or condensing two dozen more detailed volumes.

If so lately as the week before last one of the brighter scholars still professed ignorance of the meaning of "ideogramic" I must try once again to define that term, necessary to the said student if he still wishes to follow me or my meaning.

Ernest Fenollosa attacked, quite rightly, a great weakness in western ratiocination. He pointed out that the material sciences, biology, chemistry, examined collections of fact, phenomena, specimens, and gathered general equations of real knowledge from them, even though the observed data had no syllogistic connection one with another. [Nowt novel, but I think E. F. found it out for himself.]

May I suggest (not to prove anything, but perhaps to open the reader's thought) that I have a certain real knowledge which wd. enable me to tell a Goya from a Velasquez, a Velasquez from an Ambrogio Praedis, a Praedis from an Ingres or a Moreau

and that this differs from the knowledge you or I wd. have if I went into the room back of the next one, copied a list of names and maxims from good Fiorentino's *History of Philosophy* and committed the names, maxims, and possibly dates to my memory.

It may or may not matter that the first knowledge is direct, it remains effortlessly as residuum, as part of my total disposition, it affects every perception of form-colour phenomena subsequent to its acquisition.

Coming even closer to things committed verbally to our memory. There are passages of the poets which approximate the form-colour acquisition.

And herein is clue to Confucius' reiterated commendation of such of his students as studied the Odes.

He demanded or commended a type of perception, a kind of transmission of knowledge obtainable only from such concrete manifestation. Not without reason.

The whole tone, disposition, Anschauung of Confucius recommending the Odes, of Confucius speaking of music, differs fundamentally, if not from what Pythagoras meant, at least from the way the unfortunate occidental usually supposes Pythagoras to have advised an examination of harmony.

"We" think, rightly or wrongly, that Pythagoras was all out for an intellectual analysis of the relation of "harmony" and arithmetic.

Good old Richter, ripe with years and with wisdom, has the sense to interlard his treatise on theory, counterpoint, harmony with the caution that "these are the laws and they have nothing to do with musical composition which is a different kind of activity".

Let the reader be patient. I am not being merely incoherent. I haven't "lost my thread" in the sense that I haven't just dropped one thread to pick up another of different shade. I need more than one string for a fabric.

I may, even yet, be driven to a chronological catalogue of greek ideas, roman ideas, mediaeval ideas in the occident. There is a perfectly good LIST of those ideas thirty feet from where I sit typing.

I am trying to get a bracket for one kind of ideas, I mean that will hold a whole set of ideas and keep them apart from another set.

Take the whole ambience of the Analects (of Kung fu Tseu), you have the main character filled with a sense of responsibility. He and his interlocutors live in a responsible world, they think for the whole social order.

You may, by contrast, contend that Christian thought has never offered a balanced system.

You may with almost complete justice assert that greek philosophic thought is utterly irresponsible. It is at no point impregnated with a feeling for the whole people.

THE NEW LEARNING

It was mainly highbrow discussion of ideas among small groups of consciously superior persons, Curzons, etc., who felt themselves above the rest of society.

Christianity has been cursed by sectarian snobism. It escaped in the saints. As it escaped, pari passu, it gave order to Europe, it gave peace in one time or place or another, it built the cathedrals.

If, following Fiorentino, you are content to set up a mere catalogue of ideas, you will think the millenium between St Ambrose and the "renaissance" inferior to the pre-Christian era. Yet this case is by no means proved. It is a doxy, or diffused opinion.

If you squint at European thought from one angle it will appear to burrow into the schools and say farewell to reality.

If, on the other hand, you follow the good father Cairoli you will find another, and a far more vigorous current going down into the details of action.

This fibre holds strong from St Ambrose (340–397) to St Antonino da Firenze (1389–1459).

The "new" historic sense in our time demands this tradition, as it demands whole slabs of the record in latin of such men as Claudius Salmasius (and at this moment neither I nor Prof. X. Q. nor anyone else really knows their names or their number). We may know that whole beams and ropes of real history have been shelved, overclouded and buried. As in more recent times the thought of Van Buren, A. Johnson, A. Jackson and the story of Tuscany under Pietro Leopoldo, have been buried.

PART ONE

We know that history as it was written the day before yesterday is unwittingly partial; full of fatal lacunae; and that it tells next to nothing of causes.

We know that these causes were economic and moral; we know that at whichever end we begin we will, if clear headed and thorough, work out to the other.

We know that there is one enemy, ever-busy obscuring our terms; ever muddling and muddying terminologies, ever trotting out minor issues to obscure the main and the basic, ever prattling of short range causation for the sake of, or with the result of, obscuring the vital truth. Captans annonam etc. (that is to say hogging the harvest, aiding the hoggers and so forth).

The present writer like a dog turns three times round in making his bed? Very well, he turns three times round.

● ● ● ●

It is quite foolish to suppose that Heraclitus, after the quite H. Jamesian precisions of the *Odyssey*, and before the Shakespearian humour of Plato's character drawing, merely said "Everything flows", or that any one abstract statement wd. have made him his reputation.

It wd. be sheer prejudice not to suppose he and a good half-dozen of the sages tried, that is to say *tried* to correlate their thought, to carry a principle through concrete and apparently disjunct phenomena and observe the leaves and/or fruits of causation.

Yet after 2000 and more years, Fontenelle observed that not even a half-masted tyrant wd. give Plato a ten acre lot whereon to try out his republic. In contrast we hear that whenever and wherever order has been set up in China; whenever there has been a notable reform or constructive national action, you find a group of Confucians "behind it", or at the centre.

This distinction is a valid distinction. And historians of philosophy might do worse than to observe it.

Out of Zeno, out of the dogged as does it system results may have emerged. Roman senators may have fancied the doctrine, and in notable (exceptional) cases have practiced it.

But were they following the belated Zeno or Father Lycurgus? Was Zeno more than a nazi from Sparta or a dilettante naziphile?

And can we, at this distance, abstain, to any good end, from taking a totalitarian hold on our history. Can we sort out "greek thought" from the iron money of Sparta, and the acute observer who remarked that the great mass of gold in Athens served merely to assist in their arithmetic?

Are the categories hitherto used in, let us say, University teaching, in our time, and our fathers', really serviceable? Does any really good mind ever "get a kick" out of studying stuff that has been put into water-tight compartments and hermetically sealed? Didn't every sane ruler feel that Plato was a faddist? And isn't that after two millennia Fontenelle's summary of opinion?

I know, and the reader, any reader, after five minutes reflection shd. realize that any one of these "sweeping" statements of mine cd. breed a ten hour argument. Any sophomore fresh from a first reading of Plato cd. argue against me. I cd. by opening volumes I haven't seen for 25 or more years find data that run counter to what I am saying or what I shall say in the next ten pages.

I am however trying to use, not an inch rule but a balance.

In the main, I am to write this new Vade Mecum without opening other volumes, I am to put down so far as possible only what has resisted the erosion of time, and forgetfulness. And to this there is material stringency. Any other course wd. mean that I shd. quite definitely have to quote whole slabs and columns of histories and works of reference.

Socrates tried to make people think, or at any rate the Socrates "of Plato" tried to make 'em use their language with greater precision and to distinguish knowledge from not-knowledge.

And the Platonic inebriety comes to readers and Platonists when Plato's Socrates forgets all about logic, when he launches into "sublimity" about the heaven above the heavens, the pure light of the mind, the splendour of crystalline lastingness, or runs on with something a sibyl has told him.

He was deemed anti-statal. Aristotle on the other hand failed to keep Alexander in bounds.

Greek poetry as we know it flows into decadence. Any one with Gaudier-Brzeska's eye will see Greek art as a decadence. The economist will look at their usury. He will find the idea of it mixed up with marine insurance.

THE NEW LEARNING

The New Economist will say that with such *neschek* no empire-building was possible.

I offer another axis of reference: the difference between maritime and agrarian usury, the difference between 30 per hundred and 6% average roman usury.

A Russian general of high culture brought me from part of the old Slavic outlook the theory that most European history saw the fall of Rome, but failed to calculate the possibly greater loss to knowledge, learning, civilization implied in the fall of the Macedonian empire. He held that certain losses weren't again repaired till after the Italian renaissance.

At this point we must make a clean cut between two kinds of "ideas". Ideas which exist and/or are discussed in a species of vacuum, which are as it were toys of the intellect, and ideas which are intended to "go into action", or to guide action and serve us as rules (and/or measures) of conduct.

Note that the bloke who said: all flows, was using one kind, and the chap who said: nothing in excess, offered a different sort.

In our time Al Einstein scandalized the professing philosophists by saying, with truth, that his theories of relativity had no philosophic bearing.

(Pause here for reflection.)

3. SPARTA 776 B.C.

The true nature of money was comprehended in Sparta by Lycurgus, or at any rate the nature of money for use inside a given area having orderly government. The iron coin of Lycurgus was distempered so that it cd. not even serve as industrial iron or be beaten back into plowshares. We have lost time over the phrase "medium of exchange"; any generally wanted commodity can serve as a medium of exchange. The Spartan coin provided a measure. That is the statal adjunct. It is the service performed by the state when the state has power or credit, or by any individual or group of individuals inspiring confidence.

The use of the precious metals in trading was in the beginning merely the barter of a commodity.

Lacedaemon failed perhaps for not having understood the force of attraction. Statally the city existed as privilege for a shut group. It failed perhaps from disrespect of perceptions which are in excess considered, perhaps wrongly, a danger to communal life.

I do not think that HERODOTUS was the father of lies, but you might make out a fairly good case against Athens as the mother of rascality, did one not see her as the grand-daughter of a long line of markets and mediterranean trading posts. Every form of fraud flourished there in perfection, nothing is added in ingenuity.

The only novelties are matters of detail and material technique. There sat the scoundrel conjugating the verb hemerodanaidzein, lending out his shilling a day to young traders 'and taking his farden or ha'penny profit. Further along a bloke with a table performing the next grade of usury.

Ships took coin on their voyages at risk of the owner, that is of the owner and lender of the coin, and paid a composite tax covering rental and risk. The higher financiers had agents in near eastern ports, credit existed, and "bad credit".

Demosthenes argued a case wherein a bloke sailed out of Sicily, without taking the borrowed money on board, and carefully sank his ship which was worth less than the money, and was caught by the informal Lloyds' of the day. In fact the records of rascality (as conserved in fragments of law records) are so good one grudges them to the prose page, and wants to reserve them for poetry. But from all this the true function of money as MEASURE emerges.

The little gold discs were convenient. They cost labour to make. They were well made. In fact the debasement of coin really begins when the design ceased to be cared for.

These early and avid merchants carried money as we still see an occasional amateur with a couple of double eagles (20 dollar gold pieces) hung on his watch chain, as ornament and as sort of insurance that he won't be completely broke if someone pinches his pocket book.

SPARTA 776 B.C.

The difference between the gold disc and the iron one was that the gold disc cd. be carried into barbarian regions (at risk of the bearer) and it was good far beyond the reach of law, order and confidence. It was made by a difficult process. AND it was measured. The progress of minting is the progress in making the measuring more exact, the milled edge of coin was guarantee against primitive clipping. The milling consists in a series of ridges perpendicular to the face of the coin; this prevents the greedy bearer from shaving off bits of the disc without being detected, or at least he can't shave off very much. The hardening of the coin by alloy prevents or diminishes the profits of the primitive process of shaking soft coins together and gradually collecting a half ounce or half gramme of fine dust of the yellow metal.

The use of gold was convenient as a protection against counterfeit, gold being heavier than the more common metals, the fake is detectable. All this imposed the reign of gold. And all of it preceded the development of the engraving press. When paper money plus also the series of numeration etc. became harder to counterfeit than metal money, the prestige of gold was menaced. It had no longer so solid a basis in reality but only in superstition and general habits of reverence.

Another measure was there to replace it. We shall see the sense of measure, the search for a valid measure, in later operation, in the guaranteed coin of the Florentine chamber, and in moneys of account, that is in monetary units written down in the bankers' books to the credit or debit of customers and supposed to mean perfect and genuine florins, ducats, etc.

You will see that in this case the merchant did not need to ring each coin on the counter.

AS BACKGROUND

The Homeric world, very human. The *Odyssey* high water mark for the adventure story, as for example Odysseus on the spar after shipwreck. Sam Smiles never got any further in preaching self-reliance. A world of irresponsible gods, a very high society without recognizable morals, the individual responsible to himself.

Plato's *Republic* notwithstanding, the greek philosophers did not feel communal responsibilities *vide infra*. The sense of coordination, of the individual in a milieu is not in them.

Any more than there is a sense of social order in the teachings of the irresponsible protagonist of the New Testament. The Anschauung of an individual of, or among, a dominated race, however admirable from some aspects, is not the Anschauung of man who has held responsible office.

Rome was the responsible ruler. The concentration or emphasis on eternity is not social. The sense of responsibility, the need for coordination of individuals expressed in Kung's teaching differs radically both from early Christian absolutism and from the maritime adventure morals of Odysseus or the loose talk of argumentative greeks.

SPARTA 776 B.C.

You can also argue that Odysseus' hardships were very pleasant to read of, in the shelter of Pericles' court. A mechanism of escape.

Socrates was disruptive. The Athenian suspicion that thought might however have some real effect upon life is seen in their application of hemlock.

Plato had a comic sense, which shows in his character drawing. He and Balzac are perhaps adolescent enthusiasms.

Aristotle was so good at his job that he anchored human thought for 2000 years. What he didn't define clearly remained a muddle for the rest of the race, for centuries following. But he did not engender a sense of social responsibility.

This is not a stricture on what he said. You can find worthy suggestions about conduct in both Aristotle and Plato.

I don't remember 'em at the moment. Any more than I remember Plato's having thought about money, which lapse may merely mean that thirty years ago neither I nor anyone else read Plato (or Dante, or whomever) with an enlightened economic curiosity.

Aristotle left the concept of money inadequate (*vide infra*). And Cervantes has remarked on the theory of knighthood and chivalry "no man can give to another that which he hath not himself".

Whatever these worthy highbrows may have meant, their gross weight in human history has left occidental man with a belief that Aristotle was THE typical highbrow dissecting, hyperintellectual, inhuman. And Plato the great-grandfather of purple patches, of prose written as cynosure for Longinus.

The love of wisdom, or the responsibility that carries wisdom into details of action, is not a Greek glory but a Roman.

Caesar was a hi-jacker, Crassus a Wall St bloater etc. But Antoninus, Constantine and Justinian were serious characters, they were trying to work out an orderly system, a modus vivendi for vast multitudes of mankind.

They were serious characters as Confucius, St Ambrose or his Excellency Edmondo Rossoni could and would recognize serious characters.

I leave it to the next generation of historians to say whether Marcus Aurelius by comparison was a dilettante who liked intellectual toys.

In 138 A.D. Antoninus Pius was considering the difference between Roman Law and the Law of Rhodes, between agrarian usury and maritime usury, he was concerned as to whether the Roman State shd. profit by sailor's misfortune and batten on ship-wreck.

The lawcourts of Rhodes and of Athens had of course thought about equity and about justice. They had questioned whether the capitalists shd. be allowed to seize ships for debt. All that I am accenting is the foreignness of these practical matters, of these applications of high philosophic or ethical concept to "study" as Europe has known it.

For some reason philosophy has meant to the man in

the street an arid and futile quibble over abstractions. Leading to desiccation of culture.

I am not saying that this is the way my generation ought to have taken its education. I do however assert that it appears to be the way in which Europe at large for a long time has taken it. The exceptions and rebels have not been strong enough to alter this current opinion.

● ● ● ●

Building from the one volume of Claudius Salmasius that has come into my possession:

I suggest again for clarity's sake the idea of a usury axis, that is to say: the 30% racket on money rented out and risked in foreign mercantile expeditions was more than the traffic cd. bear if the traffic were to conduce to larger statal and imperial organization. Or you can say that the state of mind producing that racket was predatory rather than statal. It was the *grab-at-once* state of mind.

The racket or rental was in the circumstances justifiable in immediate aspects, far more so than the 60% money racket in our time, but it built no empire, and Alexander's mere conquests were oriental.

The Roman 6% charge, on the other hand, conduced to stability. I suggest that Prof. Rostovtzeff of Yale is unlikely to bring out evidence against this hypothesis and that his interest in Roman vicissitudes will probably confirm it, or at minimum I suggest that curiosity of future students shd. stretch out along this line of enquiry.

SPARTA 776 B.C.

I wd. go back even further and suggest that the forbidden fruit of hebrew story is a usury parable. At least that wd. make sense, the distinction between *neschek*, corrosive usury, and *marbit* (or pronounce it marbis if you prefer) is clear in the pentateuch. If you take it that the age of abundance ended when the *marbit* swelled out into *neschek* you wd. avoid a number of troublesome contradictions. And the perversion of the meaning in tradition wd. fall in nicely with old John Adams' remarks on the shamelessness wherewith the money racketeers have defaced and obliterated all monuments likely to enlighten humanity and interfere with their swindle.

● ●

Kingship, in the domain of matter and energy, is nothing other than the power to amass and distribute. Early man rightly sanctified this power, or invested it with ceremony for a pedagogic reason, as he sanctified fructification or the cycle of grain.

● ●

Bread and circuses. The first duty of the state is the maintenance of public order. If imperial thought runs to keeping that order free from inruption and disturbance jammed into it from without, the feeding problem at some point arises.

Grant tentatively that the welfare of the common people was not the first care of the emperors, it wd. still be impossible to deny the effective provisions taken time after time to establish effective and beneficent

42

order; from which the total people derived benefits greater than occidental history had known before the Pax Romana.

St Ambrose didn't rise suddenly and without fore-bears. A transition from self-centred lust after eternal salvation into a sense of public order occurred somewhere and sometime. A gradual development from a merely seditious sect to a bulwark of order indubitably occurred.

There might be a worse way of writing history than to trace the development and the going into action of a concept or set of concepts.

Equity, justice, the rights of the Roman citizen, and finally the just price emerging in canonist doctrine. The ideas of authority, of participation, of duty are as legitimate subjects of study as the phalanx, the square, the combats in chariots, and the unstill shifting of frontiers. [Nowt new but it needs repeating.]

And you can't in observing the process fix the exact point where the study pertains to philosophy, that is where one is studying thought and where one begins dealing with history (action). Action depending in so great degree on what the protagonist takes for granted.

4. TOTALITARIAN

At 3.20 this afternoon I opened an history of philosophy and "my head swam", I was submerged in a mass of nomenclatures completely unstuck from reality.

The New Learning if it comes into being at all will get hold of ideas, in the sense that it will know where they "weigh in". It will take the man of ideas when he "pulls his weight".

I am not asserting that Plato and Aristotle didn't. I am very definitely asserting that we ought to see if, how, when they (or their teaching) managed to do so.

If Plato's ideas were the paradigms of reality in Plato's personal thought, their transmutation into phenomena takes us into the unknown. What we can assert is that Plato periodically caused enthusiasm among his disciples. And the Platonists after him have caused man after man to be suddenly conscious of the reality of the *nous*, of mind, apart from any man's individual mind, of the sea crystalline and enduring, of the bright as it were molten glass that envelops us, full of light.

The history of a culture is the history of ideas going into action. Whatever the platonists or other mystics have felt, they have been possessed sporadically and spasmodically of energies measurable in speech and in

TOTALITARIAN

action, long before modern physicians were measuring the electric waves of the brains of pathological subjects.

They also evolved terminologies and communicated one with another. And there is no field where the careful historian is more likely to make an ass of himself than in trying to deal with such phenomena either to magnify or to deny them.

There is also no doubt that Platonists, all platonists every Platonist disturb or disturbs people of cautious and orderly mind.

Gemisto brought a brand of Platonism into Italy and is supposed to have set off a renaissance.

Aristotle was banned by the Church, I think because he was so discouraging. Some sort of vital instinct, down under the superficial intolerance and stupidity, felt the menace of logic-chopping, of all this cutting up, rationalizing and dissecting of reality. Not but what a man can dig a lot of acute sense out of Aristotle if he pick out what suits him in a given case or a given moment.[1]

Nothing is, without efficient cause. Rationalizing or rather trying to rationalize the prerational is poor fishing.

St Ambrose midway between Athens and the Sorbonne pulls up with a root of reality "CAPTANS ANNONAM". Hoggers of harvest, cursed among the people.

[1] These sentences of introduction had gone completely out of my mind when I wrote the later notes on pages 340-1 and I leave these repetitions so that the strict reader can measure the difference, if any, between this "residuum" left in my memory or whatever, and the justification or unustification given in detail later.

45

TOTALITARIAN

Anybody can get their teeth into that phrase. It lasts on as a "root" right up to Dr Soddy, in Butchart's collection *Tomorrow's Money*, under a shifting sea of various techniques of various conditions.

"Exactly as taxation is a forced levy on the community's money, so the issue of new money is a forced levy in kind on the wealth-on-sale in the community's marts. Just as it is unthinkable that private people shd. have power to levy taxes so it is preposterous that the banks, in the teeth of all constitutional safeguards against it, shd. by a mere trick usurp the function of Parliament and, without any authority whatever, make forced levies on the community's wealth. . . . But no one can pay taxes, or, in a monetary civilization, discharge any obligation or debt at all until there is money. The provision of the correct quantity of money shd. be the first and most important duty of the State."

The last sentence implies I take it that public order shall have been already assured; that Prof Soddy is contemplating England, and has not spread his cognizance over corporate techniques, organizations where perhaps the guilds etc. can or cd. perform functions now relegated to parliaments. These are minor varia and in no way affect Dr Soddy's main thesis.

Soddy here represents the summit of modern ethics as applicable in ordered society.

The reader who resents my introducing this question must also resent the illustrative paragraphs which terminate the second book OECONOMICORUM, say where philosophy ends and decide that it probably has nowt to do with culture and civilization.

TOTALITARIAN

Is the total man to be denied his right to discuss subjects already discussed by philosophers and theologians when such were respectable, but since abandoned by dilettantes for cosmologies about which they knew nothing, or metaphysics about which no man knows anything save what he finds out for himself. Soddy's admirable essay starts with dissociation of the "rise of man" from the myth of man's "fall". I suppose that is a philosophic issue?

The fight against unjust monopoly has never let up from the hour of St Ambrose's philipic. Jean Barral will trace it back to the Egyptian captivity. Matsumiyo with Japanese angle of incidence writes his history by dividing the year, spring, summer, autumn, winter.

No conception of culture will hold good if you omit the enduring constants in human composition.

Charlemagne fights the monopolists; he decrees a commodity denar, or a grain denar, and the significance escapes six hundred and more economists in a sequence of centuries.

A.D. 794, oats, per moggio (modio, peck) 1 denar
         barley   ,,   2 denars
         rye   ,,   3 ,,
         wheat   ,,   4 ,,

A.D. 808, oats   ,,   2 ,,
         barley   ,,   3 ,,
         rye   ,,   4 ,,
         wheat   ,,   6 ,,

the latter reading "frumento parato" and might mean superior wheat, but the rye and barley have moved in like proportion so that it wd. seem to indicate wheat as per 794 or a precaution against inferior grain.

Herein is a technical lesson in justice, there being no reasonable doubt that justice was aimed at.

Here was a lesson that David Hume had learned, presumably from some other series of observations, when he said prosperity depends not on the amount of money in a country, but on its continually increasing.

Gesell and Douglas in our time have both learned the lesson of Charlemagne's list for just prices, without any collusion.

The Catholic Church, aiming at justice, was more intelligent than professors who, in our day, fall for the stability racket, meaning a fixed set of prices, i.e. an unchanging relationship between wanted and/or needed goods and a unit of money.

The hurried reader may say I write this in cypher and that my statement merely skips from one point to another without connection or sequence.

The statement is nevertheless complete. All the elements are there, and the nastiest addict of crossword puzzles shd. be able to solve this or see this.

Having said this, perhaps the reader will believe me when I say one must begin study by method. One must be in condition to understand an author's simplest words if one wishes to understand him. A narrative is all right so long as the narrator sticks to words as simple as dog, horse, and sunset.

His communication ceases almost entirely when he writes down "good", "evil" and "proper".

TOTALITARIAN

Manifestly ideas are NOT understood, even when men write down what they themselves consider simple and unambiguous statements. C. H. Douglas remained misunderstood for years because he relapsed into algebra. I myself once printed an analytical formula in a discussion of sculpture, during 25 years I have had no evidence that that statement has ever fallen under the eye of any man who had both a college sophomore's knowledge of geometry, and an interest in sculpture.

● ● ● ●

Prof S. used to sneer at philosophy and at least contributed the statement that philosophers had worked for 2000 years and failed to define the few pieces of terminology sufficient to cover their ignorance.

My generation found criticism of the arts cluttered with work of men who persistently defined the works of one art in terms of another.

For a decade or so we tried to get the arts sorted out. (I am not leaving my narrative by this jump to the present.)

For a few years paint and sculpture tried to limit themselves to colour and form. And this did I believe clarify the minds of a small group or series of people.

We traced the "just word" back to Flaubert. We heard a good deal about using it. For the purpose of novel writing and telling of stories, the composition of poems, the evocative word, the word that throws a vivid image on the mind of the reader suffices.

We litterati struggled for twenty years on this front.

TOTALITARIAN

In the economic battle we were, after a time, confronted with the need of DEFINITION.

Definition went out in the fifteen hundreds. "Philosophy" went out in the fifteen hundreds, in the sense that after Leibniz the thought of people who labelled themselves philosophers no longer led or enlightened the rest of the thinkers. "Abstract thought" or "general thought" or philosophic thought after that time was ancillary to work of material scientists.

Some Huxley or Haldane has remarked that Galileo in inventing the telescope had to commit a definite technical victory over materials.

Before the experimental method, when men had hardly more than words as a means for transmission of thought, they took a great deal more care in defining them.

All this may be flat platitude, but one has to climb over it. The late Victorians and the Wellses were boggit in loose expression.

Every man who wants to set his ideas in order ought to be soused for a week at least in one part of mediaeval scholasticism.

5. ZWECK or the AIM

At last a reviewer in a popular paper (or at least one with immense circulation) has had the decency to admit that I occasionally cause the reader "suddenly to see" or that I snap out a remark . . . "that reveals the whole subject from a new angle".

That being the point of the writing. That being the reason for presenting first one facet and then another— I mean to say the purpose of the writing is to reveal the subject. The ideogramic method consists of presenting one facet and then another until at some point one gets off the dead and desensitized surface of the reader's mind, onto a part that will register.

The "new" angle being new to the reader who cannot always be the same reader. The newness of the angle being relative and the writer's aim, at least this writer's aim being revelation, a just revelation irrespective of newness or oldness.

To put it yet another way: it does not matter a two-penny damn whether you load up your memory with the chronological sequence of what has happened, or the names of protagonists, or authors of books, or generals and leading political spouters, so long as you understand the process now going on, or the processes biological, social, economic now going on, enveloping you as an individual, in a social order, and quite unlikely to be very "new" in themselves however fresh or stale to the participant.

The only MUST being that the reader absolutely must NOT be fooled by say Baldwin, or newspapers run exclusively by people enjoying the tyrannous privilege which accrues to the ownership of five million dollars (you can't start a daily for less).

An education consists in "getting wise" in the rawest and hardest boiled sense of that bit of argot.

This active, instant and present awareness is NOT handed out in colleges and by the system of public and/ or popular education. In this domain the individual will remain, individualism will remain, without any theoretical and ideological bulwarks. A man will continue to gain or lose his own soul. He wd. do so even were some equivalent of the grey muttony and utterly damned socialism of the Webbs and Villards to get a look-in tomorrow. It won't, but even that degraded sub-human, subthyroid disposition wouldn't wipe out the differences of awareness between John, James, Howard and William.

● ● ● ●

Run your eye along the margin of history and you will observe great waves, sweeping movements and triumphs which fall when their ideology petrifies.

You can see this best in the larger triumphs. The lesson of Mohammedan conquest and flop is the lesson for all reformers, even for little ten year and forty year movements. Ideas petrify. A koran is set up, an orthodoxy is constructed and the demand that everyone swallow it.

A national dividend, distributive economics, the obliteration of snobism, Averroes, Avicenna, a beauty of philosophical writing, a dream cut finer than Plato's, the Alcazar, the Alhambra, a thousand mosques that Keats couldn't have over described, a sense of man and of human dignity yet unobliterated. In 1906 in Tangier, you cd. see it in the walk of the Moslem.

Contempt for poverty, the pride in splendours of the mind, a sense of intellectual riches held calmly by Frobenius' arab botanist, outwardly a mere beggar.

. Knowledge is or may be necessary to understanding, but it weighs as nothing against understanding, and there is not the least use or need of retaining it in the form of dead catalogues once you understand process.

Yet, once the process is understood it is quite likely that the knowledge will stay by a man, weightless, held without effort.

About thirty years ago, seated on one of the very hard, very slippery, thoroughly uncomfortable chairs of the British Museum main reading room, with a pile of large books at my right hand and a pile of somewhat smaller ones at my left hand, I lifted my eyes to the tiers of volumes and false doors covered with imitation book-backs which surround that focus of learning. Calculating the eye-strain and the number of pages per day that a man could read, with deduction for say at least 5% of one man's time for reflection, I decided against it. There must be some other way for a human being to make use of that vast cultural heritage.

In the library of Hamilton College which then mayn't have contained more than a mere 40,000 books, mostly outside the scope of one's curiosity, the vast task of swallowing the damned lot had been less appalling.

I knew an old quaker who made tractor engines and read the *Encyclopœdia Britannica* vol. by vol. as a new edtn. appeared. That is of course one way to deal with the matter. I have never read all of Bayle, I do not travel with the four volumes in folio. Neither does anyone else.

The world had and has lost, or we illude ourselves with the belief that there once existed in France, a species of correlation of learning. I have seen old men even in my time who were supposed to "go down to the Institut" and read papers and presumably pool small parcels of learning.

And I have heard a succulent blue-stocking denounce one of the most estimable of these worthies with the statement that Monsieur R. knew everything and understood nothing, which was not quite so but did at least imply a difference of Anschauung.

It remains a fact that the anglo-saxon world has never developed a mechanism equal to that which once was, and alas is no more, in Paris.

Even in my own case I have struggled in vain for corrections, I have howled in vain for odd bits of supplementary knowledge. The eminent professor and historian G. promised me light on Mediaeval philosophy. I

sent him vainly my best set of photographs of del
Garbo's commentary on Guido. And there have ensued
years of silence.[1]

For thirty years I have trumpeted that there is no
adequate communication between scholars, men of
letters, and the damned papers, the press. We have no
standards of accuracy that an optician or a physicist wd.
recognize as other than sloppy and rascally.[2] We have
no communication system worthy the name.

And this infamy is as base in purely "cultural" or
decorative and pleasurable subjects as it is in vital sta-
tistics and fragments of history which ought to be the
common possession of every man in the street.

Properly, we shd. read for power. Man reading shd.
be man intensely alive. The book shd. be a ball of light
in one's hand.

To read and be conscious of the act of reading is for
some men (the writer among them) to suffer. I loathe
the operation. My eyes are geared for the horizon.
Nevertheless I do read for days on end when I have
caught the scent of a trail. And I, like any other tired
business man, read also when I am "sunk", when I am
too exhausted to use my mind to any good purpose or
derive any exhilaration or pleasure from using it.

There are plenty of age-old similes to show that

[1] Professor Gilson has now set Otto Bird to a thesis on Dino del Garbo.
[2] This inaccuracy was fostered by the late Col (pantalettes) Harvey
when edtr. of the *North. Am. Rev.*; it festers inexcusably in the
chronology of Untermeyer's anthologies and in Funk Wagnall's
encyclopedia.

other men have been up against the same problem. Fructus inter folia. Wheat from the chaff, and so on.

We cd. take a tip from the book-keepers. The loose leaf system is applied in effective business. Old accounts, accounts of deceased and departed customers formerly blocked the pages of ledgers.

We could make a start by distinguishing between retrospective and prospective study.

An "education" in 1938 which does not fit the student for life between 1940 and 1960 is a sham and an infamy.

"Admitted that it had nothing to do with real life but said that the course could not be changed. I therefore did not take the course."

This from a Cambridge (England) student who had thought of studying economics in that beanery.

So dense is the fugg in that department that in my student days no senior had the faintest inkling of Dante's interest, Shakespeare's interest in living.

Some of my contemporaries have suffered on visiting Schönbrun. I have seen a lady almost in tears on leaving the Venice Biennale from sheer depression at the stuff there hung on the walls.

Let us say this is hyper-aesthesia or rather let us deny vigorously that it is anything more than very high form of intelligence capable of sensing idiocy and corruption where the noseless and eyeless mind senses nothing whatever. People find ideas a bore because they do not distinguish between live ones and stuffed ones on a shelf. I mean there are ideas, facts, notions that you can look up in a phone book or library and there are others which are in one as one's stomach or liver, one doesn't have to remember them, though they now and again make themselves felt.

The value of Leo Frobenius to civilization is not for the rightness or wrongness of this opinion or that opinion but for the kind of thinking he does (whereof more later).

He has in especial seen and marked out a kind of knowing, the difference between knowledge that has to be acquired by particular effort and knowing that is in people, "in the air". He has accented the value of such record. His archaeology is not retrospective, it is immediate.

Example: the peasants opposed a railway cutting. A king had driven into the ground at that place. The engineers dug and unearthed the bronze car of Dis, two thousand years buried.

It wd. be unjust to Frazer to say that his work was *merely* retrospective. But there is a quite different phase in the work of Frobenius.

"Where we found these rock drawings, there was always water within six feet of the surface." That kind of research goes not only into past and forgotten life, but points to tomorrow's water supply.

This is not *mere* utilitarianism, it is a double charge, a sense of two sets of values and their relation.

To escape a word or a set of words loaded up with dead association Frobenius uses the term Paideuma for the tangle or complex of the inrooted ideas of any period.

Even were I to call this book the New Learning I shd. at least make a bow to Frobenius. I have eschewed his term almost for the sole reason that the normal anglo-saxon loathes a highsounding word, especially a greek word unfamiliar.

The Paideuma is not the Zeitgeist, though I have no doubt many people will try to sink it in the latter romantic term. Napoleon said he failed for opposing the spirit of his time.

As I understand it, Frobenius has seized a word not current for the express purpose of scraping off the barnacles and "atmosphere" of a long-used term.

When I said I wanted a new civilization, I think I cd. have used Frobenius' term.

At any rate for my own use and for the duration of this treatise I shall use Paideuma for the gristly roots of ideas that are in action.

I shall leave "Zeitgeist" as including also the atmospheres, the tints of mental air and the idées reçues, the notions that a great mass of people still hold or half hold from habit, from waning custom.

The "New Learning" under the ideogram of the mortar can imply whatever men of my generation can offer our successors as means to the new comprehension.

A vast mass of school learning is DEAD. It is as deadly as corpse infection.

CH'ING MING, a new Paideuma will start with that injunction as has every conscious renovation of learning.

ZWECK or the AIM

Having attained a clear terminology whereof no part can be mistaken for any other, the student might consider another point raised by Frobenius when interviewed by Dr Monotti.

"It is not what a man says, but the part of it which his auditor considers important, that measures the quantity of his communication."

STYLE, the attainment of a style consists in so knowing words that one will communicate the various parts of what one says with the various degrees and weights of importance which one wishes.

No man ever knows enough about any art. I have seen young men with most brilliant endowment who have failed to consider the length of the journey. *Anseres*, geese, as Dante has branded them, immune from learning etc.

I have heard Brancusi: la sculpture n'est pas pour les jeunes hommes.

Brancusi also said that Gaudier was a young chap who had an enormous amount of talent and *might* have done something had he lived.

Brancusi had seen only half-tone reproductions of Gaudier's work. No man except Brancusi had or has a right to such judgement. I mean no one else knows enough about sculpture to have said that in honesty and in modesty.

What we know about the arts we know from practitioners, usually from their work, occasionally from their comments. Our knowledge is sometimes second hand, and becomes more wafty with each remove.

ZWECK or the AIM

We do NOT know the past in chronological sequence. It may be convenient to lay it out anesthetized on the table with dates pasted on here and there, but what we know we know by ripples and spirals eddying out from us and from our own time.

There is no ownership in most of my statements and I can not interrupt every sentence or paragraph to attribute authorships to each pair of words, especially as there is seldom an a priori claim even to the phrase or the half phrase.

You can write history by tracing ideas, exposing the growth of a concept.

You can also isolate the quality or the direction of a given time's sensibility. That means the history of an art.

For example two centuries of Provençal life devoted a good deal of energy to *motz el son*, to the union of word and music.

You can connect that fine demarcation with demarcations in architecture and re usury, or you can trace it alone, from Arnaut and his crew down to Janequin, where a different susceptibility has replaced it.

But the one thing you shd. not do is to suppose that when something is wrong with the arts, it is wrong with the arts ONLY.

When a given hormone defects, it will defect throughout the whole system.

Hence the yarn that Frobenius looked at two African pots and, observing their shapes and proportions, said: if you will go to a certain place and there digge, you will find traces of a civilization with such and such characteristics.

As was the case. In event proved.

To illustrate another dimension of the Frobenius Institute and Afrikarchiv. Mr Butchart unearthed Stuart Mill's account of the Makute. I wished to know whether Mill knew anything about Africans. Frobenius is not particularly interested in economics. Nevertheless I enquired whether Mill was right in saying that certain tribes use the makute. According to Mill the makute was a measure of value. It was not the name of anything else. No one has seen a makute. It is not a coin. It is not a *piece* of money. It is "money of account", you swap so many makute's worth of hides for an equivalent makutage of salt.

Within a week Frankfurt sends me the names of the tribes using makutes.

Mill was right about the tribes having a money of account, that is in his main point, for the purpose of his argument. But the Makute had once existed as a straw mat. The name had lasted on long after the Portuguese had applied the name to coined units. This Teutonic thoroughness is a quality Europe can not dispense with. Compare it to the University of C. which is said to possess a manuscript of Cavalcanti. I write to its librarian. A professor of romanics, personally acquainted with the similar dept. of C. reinforces my enquiry. And the rest is silence.

Obviously the American University system is run by hirelings and by boors in great part. The last trick of the bleeders and gombeen men is to suppress learning by endowment. You give so many gothic buildings to a University that its whole income goes in the upkeep of anachronistic monstrosities.

Dr Breasted of Chicago considered a proposition for university intercommunication, such as exists in Berlin as centre for Germany, a dream above the heads of the present incumbents. Or perhaps my proposal ran a bit ahead of the quarterly Zeitschrift, perhaps I suggested that learning was not limited to men having employment in beaneries. Breasted wd. have liked to see means of communication established. He foresaw that so simple a measure wd. not come to be in his time.

Usury endows no printing press. Usurers do not desire circulation of knowledge.

Section II

6. VORTEX

John Cournos saw Gaudier's VORTEX as the history of Sculpture. I quote it, for it has been too long out of print:

Gaudier-Brzeska

Sculptural energy is the mountain.

Sculptural feeling is the appreciation of masses in relation.

Sculptural ability is the defining of these masses by planes.

The *paleolithic vortex* resulted in the decoration of the Dordogne caverns.

Early stone-age man disputed the earth with animals.

His livelihood depended on the hazards of the hunt—his greatest victory the domestication of a few species.

Out of the minds primordially preoccupied with animals Fonts-de-Gaume gained its procession of horses carved in the rock. The driving power was life in the absolute—the plastic expression the fruitful sphere.

The sphere is thrown through space, it is the soul and object of the vortex—

The intensity of existence had revealed to man a truth

of form—his manhood was strained to the highest potential—his energy brutal—*his opulent maturity was convex.*

The acute fight subsided at the birth of the three primary civilizations. It always retained more intensity East.

The *hamite vortex* of Egypt, the land of plenty—

Man succeeded in his far reaching speculations—Honour to the divinity!

Religion pushed him to the use of the *vertical* which inspires awe. His gods were self made, he built them in his image, and *retained as much of the sphere as could round the sharpness of the parallelogram.*

He preferred the pyramid to the mastaba.

The fair Greek felt this influence across the middle sea.

The fair Greek saw himself only. *He* petrified his own semblance.

His sculpture was derivative, his feeling for form secondary. The absence of direct energy lasted for a thousand years.

The Indians felt the hamitic influence through Greek spectacles. Their extreme temperament inclined towards asceticism, admiration of non-desire as a balance against abuse produced a kind of sculpture without new form perception—and which is the result of the peculiar

VORTEX OF BLACKNESS AND SILENCE.

Plastic soul is intensity of life bursting the plane.

The Germanic barbarians were verily whirled by the mysterious need of acquiring new arable lands. They moved restlessly, like strong oxen stampeding.

VORTEX

The *semitic vortex* was the lust of war. The men of
Elam, of Assur, of Bebel and the Kheta, the men of Armenia and those of Canaan had to slay each other cruelly
for the possession of fertile valleys. Their gods sent them
the vertical direction, the earth, the *sphere.*

They elevated the sphere in a splendid squatness and
created the *horizontal.*

From Sargon to Amir-nasir-pal men built man-
headed bulls in horizontal flight-walk. Men flayed their
captives alive and erected howling lions: *the elongated
horizontal sphere buttressed on four columns*, and their
kingdoms disappeared.

Christ flourished and perished in Yudah.

Christianity gained Africa, and from the seaports of
the Mediterranean it won the Roman Empire.

The stampeding Franks came into violent contact
with it as well as the Greco-Roman tradition.

They were swamped by the remote reflections of the
two vortices of the West.

Gothic sculpture was but a faint echo of the *hamito-
semitic* energies through Roman traditions, and it lasted
half a thousand years, and it wilfully divagated again
into the Greek derivation from the land of Amen-Ra.

Vortex of a vortex!!

Vortex is the point one and indivisible!

Vortex is energy! and it gave forth *solid excrements* in
the quattro e cinque cento, *liquid* until the seventeenth
century, *gases* whistle till now. *This* is the history of
form value in the West until the *fall of impressionism.*

The black-haired men who wandered through the

pass of Khotan into the valley of the *Yellow River* lived peacefully tilling their lands, and they grew prosperous.

Their paleolithic feeling was intensified. As gods they had themselves in the persons of their human ancestors —and of the spirits of the horse and of the land and the grain.

The sphere swayed.

The vortex was absolute.

The Shang and Chow dynasties produced the convex bronze vases.

The features of Tao-t'ie were inscribed inside of the square with the rounded corners—the centuple spherical frog presided over the inverted truncated cone that is the bronze war drum.

The vortex was intense maturity. Maturity is fecundity —they grew numerous and it lasted for six thousand years.

The force relapsed and they accumulated wealth, forsook their work, and after losing their form-understanding through the Han and T'ang dynasties, they founded the Ming and found artistic ruin and sterility.

The sphere lost significance and they admired themselves.

During their great period off-shoots from their race had landed on another continent.—After many wanderings some tribes settled on the highlands of Yukatan and Mexico.

When the Ming were losing their conception, these neo-Mongols had a flourishing state. Through the strain of warfare they submitted the Chinese sphere to horizontal treatment much as the Semites had done. Their cruel nature and temperament supplied them with a stimulant: *the vortex of destruction.*

Besides these highly developed peoples there lived on the world other races inhabiting Africa and the Ocean islands.

When we first knew them they were very near the paleolithic stage. Though they were not so much dependent upon animals their expenditure of energy was wide, for they began to till the land and practice crafts rationally, and they fell into contemplation before their sex: the site of their great energy: *their convex maturity.*

They pulled the sphere lengthways and made the cylinder, this is the *vortex of fecundity*, and it has left us the masterpieces that are known as love charms.

The soil was hard, material difficult to win from nature, storms frequent, as also fevers and other epidemics. They got frightened: This is the *vortex of fear*, its mass is the *pointed cone*, its masterpieces the fetishes.

And *we* the moderns: Epstein, Brancusi, Archipenko, Dunikowski, Modigliani, and myself, through the incessant struggle in the complex city, have likewise to spend much energy.

The knowledge of our civilization embraces the world, we have mastered the elements.

We have been influenced by what we liked most, each according to his own individuality, we have crystallized the sphere into the cube, we have made a combination

VORTEX

of all the possible shaped masses—concentrating them to express our abstract thoughts of conscious superiority.

Will and consciousness are our

VORTEX.

A further note of Gaudier's can be taken to augment the force of the preceding:

WRITTEN FROM THE TRENCHES [1]

I have been fighting for two months and I can now gauge the intensity of life.

Human masses teem and move, are destroyed and crop up again.

Horses are worn out in three weeks, die by the road-side.

Dogs wander, are destroyed, and others come along.

With all the destruction that works around us *nothing is changed even superficially.* LIFE IS THE SAME STRENGTH, *the moving agent that permits the small individual to assert himself.*

The bursting shells, the volleys, wire entanglements, projectors, motors, the chaos of battle *do not alter in the least* the outlines of the hill we are besieging. A company of *partridges* scuttle along before our very trench.

[1] NOTE [from *Blast*, 1915].—The sculptor writes from the French trenches, having been in the firing line since early in the war.

In September he was one of a patrolling party of twelve, seven of his companions fell in the fight over a roadway.

In November he was nominated for a sergeantcy and has been since slightly wounded, but expects to return to the trenches.

He has been constantly employed in scouting and patrolling and in the construction of wire entanglements in close contact with the Boches.

VORTEX

It would be folly to seek artistic emotions amid these little works of ours.

This paltry mechanism, which serves as a purge to over-numerous humanity.

This war is a great remedy.

In the individual it kills arrogance, self-esteem, pride.

It takes away from the masses numbers upon numbers of unimportant units, whose economic activities become noxious as the recent trades crises have shown us.

MY VIEWS ON SCULPTURE *remain absolutely* THE SAME.

It is the VORTEX *of will, of decision, that begins.*

I shall derive my emotions solely from the ARRANGEMENT OF SURFACES, I shall present my emotions by the *arrangement of my surfaces, the planes and lines by which they are defined.*

Just as this hill where the Germans are solidly entrenched, gives me a nasty feeling, solely because its gentle slopes are broken up by earth-works, which throw long shadows at sunset. Just so shall I get feeling, of whatsoever definition, from a statue *according to its slopes*, varied to infinity.

I have made an experiment. Two days ago I pinched from an enemy a mauser rifle. Its heavy unwieldy shape swamped me with a powerful *image* of brutality.

I was in doubt for a long time whether it pleased or displeased me.

I found that I did not like it.

I broke the butt off and with my knife I carved in it a design, through which I tried to express a gentler order of feeling, which I preferred.

69

VORTEX

But I will emphasize that my design GOT ITS EFFECT (just as the gun had) *from a very simple composition of lines and planes.*

GAUDIER-BRZESKA

In contrasting Gaudier's real knowledge (vide Aristotle's fivefold division later) with the mentality of bureaucracy and of beanery, note the current practices of latter and causes for.

1. Desire to get and retain job.

2. That many scholars write under a terror. They are forced to maintain a pretence of omniscience. This leads to restricting their field of reference. In a developed philological system they have to know "ALL" about their subject. Which leads to segregation of minute portions of that subject for "profounder" investigation. With corollary that any man who knows where the oil well is, is considered superficial.

The woodman's axe is still useful, but less so in New York than the spanner.

There is nothing illegitimate or contemptible in wanting to devise, contrive (rather than invent) an efficient tool kit. No man can carry an automobile factory on his back.

A great many "scholars" are as helpless as isolated mechanics wd. be were each possessed of some spare part, screw, die, lever, cog, of a huge machine.

All these bits and segments can be essential in a great works. And perfectly useless or infinitely less useful than

VORTEX

a plain wrench, a good screwdriver or a brace and bit, to the plain man in his usual avocations.

The exacerbated critic about to receive 8 and saxpence for disliking these pages, might consider the preceding points before making the definitive statement that the 40 preceding pages are as asinine as they doubtless appear to said reviewer (in a hurry, because he is paid by time and space) if he is pre-committed to the notion that I think I am inventing Mr Edison's electric light bulb.

I have been for 28 years puzzled that a good library of my time does not exist. Say my time is that of men now about 50.[1]

Arthur Symons wrote *Spiritual Adventures* (there is I fear no second edition). Carrying on from Balzac's *Louis Lambert* Symons gave us a series of studies in special sensibility, as for example the actress who as child in the ghetto watched people's hands and their way of moving. As culture this book is worth all the freudian tosh in existence.

Walter Rummel's brief preface to his edition of troubadour songs, Arnold Dolmetsch's manner of writing in his *Music of the XVIIth and XVIIIth Centuries* and even Antheil's incisiveness when not writing for publication might give basis for belief that music is excellent discipline for the writer of prose.

Considering the curious segregation of musical acti-

[1] "Greek" sez Doc. Rouse, "necessity of civilized life". Loeb Library O.K. for gk. and latin, but there are other necessities.

vity, especially the composition of music from all other kinds of intellectual action, this clarity, when they do use words, must come from a habit of making distinctions—as between one tone, half tone, and another, or between durations of notes almost equal? I leave this in the form of a question.

7. GREAT BASS: PART ONE

I assert at this point one thing without which I can not see music rightly received.

I have put it in a dozen forms, I have printed it in one form, and sent it out by private letter more briefly.

Certain sounds we accept as "pitch", we say that a certain note is do, re, mi, or B flat in the treble scale, meaning that it has a certain frequency of vibration.

Down below the lowest note synthesized by the ear and "heard" there are slower vibrations. The ratio between these frequencies and those written to be executed by instruments is OBVIOUS in mathematics. The whole question of tempo, and of a main base in all musical structure resides in use of these frequencies.

It is unlikely that great composers neglected this basis. I am convinced that it is unwise to wander into musical study without taking count of it.

●　●　●　●

At least two kinds of statement are found in philosophers. Spinoza writes:

The intellectual love of things consists in the understanding of their perfections.

Swedenborg, if you permit him to be called a philosopher, writes: I saw three angels, they had hats on their heads.

73

Both carry conviction. One may be a bit in the dark as to what constituted Swedenborg's optic impressions but one does not doubt that he had such impressions.

The standard of conduct among angels in his third heaven furnishes an excellent model for those of us who do not consider that we have entered that district.

● ● ● ●

Weighing it by and large Leibniz was the last philosopher who "got hold of something", his unsquashable monad may by now have been pulverized into sub-electrons, it may have been magnified in the microscope's eye to the elaborate structure of a solar system, but it holds as a concept.

If you let go of it, you are wafted out among mere nomenclatures.

Or if you like, try it another way. Up till Leibniz you can find men who really struggle with thought. After Leibniz, the precedent kind of thought ceased to lead men. Before we had much material science, or during the two thousand years' lapse between the mislaying of what greek science there had been and the new science of Galileo and of the renaissance, the defining of terms, speculation, the measuring and testing of one thought on another and the attempt to lock thought in words HAD led men, it had even conduced to material science. Afterwards it was a result of one "scientific discovery" or another.

Philosophic argument was flooded with a new batch

of similes. In our time the wireless telegraph has pro-
duced a new outbreak of antient speculations.

• •

Take it that Leibniz was the last serious character to
worry about the reconciliation of churches. He and Bos-
suet ran onto the snag of "authority", shd. one accept
Church authority when it was against one's own con-
science?

I repeat: the Catholic Church went out of business
when its hierarchy ceased to believe its own dogma. Leo
X didn't take Luther's thought as a serious matter. He
didn't expect others to do so.

Scotus Erigena held that: Authority comes from right
reason. I suppose he thought himself a good catholic.

This page can stand in lieu of an Agony Column. I
still invite correspondence as to the trial of Erigena and
his condemnation centuries after his death.

I can still see a Catholic renaissance or the Church
"taken seriously once again" if Rome chose to dig up
the records, if Rome chose to say the trial was a mistrial,
if Rome chose to say that Scotus was heretical because
of some pother about the segments of the trinity but
that on "Authority" he was sound, a son faithful etc.

• • • •

*These disjunct paragraphs belong together, Gaudier,
Great Bass, Leibniz, Erigena, are parts of one ideogram,
they are not merely separate subjects.*

8. ICI JE TESTE

Next week or the year after I expect several cardinals to admit that during the XIXth, or most infamous, century the Church's best friend was Cavour. The immeasurable ascent of the Church of Rome between the time of Cardinal Antonelli and our time (our time being also the time of the Concordat) very nearly proves Cavour's contention as to the effect of the Temporal Power.

Quadrigesimo Anno and the other economic passages from the Encyclicals have put the Church on the map for thousands of people who had and have "no religion". Those few pages of honesty count to non-church population more than all the preachings on sundays.

The answer coming to me from Canada: If the Church is against usury why are all Canadian churches mortgaged?

Perhaps the Vatican needs a few more Cavours.

Given a free hand ·with the Saints and Fathers one could construct a decent philosophy, not merely a philosophism. This much I believe. Given Erigena, given St Ambrose and St Antonino, plus time, patience and genius you cd. erect inside the fabric something modern man cd. believe.

The question is: how much more wd. Rome try to load onto you?

ICI JE TESTE

This much I believe to be also true: there is more civilization lying around unused in the crannies, zenanas, interstices of that dusty and baroque fabric than in all other institutions of the occident.

The utter paucity, falsity and vulgarity, together with sheer rascality of anglicans à la Baxter (the swine who sold his king and his church to the usurers) are beyond my vocabulary.

Grosseteste was a serious character, Albert de la Magna was an intellect. There were centuries of honest work done inside the building. Aquinas lacked faith.

The syllogism, time and again, loses grip on reality. Richard St Victor had hold of something: sic:

There are three modes of thought, cogitation, meditation and contemplation. In the first the mind flits aimlessly about the object, in the second it circles about it in a methodical manner, in the third it is unified with the object.

That is something a man can check up on. It is a knowledge to be verified by experience. I mean ours with St Victor's.

Grosseteste on Light may or may not be scientific but at least his mind gives us a structure. He throws onto our spectrum a beauty comparable to a work by Max Ernst. The mind making forms can verbally transmit them when the mental voltage is high enough. It is not absolutely necessary that the imagination be registered either by sound or on painted canvas.

Out beyond that, the so called rational statements

attempt to prove what can not be proved; attempt to lift zero by its own bootstraps. A man sits still and claims that he moves by interjecting a "therefore". The Descartian hat trick. His grandfather was Aquinas.

Descartes did however invent a geometry.

Or shall we say he introduced us occidentals to the Chinese five pointed compass: North, East, South, West, AND THE MIDDLE.

● ● ● ●

I will try it another way: Up till Leibniz' time men could struggle with words, they cd. "speculate" without hiding from anything. They were not being merely lazy. After Leibniz' time the professional philosopher was just a bloke who was too damned lazy to work in a laboratory. He was too lazy even to work at an art. Or else he was, like 89% of the since writers on philosophical subjects, just a dud or a half wit, who didn't know what had happened.

In this stricture I do not include the mathematicians who worked at determinants and/or who carried on into mathematical physics.

(And somewhere on that front I get out of my depth. Though I assert that there are immoral mathematics. My brick is for those who thought they were being philosophers.)

9. TRADITION

I reiterate our debt to Frobenius for his sense of the reality in what is held in the general mind. Dr Rouse found his Aegean sailors still telling yarns from the Odyssey though time had worn out Odysseus' name, down through O'ysseus, already latin Ulysses, to current Elias, identified with the prophet.

Of the seven sages we in like manner conserve a few maxims: Heraclitus' "Everything Flows", somebody's "nothing in excess" and with effort of memory from the school list "Know thyself".

The Christian examination of conscience is not much better. Saving one's soul may be of interest *in a system*, but in ignorance of that system, in default of a motto that Yeats once printed in an early volume of poems, and had, when I cited it to him, forgotten: God hath need of every individual soul. . . . , your Xtian examination degenerates into mere cerebral onanism. As hell-dodging it is a personal matter, and as pie in the sky it is merely a greed system with imbursement delayed.

The greek injunction is glib whereas the Confucian Great Learning, the examination of motivation, is an examination with a clear purpose.

It is a root, the centre of steadily out-circling causations from immediate order to a whole series of harmonies and good conducts.

CIVILIZATION, to define same:

1

To define it ideogramicly we may start with the "Listening to Incense". This displays a high state of civilization. In the Imperial Court of Nippon the companions burnt incense, they burnt now one perfume, and now another, or a mixture of perfumes, and the accomplishment was both to recognize what had gone materially into the perfume and to cite apposite poems.

The interest is in the blend of perception and of association.

It is a pastime neither for clods nor for illiterates.

2

They say when Younghusband finally got to Lhassa he found a man from Connecticut selling stove pipes. Commerce precedes. But after Fenollosa, among my honoured compatriots in the higher exploration I shd. propose for distinction Katharine Carl. It appears that the St Louis exposition of sometime or other desired the Dowager Empress's portrait, and sent out a lady who appears to have passed the rest of her time doing squashy water-colours in the St Louis style of that period. Under the insistence of the Empress she turned out what appears in reproduction to be an excellent work of art, in the course of producing which she observed the Dowager charming birds, definitely luring at least one down from a tree when the court ladies couldn't. Mrs Carl also describes the old lady painting or writing the ideograms, writing them large and with great and delicate perfection so that they were prized by recipients.

This book[1] records a high degree of civilization. Fenollosa is said to have been the second European to be able to take part in Noh performance. The whole civilization reflected in Noh is a high civilization.

The ghost of Kumasaka returns not from a grudge and not to gain anything; but to state clearly that the very young man who had killed him had not done so by a fluke or slip, but that he had outfenced him.

The play Kagekiyo has Homeric robustness. The Noh is not merely painting on silk or nuances *à la* Chas. Condor.

3

Let me set it down as a matter of record, in case this book lasts fifty years, that men of my generation in the occident have witnessed the belly-flop or collapse of a number of kingdoms and empires, all of them rotten, none of them deserving any pity or two words of regret. Among putridities it is difficult to make a just estimate. The Grand Dukes stank no worse than Basel, the Banque de France, or other politcal producers. They sold their country. They had no moral splendour.

[1] *With the Empress Dowager of China*, by K. A. Carl, Century Co., N. York, 1906.

TRADITION

Their flop did however for a few years enrich bohemia or la vie humaine des littérateurs by a dispersal of fragments.

During the downshoot of XIXth century forms there remained a species of surface. A sort of immense cardboard raft intact on, as it were, a cataract of stale sewage. A room of Madame Tussaud's as it might have been.

I am not merely taking a pot shot at something I, personally, loathe, I am contrasting the fine flower of a civilization with a species of rot and corruption.

The denizens somewhat hushed, but not conscious, as it were perhaps semi-asphixiated but still smiling, shall we say with a touch of stiffness.

Men of my time have witnessed "parties" in London gardens where, as I recall it, everyone else (male) wore grey "toppers". As I remember it even Henry James wore one, and unless memory blends two occasions he wore also an enormous checked weskit. Men have witnessed the dinner ceremony on flagships, where the steward still called it "claret" and a bath oliver appeared with the cheese. (Stilton? I suppose it must have been stilton.)

Such activities may be called natural phenomena, to be distinguished from more numerous "efforts", by which I mean social events whereunder one sensed a heave, an unhabitual outlay.

I isolate social habit, custom indicating high culture, from exceptional individuals, let us say those who made history or have at least appeared in the story.

Apart from things seen, and more pertinent to my

ideogram at this moment: von X. had never been out of uniform from the time he was six until the end of the "war" (1919).

I am not in these slight memories, merely "pickin' daisies". A man does not know his own ADDRESS (in time) until he knows where his time and milieu stand in relation to other times and conditions.

Countess M. (an italian title) counted her high water mark a wedding at the court in St Petersburg. My most prolific Urquell, source of these notes, has been an ex-diplomat, ex-imperial staff officer, reduced along with dukes k.t.l. to flats, restaurants and intercourse with untitled humanity.

Comfortably at the Régence he remarked that if you are covered with brass chains, a sword, etc.; if your sartorial sheath is rigid and every time you move something jangles you naturally do not loll, you sit still and upright. Considering simply the phrase "good society" it appeared that he had seen some, for example the Duchess of D. never spoke. She nodded. She had the dignity of a temple image, and various nods and bobs eliminated all need of verbal expression.

It being then 1925 I asked if any remained. He meditated and finally thought there was some left in Spain.

"Is it a society in which you wd. care to spend much of yr. time?"

"Good GOD, no!!" said the general.

TRADITION
4

Against this a few evenings in Brancusi's old studio, wherein quiet was established.

"The quality of the sage is like water."[1]

I don't know the source of Allan Upward's quotation.

A few evenings in the Palazzo Capoquadri listening to Mozart's music.

I am setting down "social" as distinct from personal events. I am not counting "spectacles", people brought somewhere to see or to hear a show.

In attempting to discover "where in a manner of speaking etc. we have got to" (ref. H. James plus Madox Ford's exegeses) one can use allegory or data, trifling or grave things seen. The Goncourt insisted that the top belongs to reality no less than the bottom. H. J.'s excuse for some of his characters was that "if they didn't exist and if no counterparts existed we, still, ought for the honour of the race to pretend that they existed". Landor finding no good conversation had to pretend it had sometimes existed.

If one is to measure merely by brilliance, the maximum I have known was at Picabia's of a Sunday about 1921 or '22.

[1] This text is interpreted in various manners.

PART II

Section III

10. GUIDE

The present opusculus is listed even in the early business arrangements between my agent and publishers as "A guide to Kulchur" (verbatim), "to be known provisionally as a Guide to Culture", sic. the contract. To avoid mysterious carriage of body designed to conceal defects of the intelligence.

A definite philosophical act or series of acts was performed along in 1916 to '21 by, as I see it, Francis Picabia. If he had any help or stimulus it may have come from Marcel Duchamp. Picabia may have been touched up by Eric Satie. I know of no other intelligences implied in the process. There were participants in a "movement" but they were, so far as I know, not sources of movement.

Bayle and Voltaire used a sort of *reductio ad absurdum* for the destruction of hoakum. Picabia got hold of an instrument which cleared out whole racks full of rubbish.

"Europe exhausted by the conquest of Alsace Lorraine." The transposition of terms in idées reçues. The accepted cliché turned inside out, a, b, c, d; being placed
        b, d, c, a,
        c, b, d, a, etc., in each case

expressing as much truth, half truth or quarter, as the original national or political bugwash.

That anyone shd. have tried to use Picabia's acid for building stone, shows only the ineradicable desire of second-rate minds to exploit things they have not comprehended.

After Dada there came a totally different constructive movement. Based on the inner need of a couple of painters to paint; in certain permanent facts of human mental existence and sprouting in a field utterly unconscious (as far as one cd. see) of ancestry and tradition.

The young frenchmen of 1920 had NO elders whom they cd. in any way respect. Gourmont was dead. The war had thrown up a few stuffed monkeys, third rate gallic effigies, cranks who hadn't even the excuse of being British to account for their holding the tosh of Manchester they emitted, the bunk of a Romain Rolland, the vacuity of a Gide.

Apart from the unclean daily press of Barrès etc. etc.

The stream of thought that had made the *Mercure* in the beginning, trickled out into the sand. A concept of literary integrity remained among weaker brethren who have finally been gathered into their graves. France rose after 1870 and almost disappeared after 1918. I mean to say that anything that cd. have caused Henry James' outburst of devotion to France, anything that cd. have made Paris the focus of human respect and intelligence and of "respect for intelligence" entered a phase of non-being.

A few more than middle aged gents had reminiscences.

GUIDE

Hennique remembered Flaubert and Maupassant. Men distinctly of the second line conserved this, that or the other.

A new boiling of french talents was as grossly avid and as vulgar as Lorimer, without even the natural American gusto and genuine unconsciousness of all civil values. Lorimer honestly didn't know that there ever had been a civilization.

The post-war frogs *à grand tirage* were a set of perruquiers. They differed from the yankee and cockney shekel chasers only in being more cheaply for sale.

"I thought I was among men of letters," said Z. "and suddenly saw they were garage assistants." You can get the meaning of this from Willy's pharmacien. Willy's figures of fun were inheriting the seats of the serious. Willy and the earlier Abel Hermant are the recorders of an epoch and of part of an epoch preceding. A civilization definitely runs down when for its best you go *away* from serious books to the comics, from comics to the theatre, from the theatre to the cult of the music-hall.

Which is not to sneer at the music-hall or at Mr Eliot's obit for Marie Lloyd. At a given point the word ceases. The observer inexpert in music-hall technique finds more *literary* sense in George Mozart than in the British novelists of 1919.

Ellen Terry said to me that she wasn't clever enough to have made a success in the halls. There is a distinct decadence when interest passes from significance— meaning the total significance of a work—into DE-TAILS of technique.

GUIDE

That sentence must not be taken to contradict my sentence of 30 years ago that technique is the test of a writer's sincerity. The writer or artist who is not intolerant of his own defects of technique is a smear.

But the aim of technique is that it establish the totality of the whole. The total significance of the whole. As in Simone Memmi's painting. The total subject IS the painting.

When the usurer climbs into the saddle you have attention absorbed by the detail, colour, lighting etc. to DETRIMENT of the total reason for the work's coming to be.

11. ITALY

There was and is a higher civilization in a dozen, or a hundred or two hundred Italian writers, who will never achieve any celebrity, than in the much published and touted names.

A man's character is apparent in every one of his brush strokes. There are I believe scattered chapters in novels by F. M. H. which show civilization. Fox of the Forschungsinstitut picked up a Japanese letter from my desk, and bowed to its civility. I have known a local Italian librarian to attain great elegance on a post card in four or five simple phrases.

There are passages in what's-his-name's *Glaucus* and in his *Ixion*. Tozzi is perhaps not an illustration of what I am after, but merely a serious novelist. An unknown Monti, wrote a few civil chapters.

12. AESCHYLUS and . . .

The triumph of total meaning over detail is nowhere so demonstrable as in the common phrases "greek tragedy" or "greek drama". Those phrases carry a definite and freighted meaning to every literate auditor. That is to say they carry meaning to a vast multitude, 99% of whom have never read a line of Sophokles or of any greek writer.

There are, to the best of my knowledge, no translations of these plays that an awakened man can read without deadly boredom.

Eliot's interment of Murray might have been the last word: "erected a barrier between Euripides and the reader more impassable than the greek language".

After which or concurrently I asked Eliot to have a shot at the *Agamemnon*. He didn't. Or rather he sat on it for eight months or some longer period.

I then took over. If one greek play can claim preeminence over the best dozen others (which it probably can not) that play wd. be the *Agamemnon*. (I take it my delight in the *Prometheus*, as in *Pericles Prince of Tyre*, is a personal variant on best critical preference. I shouldn't ever try to get a committee of good critics to follow me into it.)

At any rate THE *Agamemnon*. I twisted, turned, tried

every elipsis and elimination. I made the watchman
talk nigger, and by the time you had taken out the rem-
plissage, there was no play left on one's page.

There was magnificence; there was SENSE of play,
the beacon telegraph stuff is incomparable. Nobody but
a fanatic like myself wd. have the crust to insist that
the greek writers were on the down grade AFTER
Homer. But the translation is unreadable. No one with
a theatric imagination can conceive it holding now as a
stage play IF you leave in all the verbiage. But as an
entity it stands rock-like.

H. D. in her *Ion* has tried various wheezes. She has
certainly pared down as much as the Genevan pacifist
has upholstered and straw-filled.

I wdn't. condemn a mad dog·on the strength of Gbt
Murray's evidence. But the opposite system doesn't
work either.

Yet greek drama exists. Cocteau by sheer genius has
resurrected it.

Antigone "T'as inventé la justice" rings out in the
Paris play house with all the force any man ever imag-
ined inherent in greek originals.

There is neither anything past, nor anything less than
the maximum charge, in the contest of Cocteau's Anti-
gone with his Creon.

Pirandello was worried at the news that Cocteau was
trying an Oedipus; for a moment he "feared" or "had
feared" that M. Jean wd. fall into psychoanalysis, and
caught himself the next moment with "No, he won't fall
into that mess. Il est trop bon poète."

AESCHYLUS and . . .

The *bon poète* of sheer crystalline genius leaps out again in the dea ex machina, the oracle speaking in numbers,

> huit, sept, trois,
> cinq, huit, dix,

or whatever. But the numbers Athena wd have used. The closed speech, the riddle, the absolute.

Done once, immortally, and not to be undone or followed.

● ●

There is your "aesthetic criticism" or whatever you want to call it, now that the word *culture* and the word *aesthetic* are both damned, faded, meringued in our language.

There are old Byzantine panels that you can chip, scrub, deface, fill full of worm holes, and the fact of their force remains. There are Madonnas whose blue has gone black with no more deterioration of their totality than is implied in the beholder's supposing they were painted black in the first place, until some expert explains to him this, that and etcetera.

Musical moralists have damned in my presence that very tough baby George Antheil. He has gone to hell and to Hollywood a "sub-Medean talent", he has made himself a motley and then some. He was imperfectly schooled, in music, in letters, in all things, but he nevertheless did once demand bits of SOLIDITY, he demanded short hard bits of rhythm hammered down, worn down so that they were indestructible and unbendable. He wanted these gristly and undeformable "monads", as definite as the

    All the angels have big feet.

    Hump, diddywim tum. . . . Hump, bump, stunt.

This is in accord with, though not contained in Jean's *Rappel à l'Ordre.* Cocteau there demanded a music to be like tables and chairs.

That goes with Mantegna's frescoes. Something to be there and STAY there on the wall.

If I am introducing anybody to Kulchur, let 'em take the two phases, the nineteen teens, Gaudier, Wyndham L. and I as we were in *Blast,* and the next phase, the 1920's.

The sorting out, the *rappel à l'ordre,* and thirdly the new synthesis, the totalitarian.

13. MONUMENTAL

I am not dealing with Mr Joyce in this volume. I have small doubt that no reader will have taken this book, up to this moment, for anything save an universal receptacle, yet it has limits, and its edge is a demarcation. In 1912 or eleven I invoked whatever gods may exist, in the quatrain:

> Sweet Christ from hell spew up some Rabelais,
> To belch and . . . . . and to define today
> In fitting fashion, and her monument
> Heap up to her in fadeless excrement.

"Ulysses" I take as my answer. Yet ten years later when Brancusi inveighed against the "monumental", I did not at once grasp his meaning. "Ulysses" is the end, the summary, of a period, that period is branded by La Tour du Pin in his phrase "age of usury".

The reader, who bothers to think, may now notice that in the new paideuma I am not including the monumental, the retrospect, but only the pro-spect.

The katharsis of "Ulysses", the joyous satisfaction as the first chapters rolled into Holland Place, was to feel that here was the JOB DONE and finished, the diagnosis and cure was here. The sticky, molasses-covered filth of current print, all the fuggs, all the foetors, the whole boil of the European mind, had been lanced.

Section IV

14. THE HISTORY OF PHILOSOPHY IS . . . ?

At the start the record of various guesses made about the nature of the universe, various obiter dicta as to how people ought to behave. Some effort to work out the particular guess so that it shouldn't be self-contradictory, or produce contradictions inside the structure built up on it. In this game a very considerable technique can be developed without the guesser and figurer learning anything about exterior nature.

It is perhaps Aristotle's glory that he did try to sort out the cosmological guesses, and the various kinds of obiter dicta, and that he did mildly recommend some sort of observation of exterior fact. After which the guessing pretty well set in again, down on through the ingenious Arabs, to the renaissance.

Any man with the kind of mind that takes an interest in this sort of thing ought to be able to guess for himself.

Obviously communication in this sphere is impossible without terminology.

The earth revolves round a central fire. All is from number. Numbers are the source of all things. All things

97

are created in accordance with number. Water is the source of all things. He don't mean that kind of water. He means a special dampness. Nothing exists. All is from a rain of atoms. If anything did exist it wd. be ununderstandable and if understandable wd. be incommunicable.

"Gorgias debunks the logical process."—Headline on Athenian bill-board.

All knowledge is built up from a rain of factual atoms such as:

Frobenius forgets his note book, ten miles from camp he remembers it. Special African feast on, and no means of sketching it for the records. No time to return to camp. No matter. Black starts drumming. Drum telegraph works and sketching materials arrive in time for the beano.

Culture possessed and forgotten. Also flute music with definite language of motifs.

"Erlebte Erdteile" not very specific as to whether this language of music has grown from association of words with tunes and fragments of tune.

Such is the parody of Chevy Chase, ta ta tata tata tum, tatum, taTUM ta to dy. The tum tum TUM thereafter as it were meaning "riding on" and the "ta ta tum" meaning "come (came) to town". Etc.

Or whether the drumming language was worked out like a morse alphabet.

I suspect that the error in educational systems has been the cutting off of learning from appetite.

Knowledge is to know man. Mr Alexander Pope rubs

it a bit too smooth. If you translate him, the proper study for man is anthropology, you get nearer the source of error. Every word ending in -ology in English implies reading generalities. It implies a shutting off from particulars. It is a thousand miles remove from POLLON D'ANTHROPŌN IDEN.

Real knowledge goes into natural man in titbits. A scrap here, a scrap there; always pertinent, linked to safety, or nutrition or pleasure.

Human curiosity survives and is catered for, by the twopenny weeklies, 24 lines on chromosomes, six lines on a three-headed calf.

THE POINT OF HIS AIM

I believe (on inadequate knowledge) that Mme Montessori has tried to apply this principle in the teaching of infants.

A mean might be discovered. No man can contemplate the point of a candle flame for how long is it?? If however an underlying purpose or current cd. be established beneath a series of facts (as is done by Edgar

Wallace even in some of his craziest stories) education might be more rapid. Without going to excess?

One does not eat exclusively soup for one week, fish for one week, meat for one week, and ice-cream for the fourth week. Up to a point the process might toughen one?

The process may have gone too far in dealing with mental nutriment.

Discoveries are made by gluttons and addicts. The man who forgets to eat and sleep has an appetite for fact, for interrelations of causes.

The endurance test in vacuo does not fecundate. It may lead to fakirism, which will in turn be harnessed, as in Singapore where the fakir does the penance for the usurer, sticks himself full of knives etc. and gets paid for it. To the glory of Shiva?

The sheer physical enduring had a use in primitive conditions. There is no doubt about that. The fighter who is not rattled by pain is a tribal asset.

And the last thing one is taught in school is to watch other human beings.

The weak watch and take vengeance. The intelligent lads are the youngest in the class and if they play games are at a disadvantage in weight and in muscle.

Give 'em tennis rackets with shorter handles, and make 'em play with the left hand most of the time? half the time?

In any case, *-ologies* come out of greek separation and dilettantism. "Occupy leisure with the arts." For Kung and co. the arts included riding horses and using the bow and arrow. Kung "fished occasionally with hook and line, never with a net. He used a bow now and then but not snares to take birds."

What China is and came out of, can be divined from the 187th ideogram (MA) meaning horse, 22 pages double column of Morrison of words with the radical horse, and "all of 'em doin' wiff 'orses, sir" unless I have missed an exception.

PART III

Section V

15. VALUES

To establish some table of values as among men I have seen and talked with.

Brancusi in some dimensions a saint.

Picabia a brilliant intellect.

Gaudier had and Cocteau has genius.

Mussolini a great man, demonstrably in his effects on event, unadvertisedly so in the swiftness of mind, in the speed with which his real emotion is shown in his face, so that only a crooked man cd. misinterpret his meaning and his basic intention.

Arthur Balfour, a fake. The effect shown in his disciples, in the states of mind which he left behind him in British govt.

Arthur Griffith I think a great man. Again the droiture, the sincerity and frankness of his reactions. Both he and Mussolini instantly carrying their thought unhesitant to the root. The one: "Can't move 'em with a cold thing like economics."

The other: "*Perchè vuol mettere le sue idee in ordine?*"

"Why do you want to put your ideas in order?"

By genius I mean an inevitable swiftness and rightness in a given field. The trouvaille. The direct simplicity in seizing the effective means.

I have seen honest men, patient men, honest workers, good, as you might say, watchmakers, patiently hunting for and applying their words.

A volcanic and disordered mind like Wyndham Lewis's is of great value, especially in a dead, and for the most part rotted, milieu. The curse of England is fugg. A great energy like that of Lewis is beyond price in such a suffocated nation; something might come of disorder created by Lewis "As the giant plough is needed to break intractable soil". (I may err here in agricultural metaphor. Shallow ploughing is useful in proper conditions.)

"Human Greatness" is an unusual energy coupled with straightness, the direct shooting mind, it is incompatible with a man's lying to himself, it does not indulge in petty pretences.

16. EUROPE OR THE SETTING

The *De Vulgari Eloquio* is still the best guide to the troubadours, not that Dante was writing Essays in Appreciation. His Paideuma was strictly factive. He had needed the knowledge for himself and set down a memo.

Petrarch, I believe, did not use it. Whether anyone between 1321 and 1905 in the year of our Lord considered that treatise as text book I as yet know not. Or rather Chaytor did use it as text book (*The Troubadours of Dante*) but if he practised the art, I know not. But at any rate he knew where to look for the knowledge.

Real knowledge does NOT fall off the page into one's stomach. Allow, in my case thirty years, thereabout, for a process which I do not yet call finished, the process of gradually comprehending why Dante Alighieri named certain writers. Sordello he might also have touched in spoken tradition. Cunizza, white-haired in the House of the Cavalcanti, Dante, small gutter-snipe, or small boy hearing the talk in his father's kitchen or, later, from Guido, of beauty incarnate, or, if the beauty can by any possibility be brought into doubt, at least and with utter certainty, charm and imperial bearing, grace that stopped not an instant in sweeping over the most violent authority of her time and, from the known fact, that vigour which is a grace in itself. There was nothing in Créstien de Troyes' narratives, nothing in Rimini or in the tales of the antients to surpass the facts of Cunizza, with, in her old age, great kindness, thought for her slaves.

Whether or no the next student of troubadours will understand their tones of voice more quickly than I have, there is chance that young perception will follow one of two roads, either it will seize first what is easiest, or it will take the tip from the *De Vulgari Eloquio* or the *Commedia* and look harder at what Dante indicates.

Arnaut Daniel has merits that can be argued; that can be picked out, demonstrated, explained even to people who will never, or will not in thirty years, have direct perception of quality.

Only after long domesticity with music did I, at any rate, see why Dante has mentioned Sordello, or has he even done so in *De Eloquio*?

Above other troubadours, as I feel it *now*, Sordello's hand (or word) "deceives the eye" honestly. The complete fluidity, the ease that comes only with mastery in strophes so simple in meaning that they leave nothing for the translator.

Of his age, that just before Dante's, we have concurrently a fineness in argument, we have the thought of Grosseteste, and of Albertus. We have a few fragments of enamel, and a great deal of stone work.

A PAIDEUMA carried on, out of Byzantium, or, at least as I see it, the romanesque building and the arab building in Sicily, was Byzantine or late Roman *struc-*

ture, the difference being merely in expensiveness. With
the break down of Constantine's and Justinian's eco-
nomic system, no one cd. cover church walls with gold
mosaic.

Those of us who remember the beginning of the new
Westminster Cathedral recall a beauty of stone and
brick structure, before the shamrocks (mother of pearl)
and the various gibblets of marble had been set there to
distract one.

Modena, San Zeno (Verona), St Trophime (when did
cloisters become an habit?) the churches in Sicily and the
other Veronese structures add nothing that wasn't there
in St Apollinaire (Classe, Ravenna).

Mohammed was against usury. There is the like fine-
ness of outline in Cordova (the Mosque) in AlHambra,
and AlCazar (Sevilla). Plus the honey-comb plaster.

For European architecture a development occurs in
St Hilaire (Poitiers) and the Hall of Justice of Poitiers.
Here the architect has invented. The cunning contriv-
ance of lighting and the building of chimneys is, at least
for the layman, something there invented, something
that has no known fatherhood. In the sense that roman-
esque forms have a known fatherhood.

This total PAIDEUMA is anti-usura. A tolerance of
gombeen men and stealers of harvest by money, by dis-
tortion and dirtiness, runs concurrent with a fattening
in all art forms.

I have not deflected a hair's breadth from my lists of
beautiful objects, made in my own head and held before
I ever thought of usura as a murrain and a marasmus.

EUROPE OR THE SETTING

For 31 years I have carried in my mind as a species of rich diagram, the Prado as I saw it, and heaven knows if my readers will see it ever again. In the long gallery you turned after a time to the left. On your left hand in the great room, Las Hiladeras, the spinning girls, with the beamed light, and the duskiness, in the separate smaller room Las Meniñas, the young princesses or court ladies, the mirror with glimpse of Velasquez by the far door painting the picture.

On the wall facing the great canvas, alone, his self-portrait. In the great room Don Juan de Austria, the dwarfs, high at the end facing the door, the Virgin enthroned, differing greatly in workmanship, designed shall we say for Church lighting and not for a palace. The Surrender of Breda with the spears, new for the american visitor, only years later in Avignon did one see that this composition was not invented ex nihil and ex novo, but had been in fresco.

On the right wall Baldassar Carlos, Philip on foot with his hunting gun, Philip on Horseback, the horse's foot having been done first in a different position. Again by the door Mercury and Argos, and below it the Drinkers.

At first go one wondered why Jimmy Whistler had so insisted. A dozen returns and each time a new permanent acquisition, light, green shadows instead of the brown as in Rembrandt, who has steadily declined through 30 years in his power to rouse enthusiasm. I don't mean ceased, I mean that the current in our past three decades has been toward the primitives, WITH a forward current, via Velasquez and, for a surprisingly small number of people if you consider the vast pother and blather about painting that has been used to red-herring thought in our time, a surprisingly small number of people who saw the light, via Manet (as in the "Bar of the Folies Bergères", or the fragments of the Execution of Maximillian). So the background of Don Juan de Austria, the fire, that is there with two strokes or perhaps ONE of the brush.

Où sont . . .? God knows where this canvas has got to. Russia shall not have Constantinople etcetera.

Our husky young undergraduates may start their quest of Osiris in a search for what was the PRADO. . . .

In 1938 let us say, a bloke with small means wants the best of Europe. Once he cd. have done a great deal on foot. I dare say he still can. In 1911 there was an international currency (20 franc pieces) twenty such in jug-purse and no god-damned passports. (Hell rot Wilson AND the emperor, I think it was Decius.) If a man can't afford to go by automobile, and if he is content with eating and architecture, the world's best (as I have known it) is afoot from Poitiers, from Brives, from Périgord or Limoges. In every town a romanesque church or château. No place to stay for any time, but food every ten miles or fifteen or twenty. When I say food, I mean food. So, at any rate, was it. With fit track to walk on.

I do not say walk in Italy. The sane man will want his Italy by car. Even if it is public omnibus. The roads go over the Appenines, they go over the Bracca. They go over, where trains bore through. It is not a country to walk in because food is a FRENCH possession, when on foot one wants it.

In the territory of the Exarchate there is still some remains of this form of civilization. In twenty and forty and I suppose 400 small towns of France there is the ex-chef of the House of Commons, the ex-chef of the Duke of Bungle, the ex-chef of MiLord of Carogguh, and so forth. And there is food that its concocter respects.

In Italy there are perhaps two dozen restaurants, whereof no man knows more than eight. Inclusive or exclusive of a few stunt places where the boss makes one dish.

Le Voyage Gastronomique is a French paideuma. Outside it, you can get English roast beef in Italy (if you spend 25 years learning how), you can find a filetto of turkey Bolognese. You can get fish in Taormina which (after 30 years absence) may seem as good as American shad. I am writing of civilization. The Chinese have civilization. The Nihon Jin Kwai (London) had a cuisine. Brancusi cd. cook on occasion and Gurdieff made Persian soup, bright yellow in colour, far more delicate—you might say Pier della Francesca in tone, as compared with a bortch (tinted Rembrandt). If he had had more of that sort of thing in his repertoire he cd. had he suspected it, or desired it, have worked on toward at least one further conversion.

The dust on Italian roads, the geographic or geological formation of the peninsula all say go by car. Don't try to walk it. You have enough foot work when you get to the towns. You have a concentration of treasures that will need all your calf muscles, all your ankle resistance. Perugia, the gallery of the Palazzo Pubblico, Bonfigli and co. in a dozen churches. Siena, likewise the gallery, newly set. Cortona, Fra Angelico, in six or eight churches.

Ravenna, mosaics. A less known gallery, and three churches in Pisa. San Giorgio Schiavoni for Carpaccio's, Santa Maria Miracoli, Venice, and a few pictures here and there, a Giovan Bellin' in Rimini, Crivelli in Bergamo, the walls of La Schifanoja (Ferrara), Mantegna's portraits of the Gonzaga (Mantova). Botticelli in Firenze, and the Davanzati if it still be open, Firenze the most damned of Italian cities, wherein is place neither to sit, stand nor walk. The highest aristocracy have or had one very high club, with it wd. seem no windows. The conti and marchesi project from the main portone, the most senile is privileged to the concierge's wooden chair.

Truly this town cast out its greatest writer, and a curse of discomfort has descended, and lasted six hundred years. Don't miss the Bargello. Don't miss the Palazzo Pubblico in Siena.

For fish, try Taormina, for the glory that was Greece try Siracusa, though the Roman marble or white stone is as good as any Hellenic monuments.

So near to a full catalogue, I may as well finish it.

Some good Egyptian sculpture in the British Museum (none in The Louvre though there is a small bit called portrait of Chak Mool or something, with something half like a chinese inscription). There are, the most hurried tourist has heard it, pictures in the Louvre, the

EUROPE OR THE SETTING

National (and less touted in the National Portrait) Galleries (Paris and London), the early Italians in London, missing their natal light. If any man or young lady will first get this eye-full, this ideogram of what's what in Europe, one will not need greatly to instruct 'em as to why some very great works of art are from it omitted.

Goya, yes Goya. The best one I know is in New York.

How to see works of art? Think what the creator must perforce have felt and known before he got round to creating them. The concentration of his own private paideuma, whereof the shortcomings show, my hercules, in every line of his painting, in every note of his melody (I say melody . . . vide De Schloezer's *Strawinsky* for context). You can cover it up more or less in symphonic or "harmonic" writing, you may even be able to camouflage it a little, a very much lesser little in counterpoint by patience and application of process. But you can't damn well learn even that process without learning a great deal by the way.

A fugue a week for a year wd. teach even a bullhead something.

Loathe the secolo decimonono. What was good from 1830 to 1890 was a protest. It was diagnosis, it was acid, it was invocation of otherness. Chopin carried over precedent virtue.

17. SOPHISTS

Somewhere amid copybook maxims was the sentence: Suretyship is the beginning of ruin. In an effort to remember the table of what the seven sages had stood for. I am drawn to wonder whether this motto was among them . . . philosophers overlook it. The one history we have NOT on the news-stands is the history of Usura. Salmasius (who may have been the bloke who got into a shindy with Milton) wrote *De Modo Usurarum*, which he intended to get into three volumes, whereof only the second has yet come into my hands. This treats of terminology and of usurer's habits, and of laws regulating his process. But the history of where such and such tyrant, dupe, idiot, bewigged pustulent Bourbon, bewigged pietist diseased Stuart got his money and how, from Caesar's time (despite Rostovtzeff and the unreadable and dull Ferrero) to our own is not clearly written. Who paid for such and such wars, what save poverty prevented so and so from making more wars, with more splendid equipment? Malatesta and the late condottieri, their mouths watering over the designs, in Valturio, of war engines, tanks, superior catapults, as damn'd froust now letches after a Vickers' advertisement or a farm boy over automobile ads.

All this is still blank in our histories. "Wars are paid

for by depreciation of currency", wars are paid for in blood and carnage. Indiscriminate murder is respectable, discriminate murder is criminal, and so forth, so weiter, etcetera.

We know where the Pope got his money for one war. But that was in 1400 and something. Two weeks ago *Reynolds* asserted that a true opposition had risen. That the opposition really meant to oppose. I wonder has it (this day 2nd March 1937, anno E.F. XV.)?

Suretyship is the beginning of ruin. Don't borrow money. Every dollar is worth a dollar and six cents to any intelligent man. That much was current prudence, not taught in the day-schools but current in America in 1895. The epitaph "he signed too much paper" was held up as a warning, meaning that so and so had gone surety for another and lost in the process. But there ended the instruction.

The new curiosity will not accept such termination. Historians like Buchan and Thayer and Bell are no longer counted first-rate historians, or rather Thayer still is because he is dated.

No biography of a public man or of a ruler or prime minister can henceforth be accepted as valid unless it contains a clear statement of his finances, of his public acts in relation to public financing. Did he or did he not aid in, or connive at, swindling the people into paying two dollars taxes for every dollar's worth of services rendered the public, for every dollar's worth of material bought for the public?

That is distinctly what we want to know from now

on about any man in public authority. It is the first thing we want to know (after which the news-stands of the world can circulate his bedchamber romance, his flirtations with the housemaid or the duchess as fancy took him).

Peace movements financed by war-profiteers who are still in the bank and gun business or whose subsidy is derived from munitions' sales are unlikely to conduce to the new paideuma. Pacifists who refuse to examine all causes of war, from natural fitfulness on through the direct economic causes, are simple vermin, whatever their level of consciousness, their awareness or un-awareness of the nature of their actions and moti-vations.

All this is aeons away from Anaximandros 610 av. J. C., of Miletus, who held that all comes not from water (à la Thales) but from primitive matter, and from his successor Anaximenes who said that all is from air, pro-ceeding by condensation and rarefaction, PUKNOSIS and MANOSIS, all of which forms nice background to mediaeval writers on light and diaphana.

The "being" of Parmenides is, philosophically, as valid as Zenophanes' God, but one shdn't believe that it is a speculative concept without admixture of sensuous intuition (this wd. be fifty or sixty years later, i.e. after Anaximenes).

"The Parmenidean 'being' is the sensible real (per-ceptible), the plenum filling space, the division between corporeal and incorporeal not yet existing, this 'being' is the substratum of change, the corporeal substance which endures while qualities alter. Abstraction in it (the being?) in him, Parmenides, does not go further than sensible intuition, and conserves trace of it."

It will be seen that even in the translation of the commentator's comment on commentator there is chink for two interpretations.

Zeffer, Uberweg, three thousand Germans enjoyed themselves along with Schleiermacher, Marsten and Bertini in sorting out what so and so thought so and so meant. "Truth from opinion" etc. . . .

"Aristotle considered Zeno the father of dialectic." 23 years younger than Parmenides, Zeno also took part in public business.

Zenophanes was, they tell us, a troubadour who went about in Hellas and Sicily, possibly a white liar as to his age, settled down at 92, to propagate a doctrine more religious than philosophic, with the humour to say "African gods have snub noses, the Nordic gods are blond with blue eyes. If lions and oxen cd. paint" (If horses cd. sing Bach, mother) "we shd. doubtless see them also making Gods in their image."

Heraclitus: You can not dive twice in the same water. Empedocles counted four elements, the three "before mentioned" fire, air, water; and earth, "which however he didn't call *stoikeion* (as Plato did in our scientific sense) but the four roots of all things, *panton hridzomata.*"

"Democritus who postulated the world due to chance."

Nunc et Anaxagorae (says Lucretius) I suppose men still can read Lucretius. I prefer to respect him. There, biGum or bah goom, is my limit. I admit it is all very interesting; "He called, that is Anaxagoras called, the beginning of all things *homoeomeriam*, or bones and, *pauxillis minutis*, particles."

And SO forth till Gorgias cleared up the lot with:
"Nothing is. Were it it wd. be unknowable and if knowable, incommunicable."
Someone having "proved" that nothing can become, and yet becomes etc. Gorgias was at least for a few moments, entertaining.
The reader will still be looking round for the bloke who attributed all being to fire.
Mechanism, how it works, teleology, what it's aimed at, the soul of the world, the fire of the gods, remembering of course that the "history of philosophy", when dealing with the greek start, now flickers about among fragments, and that every word is used, defined, left undefined, wangled and wrangled according to the taste of the wrangler, his temperament, his own bias.

SOPHISTS

Fiorentino tries to whitewash Aristotle's character. Like Cunizza, later, he freed his slaves, but by testamentary disposition. She did it while living, but circumstances etc. . . .

Marx sold a pup by the Sadducees.

The question whether Arry Stotl was a good guy or the opposite is vexed. A man who suffered fools as badly as he, must have been unpopular even during the decadence of greek institutions. For the rise and fall of the various cities, vide the record of Olympic winners that used to be printed as appendix to fine folios of Pindar's racing reports. Greek cities that cdn't. keep up in athletics, declined, or vice versa, pari passu etc.

Battle of Cheronea, END of Liberty, Achaia a Roman province. Headline or whatever. B.C. 146.

In a sense the philosophic orbit of the occident is already defined, European thought was to continue in a species of cycle of crisis: grin and bear it; enjoy life; variants of Gorgias' dadaism. Or as they say: Originality of speculative research (guess work) was exhausted with Arry Stotl. If one interpret Fiorentino's dicta in a terminology that he did not use, one wd. say that in his view this next circuit showed a frittering away of the totalitarian concepts: "Ethics and politics are no longer one" (? if that is the right way to translate *La Morale e La Politica*). Knowing is no longer the basic problem "of philosophy", "religious tendency" and concern with practical end sprout, and prevail over curiosity.

SOPHISTS

The interest in Fiorentino's comment is, at this point, his dissociation and contrast between the three concerns.

Down underneath the whole greek time had been a mythopoeic sense, and concern with the un-named. Kung did not pester his son with questions. It is recorded that he once asked the boy had he read the Odes. Pythagoras imposed five years silence. Can't write a book about that.

The reason for reading the Book of the Odes, the books of poetry, that is the books of basic poetry whether in Ideogram and collected by Kung (B.C. 500 or whatever) from the 15 hundred years before his time, or by me or even by Dr. Ward (English Poets) is that poetry is totalitarian in any confrontation with prose. There is MORE in and on two pages of poetry than in or on ten pages of any prose save the few books that rise above classification as anything save exceptions. Apart from the Four Classics: *Ta Hio* ("Great Learning"), *The Standing Fast in the Middle*, the *Analects*, say the three classics, or tack on Mencius, and Papa Flaubert, certain things are SAID only in verse. You can't translate 'em. The man who hath not . . . in his soul (yrs. Bill Shxpeare), Man gittin' Kulchur had better try poetry first. If he can't get it there he won't get it anyhow, though he may be a good sanitary engineer or succeed as a funeral director.

But nice men dislike bad poetry. Ho yuss! vurry true.

A defence of the Stoics might be built on these lines:

I. That Zeno excogitated a system of conduct that cd. be followed, or at least he himself was reputed to have practised his own injunctions (somewhere between birth, about 334 B.C. and demise *circa* 262).

There must have been some fibre in the teaching, as the "school" persisted, with various respected names emerging, Crisippus, Laelius, Scipio, Cicero more or less, Mucius Scaevola, Cato the younger. If Chemon didn't make a very good job of young Nero, he may have exceeded Zeno's prescription, or may have been a bad Stoic, at any rate the teaching left a trace, till it petered out in Marcus Aurelius.

II. It was a system of ethics with logic and cosmology as periphery.

They, the Stoics, did have some respect for terminology or "representation" which gathered or seized the object with clarity.

SOPHISTS

WITH emphasis on the individual object "reality existed only in the particular", "universals were to them subjective concepts formed by abstraction".

The syllogism was counted as "merely a grammatical form". It didn't pull any weight. Was merely useful for hypothesis and dissociation. Didn't PROVE anything. In that position lies the intellectual greatness of the school of the Porch. That the syllogism was not apodictic but anapodictic. After all the greek blather. Here they got their teeth into something.

Their four categories were: 1 the substratum, 2 the general quality, 3 the determined modification, and 4 the relatively determined modification. Each presupposing the one named before it.

I don't know that they need any plus marks here:

"Scientes quia rationale animal homo est, *et quia sensibilis anima et corpus est animal; et ignorantes de hac anima quid ea sit, vel de ipso corpore perfectam hominis cognitionem habere non possumus; quia cognitiones perfectio* uniuscuiusque terminatur ad ultima elementa", says Dante, continuing, "sicut magister sapientum in principio Physicorum testatur."

They (the Stoics) maintained a dualism between matter and energy, reminiscent of Aristotle's between matter and form, but did not feel them so separate. Their God was the active principle intrinsic in the world; their characteristics labelled by one of our german luminaries (Zeller) materialism, dynamism, pantheism.

God and soul, not immaterial "*noos*" (mind) but more subtle corporeal substances.

SOPHISTS

(Here we hook up with a good deal of mediaeval physics, arabic, and italian.)

God the architectural fire, *pur texnon*. Cicero says: all life is in this warmth, every animal, all that liveth, tho' earth-born, lives because in this warmth (calorem). From this principle the kinship of all things.

This cuts off Stoicism from Aristotelic God as pure form, the thought of thought, coming from without into the soul.

Out of fire, back to destruction by fire, i.e. to origin, this orbit, and start again. The soul a blob of the first fire, apospasma, a torn-off shred, stuck in the human chest whence the voice proceeded, the word a creative force.

The one individual soul an instrument of the world-soul lasting while the world-soul lasts, and after a new ekpyrosis to be again frayed off from the pneuma.

The body a dwelling-place. Fate acc. Seneca an inwoven series of causes. Predestination, prophesy etc.

Somewhere about here we bump into Kant and Calvin, and somewhere, in the lines preceding, we slip out of

"Knowledge is to know men."

Scaevola, pontifex maximus (died 82 B.C.), said there were three theologies: the poet's anthropomorphic and false, the philosopher's rational and true but not for use, the statesman's built on tradition and custom.

Herein self-proclaimed the defeat or defect and/or limit of the school.

For the gods exist. I am looking for decree of the Roman Senate (161 B.C.) which forbade the entrance of Stoics along with other exotic philosophies. Was it wisdom or mere bull-headed provincialism? I prefer to think it intuitive.

A wisdom built of the first and third theologies. We do not marry young ladies to trees. But there is truth in the custom. It has taken two thousand years to get round again to meditating on mythology.

Scaevola's phrase shows the leak, the point at which, for all the magnificence of their metaphysic (which they call physics) we have not

in the Stoics "logical, not for use".

SOPHISTS

The flaw in the lute, the crack in the ointment, the fly in the fly-wheel.

On this we can wrangle till doomsday, and eleven thousand volumes and eleven thousand virgins of Cologne, made out of eleven soldiers of the Xth legion etc.

Without gods, no culture. Without gods, something is lacking.

Some Stoics must have known this, and considered logic a mere shell outside the egg.

18. KULCHUR: PART ONE

When you don't understand it, let it alone. This is the copy-book maxim whereagainst sin prose philosophers, though it is explicit in Kung on spirits.

The mythological exposition permits this. It permits an expression of intuition without denting the edges or shaving off the nose and ears of a verity.

Byron regretted that Kung hadn't committed his maxims to verse. (This was a little hurried on B's part.) Any wise man knows a great deal he can't impart to a man of mediocre intelligence. Nevertheless all professors of philosophy tend to cut corners. A summary like the present sins worse than the professoriate, who however neglect Kung's first method of instruction (whereof 4 strands). Literature, practice of virtuous actions, no faking, fidelity. Kung's insistence on the ODES lifts him above all occidental philosophers.

It avoids the blather of rhetoric and the platonic purple patch (i.e. inferior poesy). Vide in our time Ogden's scholars,[1] often lucid in sentence, but feeble in concrete illustration. I mean they talk of language, of style etc. and don't know it when encountered. I am not *even* guying the whole Stoic show, or all attempts at "philosophic expression". I might, under duress, admit

[1] Basic English. "Psyche", etc.

that even "abstract", that is to say generalized, statement has, or might have, uses.

Plato the purple swine advocated the expulsion of "poets" (he may have meant Eddie Marsh's gang or the blokes who write in the *Observer*) from his projected republic but he failed to *specify* that he meant sloppy poets. He was, as I have already said, a "prose poet", that is a rhapsodist who shirked verse technique (musical technique).

In return I point out that even the Stoics were lured "out on the limb", they end up by talking about ekpyrosis, about which they knew no more than you, me or Heraclitus.

"From god the creative fire, went forth spermatic *logoi*, which are a gradual and organic distribution of an unique and spermatic word (logos)."

That's all very nice, and it even contains a provision against the process being merely mechanistic, but like all other generalized statements it tends *toward* mechanistic. Cadmus, or any other myth, knows where to stop, in the sense that the maker of myth don't try to cut corners, he don't try to level out all differences and state what he doesn't know.

On the other hand we also err in trying to FORCE abstract or general statement. We err in supposing that insincerity is peculiar to the man speaking. In nine cases out of ten we find an insincerity of the auditor, of the man who does NOT want to hear.

(e.g. Colonel X. indignant with foreign policy of his infamous government, but shuddering like babe before bogey-man, in the presence of the mildest economic truth. Definitely making protective gestures to avoid knowledge of what is known. Definitely putting a piece of paper from him, "as devil wd. avoid holy water".)

An imperfect broken statement if uttered in sincerity often tells more to the auditor than the most meticulous caution of utterance could.

The popular novelist H.: "I cdn't do anything like that. I got no depth."

Gorgias' *dada* has made men think. As the present is unknowable we roust amid known fragments of the past "to get light on it", to get an inkling of the process which produced what we encounter.

At immense remove from popular novelist, Binyon in 1908 or 1909: "I cdn't do that. Never can do anything QUICK." Later, in, I think, *The Flight of the Dragon*, or it may have been in the same conversation, "Slowness is beauty."

The sincere reader or auditor can find in those words a very profound intuition of verity. It is a personal aesthetic. The bare "wrong" phrase carries a far heavier charge of meaning than any timorous qualification such as "We admit that beauty can't be hustled, it cannot be scamped for time".

Again I reiterate that if my respected pubrs. expect of me, in accord with contract, a chronological exposition, they will have to wait for tables and an appendix, I have no intention of writing one HERE. Mr Matsumiya is doing his history of Japanese poetry as spring, summer, autumn, winter. J. J. in Ulysses treats his matter as in 24 hours.

I see no reason why the unities shd. be restricted to greek stage plays and never brought into criticism.

● ● ● ●

As to this morning's prod about mathematics? All right mathematics, apart from technical exposition: Arithmetic, Euclid and the Arabs (with Monsieur Ptolemy somewhere) or why Ptolemy?

"L'année julienne chez un peuple si éloigné des nations européennes, est à une époque qui remonte à 2,357 ans avant notre ère," at which time the Emperor Yao desired to regulate terrestrial law on heavenly model and therefore wished to know how the stars moved.

Also Descartes, and the blokes who worked on determinants, leading to mathematical physicists, radio, television, but awaiting opportunely an age of ethical degradation, the sewage of the nineteenth century, for their departments to go in extensively for immoral geometries, thereby depriving mathematics at least temporarily of that probity which it had hitherto possessed.

For up till now it had been the research into reality. But with the peculiar filth of the present age even mathematics shot out into unreality. No other mathematical basis being compatible with a public instruction that tolerates deliberate falsification of economic studies.

As an example of this time-spirit in this latter vein, one of Roosevelt's gang, now happily ex-, in a slimily flattering preface drew F. D.'s notice to F. D.'s greatness and then slithered from a discussion of dollars into one of pure numbers, as if . . .

A dollar being at that moment an elastic unit of no regular value. Whereas 1, 2, 3, 4, 5 do at least maintain a regular proportion between themselves, and stand as nomenclature for a determinate series.

This dogfish was probably unconscious, and merely compliant to the standards of bankery, whiggery and like spawn of usura.

The utter dastardliness of this age is nowhere more apparent than in X.'s falsification of a Douglas equation containing a time element. X. printed the statement with no element of time included, as if his (X.'s) statement were Douglas's.

Judas had the decency to hang himself. But no member of X.'s sect has even had the cleanness to apologize or repudiate.

And, quite naturally, millions starve or are kept on health-destroying short rations, diluted foods, Ersatz and offal.

> Gehazi by the hue that chills thy cheek
> And Pilate by the hue that sears thy hand
> . . . thy soul a manslayer's.

Mr Swinburne did not admire the use of the knout and other characteristically Russian methods of the Romanoff government, but future historians will find more excuse for Romanoffs than for the men who governed France and England from 1920 to 1937. During the period of infamy, the reigns of Harding, C. Coolidge, H. Hoover, America was largely acephalous. Russia is a barbarism. Spain is a barbarism. But France and England have not even these partial alibis, their government an usuriocracy, that is foetor, and its protagonists rotten.

19. KULCHUR: PART TWO

Without bothering about Mr Maeterlinck's *The Bee* or insisting on one's preference for Gourmont's method of conveying biological information one might, in considering the localization of sensibility either in apiary or human hive remember—"*gli uomini vivono in pochi*".

The rest regret elegiacally. Dr C. said: Think of what that wd. have meant. To have been able to study under Stevenson. (R. L. S. having been denied not university preferment, but a place on the lowest rung of it in America when he was broke in that godawful country during one of its stinkingest epochs.) G. Rogers used to tell of the gt. joke on himself. He fired Kipling, I think before he had even taken him on to a Philadelphia daily abomination. G. R. was on the *Inquirer* when I met him.

It is or has been said that the Florentines of the renaissance had the sense to let Raphael choose designs for a new town gate despite his youth (aetat 16). If true this indicates a high state of culture. I use "high state" in the laudative sense, not as we have it in D. C. Fox's ironic: "we have cannibalism among the high cultures" —apropos Helmut Petri's *Geldformen der Sudsee*. Fox continues: "You will find much of interest in it—even inflation when the whites imitated the native tokens with a factory product."

KULCHUR

As to the localization of sensibility, vide *Blast*. Vide the 1917 productions of "dada", vide the publications by Picabia from N. York of that time or about that time.

Form-sense 1910 to 1914. 15 or so years later Lewis discovered Hitler. I hand it to him as a superior perception. Superior in relation to my own "discovery" of Mussolini. I was after all living in Italy where, however, the decayed upper bourgeoisie and pseudostocracy in great part, and the weakling litterati, sic "not wops, mcrc pseudofrogs", did NOT sense the resurrection. Lewis on the other hand still retained London residence, that is to say inhabited for years at a time, and between foreign expeditions, the most sodden herd-sink known to humanity. (The vast running sore which crosses England on the meridian of Manchester is not known to humanity.)

"o'er dull and speechless tribes."

So far as I know Ford Madox Ford is the only living communicator of the Manchester Anschauung to the domain of outer-world consciousness. Ford has mentioned it in a book that a human being can read. I have forgotten what book. It may have been told me viva voce.

RAPPEL A L'ORDRE

Knowledge is NOT culture. The domain of culture begins when one HAS "forgotten-what-book".

Boccherini, Op. 8 N.5 (as played by the New Hungarian Four) is an example of culture. Bartok's Fifth

PART TWO

Quartet under same conditions (March 5th, 1937, Rapallo) is the record of a personal struggle, possible only to a man born in the 1880s.

It has the defects or disadvantages of my Cantos. It has the defects and disadvantages of Beethoven's music, or of as much of Beethoven's music as I can remember. Or perhaps I shd. qualify that: the defects inherent in a record of struggle.

Man is an over-complicated organism. If he is doomed to extinction he will die out for want of simplicity.

The Analects have endured. I don't know how many purgatories a man need pass through before he comes to ask himself; why?

The plainness of some of the anecdotes and reported remarks seems almost void of literary merit. They are simpler than the jokes in Boccaccio.

Kung said: "This music is utterly beautiful but . . ." and so forth.

Very well, the Boccherini Op. 8 N.5 was, on the day before yesterday's evening, utterly beautiful. No trace of effort remained.

It was impossible to "marvel" at the cleverness of the performers. By contrast the Bartok was "too interesting". Given the fact that "no one" cd. grasp the whole work at a first or even a second hearing, one did wonder what "in hell" wd. occur if any other musicians attempted to play it. Koromzay says the "Kolisch" have played it. He says they were marvellous. That makes two organizations of four men each who can deal with this new musical situation.

KULCHUR

That is no more a "culture" than the invention of a new smelting process is "culture". It is, or may be, a link in a chain of causation.

Culture, "A" culture was. An age of infamy, usury and the hyper-usura of the money racket, was and is not yet burnt out of a carious Europe.

The Vth Quartet may "go into a culture", as gold dust may go into a coin.

The old guardian at Sta Maria dei Miracoli says of the carving "It just seems that nobody *has* been able since . . ."

That refers to a culture. The perception of a whole age, of a whole congeries and sequence of causes, went into an assemblage of detail, whereof it wd. be impossible to speak in terms of magnitude.

Boccherini is "late". I haven't the latest massed catalogues of the music trade, but I imagine one must still say of his Quintets, as at the date of Lavignac's consummate manual, *Musique et Musiciens*, "*Beaucoup sont encore inédits et le resteront probablement.*"

20. MARCH 12th

A civilized man is one who will give a serious answer to a serious question. Civilization itself is a certain sane balance of values.

The VOU club supplies me such an answer, not only to my particular question: what is young Japan doing? but to a half dozen others whereon a deal of occidental ink has flowed vainly. The club was started by some admirers of "that great harmless artist Eric Satie". Katue Kitasono writes me:

"Now the most interesting subject to us is the relation between imagery and ideoplasty. Contemporary young poets are all vaguely conscious of, and worry about this. Some of them went over again to its extremity and returned. Others gave up exploration, and found out a queer new country, remaining only as amateur thinkers. But anyone whose standing ground is in literature, can do nothing for it if he ignores the system of literature.

"The formation of poetry takes such a course as:

A. language   B. imagery   C. ideoplasty

That which we vaguely call poetical effect means, generally, ideoplasty which grows out of the result of imagery. Man has thought out to make a heart-shaped space with two right angles.[1] This great discovery in plastic, also that of the conics in mathematics are two mysteries brought by man's intellect.

"The relation between imagery and ideoplasty makes us suppose the heart-shaped space which is born by the connection of the same mysterious two curves. We standardized these two curves and got a necessity.

"What we must do first for imagery is (in this order) collection, arrangement and combination. Thus we get the first line: 'a shell, a typewriter and grapes' in which we have an aesthetic feeling. But there is not (in it) any further development. We add the next line and then another aesthetic feeling is born. Thus all the lines are combined and a stanza is finished. This means the completion of imagery of that stanza and then ideoplasty begins.

"This principle can be applied to poems consisting of several stanzas. In that case ideoplasty is formed when the last stanza is finished.

"Though it cannot be allowed as orthodox of poetry that imagery is performed by ideoplasty."

● ●

This is where the present commentator suggests that his reader pause for reflection.

● ●

"This violence is dared often by religionists, politicians,

[1] Point where the occidental pedlars of imaginary geometries fell down.

and satirists. Morality poems, political poems and satirical poems are written, almost without exception, with such an illogical principle.

"The phenomena in our life proceed, through our senses to our experiences, perceptions, and intuitions. It is intuition rationally that provides the essentials for imagery, and it is the method of poetry that materializes intuitions perceptively and combines. Consequently, exact imagery and ideoplasty are due to an exact method. Pure and orthodox poetry cannot exist without this theory."

Jan. 6th (or thereabouts), 1937.

Mr Kitasono has arrived at a clearer and gentler statement than I had seen before the arrival of the brief essay here quoted. What he says is not alien to something I once wrote re Dr Williams' poems, nor is it contrary to Gaudier's sculptural principles. I do not for a moment suppose Mr Kitasono wd. insist on the "theory" being *consciously* held. Intuition may even provide the essentials in this domain.

Against this is set the sickly and pasty-faced appearance of the lower deck men as seen some years ago, here, Rapallo, when the British fleet used to put into this harbour. "Can't have 'em always around on deck," said the chaplain.

A veteran submarine commander described to me the as he called it ludicrous appearance of himself and companions (with mimicry) "like dogs with their tongue hanging out", when the oxygen was exhausted.

He finally went aground on the base of a lighthouse

after all night steering blind by instruments, an error of say four yards at a harbour entrance. Then he couldn't blow out the bottom of his boat because the shells weren't geared to explode so near the point of discharge. One of the lot has a national monument. The comandante remarked of the old navies: "The sick-bay where Nelson died was about four feet high, so that Nelson was the only one there who *stava un poco ad agio*."

21. TEXTBOOKS

I have just sent out a note on this year's Italian textbooks. It is unlikely that the "advanced" will look into these textbooks. These books won't do very much harm. The one designed for children of eleven might even reveal the reason why Christianity has not, as a rule, in Italy degenerated into that pest, eccentricity, accompanied by oppressions, witch-burnings, that it has so often become in countries not built on a "classic" basis. The Mediterranean moderation appears in a Prayer for Rain:

> *O God, in whom we live and move and are, concede a restoring rain, so that we, aided sufficiently in our earthly needs, may reach up with great trust to eternal things. So be it.*

Cosi sia, is less rhetorical than Amen. It is also Italian.

A prayer for serenity (that is fair weather):

> *We implore, omnipotent God, thy clemency, so that thou having made to cease the flooding rain, shalt show to us through the calm sky the hilarity of thy face. In the name of Jesus Christ our Saviour. So be it.*

Hilarity. The italian is just that: *l'ilarità del Tuo Volto.*

These seem to me to belong rather to the universal

141

religion of all men, than to any sect or fad of religion. This universality was, and perhaps still is, one of the ideals of the "Church".

After these and a few more prayers I find *Il Cantico del Sole* of St Francis; here and there a verse quotation, Fogazzaro on the bells, a bit of Manzoni, "*I Templi*" of Silvio Pellico, a bit of psalm and a rather beautiful passage from the Mass translated into Italian, so that the Mass shall not be mere mumbo jumbo in latin. St Francis' poem is, or shd. be, in any early Italian anthology. The anecdotes of the few Saints are such as cd. be in any school reader. They are of commendable human actions, not of eccentricities or excesses. It is impossible to tell everything in one school-book, if Mazzini is not attacked for fanaticism, his constructive acts are recorded, and Cavour is praised with masterly succinctness: through deep study and long travels he came to understand the needs of the Italian people. . . . As head of the govt. he improved with wise provisions the condition of agriculture, industry and commerce. . . .

Space does not permit me to give an exhaustive study of the Italian school system, but I do not think the régime has anything to fear from equanimous examination of it . . . until one gets up to the somnolent universities, and there IF you compare 'em with those in our own "blessed" etc. country. . . .

I have no idea where "the textbook racket" has now got to in America. I do know that I have on my desk an Italian child's schooling for a grade, contained in one book, eleven lire, 648 pages plus a geographical supplement. Illustrated, with not very brilliant half-tones of a nature to interest anyone: cathedrals, paintings, savages, farm machinery, animals, magnets, fossils, an appalling amount of arithmetic aimed at practical life.

Italy, a.d. 1937, anno XV, 52 million lire in fines on financial traitors, 5 million lire in gold seized from a gang of financiers engaged in smuggling gold and bonds.

22. SAVOIR FAIRE

To act on one's definition? What concretely do I myself mean to do? I mean to say that one measure of a civilization, either of an age or of a single individual, is what that age or person really wishes to *do*. A man's hope measures his civilization. The attainability of the hope measures, or may measure, the civilization of his nation and time.

I hope to know the *Odyssey* better. I hope to read the *Odyssey* and the *Ta Hio*, someday, without need to look into dictionaries, and, beyond the *Ta Hio*, the Odes, on Kung's recommendation. The first two I have by me, with such books of reference as allow me to get a good deal of their meaning. For the third, sic: the Odes, the English cribs give me NOTHING, or else a mere annoyance. Beyond the dead English something extends, per forza, extends or Kung wd. not have told his own son to read the old poems.

Great intelligence attains again and again to great verity. The Duce and Kung fu Tseu equally perceive that their people need poetry; that prose is NOT education but the outer courts of the same. Beyond its doors

144

are the mysteries. Eleusis. Things not to be spoken save in secret.

The mysteries self-defended, the mysteries that *can* not be revealed. Fools can only profane them. The dull can neither penetrate the secretum nor divulge it to others.

Science is hidden. The layman can only attain conic sections by labour. He can only attain the secretum by greater labour, by an attrition of follies, carried on until perception is habit. Every knowledge in our time has its outer courts and its portals. The pons asinorum is but one bridge of many.

"*Il sait vivre*," said Brancusi of Léger. This must also be said of the catechumens before they pass the third door. It is quite useless for me to refer men to Provence, or to speculate on Erigena in the market place.

"Peasants or Pheasants?" said the Editor, "Oh, a gloomy cus', was he (Verhaeren) I don't think we'd better touch it."

Editor all right in his place, but not a man with whom to talk of John Donne.

No, I do not regret not having learned greek better in school. A fellow named Spenser recited a long passage of *Iliad* to me, after tennis. That was worth more than grammar when one was 13 years old. Three of the most "passionate hellenists" of my acquaintance knew almost no greek before they were 19 or 20. Dr Rouse on the other hand knows the *Odyssey* backward, but perhaps private correspondence wd. show that his latest stimulus to know more of it, has not come from greek scholars.

SAVOIR FAIRE

If this be the case, it will surprise no one whomsoever. E. A. said to me long years ago, to tease me, that of course if I had to look up words in the dictionary I might find more meaning than he had.

As perhaps every great line of Homer has had its comment and praise, it is footless to say such and such commendation has been withheld from the *Odyssey*, or that such and such qualities have passed unnoticed.

Yet in rough average I shd. say that its lessons for novelists may have recd. insufficient attention. The imaginary spectator, the study in moeurs, Castiglione's Il Cortegiano element, the knowledge of the whole life has been hammered by dozens of critics but perhaps not been sufficiently probed. The things that the *polumetis* knew were the things a man then *needed* for living. The bow, the strong stroke in swimming, the how-to-provide *and* the high hat, the carriage of the man who knew how to rule, who had been everywhere, Weltmensch, with "ruling caste" stamped all over him, so that a red, cracked skin and towseled hair as he came out of the underbrush left him "never at loss". He might as well have met Nausikaa in gibus and opera cloak.

And as Zeus said: "A chap with a mind like THAT! the fellow is one of us. One of US."

I hope that elsewhere I have underscored and driven in the greek honour of human intelligence

"Who even dead yet hath his mind entire".

Even roughnecks like Kipling and Hemingway have, in their obscure way, paid tribute to intelligence. I admit

146

they don't keep that flag up much of the time. But you cd. at least in Hemingway's case get him to admit that mind has its uses. The careful and alert reader will find admission in Hemingway's writing.

The stupidity of my age is nowhere more gross, blatant and futile than in the time-lag for getting Chinese texts into bilingual editions. The *Ta Hio* is so edited. It may even have been so pirated, and if so piracy is lesser sin than the continued blithering of University presses, the whole foetid lot of 'em, men with NO human curiosity, gorillas, primitive congeries of protoplasmic cells without conning towers, without nervous organisms more developed than that of amoebas.

Fenollosa died in 1908.

Perhaps Tokio will take pity on us, perhaps the best hundred books in ideogram will be provided with an english (or european) crib before we are many more decades deader, older, stupider and void of perception. At least we shd. have in current editions the Odes, the *Ta Hio* and the Four Classics, *Li Po* (Rihaku) and at least 400 pages of the post-Confucian great poets, and a few dozen Noh dramas. We shd. have AT *least* an anthology of the Japanese writers now living. We shd. NOT be at the mercy of single translators. We shd. have bilingual editions of this lot and MORE done better than the few pages in my last edition of The Chinese Written Character, but on that system. The ideogramic text, and under or beside each ideogram an explanation. Or in case of very common words, an interlinear translation with notes on the less familiar signs.

SAVOIR FAIRE
AND

We shd. get on with microphotographic editions of the vast treasure of music now lying hid or monopolized in our libraries, as for example the mss. of Vivaldi and Boccherini, and even of the masters now "published" but in editions which leave every good musician in doubt, when one gets back to ciphered bases, abbreviations, things left to interpretation of performers contemporary with the composers.

● ● ● ●

To the best of my knowledge young Bridson was the only poet to try constructive criticism on my *ABC of Reading*, he asked why particular authors (naming them) were omitted and whether someone or other cdn't. replace something else. This, the careful student will observe, is the kind of answer I asked for.

I did not speak of Shakespeare in that opusculus, and still believe the bard is both read and ably discussed by others almost sufficiently. The VOU club thought that my meaning was clear and that they at least were sufficiently conversant with Elizabethan drama not to be led astray by my indication of other peaks in our poetry.

Whether England yet or still reads Shakespeare adequately as poet, I do not know. Certainly in my time few read him adequately either as poetic technician or as knower of knowledge as in his own day available.

The sonnets as technical prelude, exercise ground preceding the plays? The opening fanfare in *Pericles* perhaps better than any sonnet? Or perhaps this query

148

indicates merely my component of error, my human frailty in marking out my own particular garden where contemporary criticism pullulated less abundantly.

Lombard law behind Venetian penalties against mayhem. The ethical barrage versus usura. The undercurrents in the *Merchant of Venice*, glossed over in Victorian treatment and popular acceptance of that play, in the low and vile era "of usury" the century of Victoria and Franz-Josef reaching its maximum squalor in such administrations as that of U.S. Grant, Herbert Hoover and Baldwin. For we are not yet out of this filthiness by a long chalk.

"Is your gold rams and ewes?"

I suppose a man might still learn from Hesiod if he had no other access to agricultural knowledge. The civilized farmer will want to compare today's knowledge with Hesiod's, the civilized merchant will want to compare monetary practice with what Shakespeare and Dante and/or Demosthenes knew. "Usury as Mahomet forbade." The evil wrought on the arts by pustulence in the system of money. All these are part of the
POLLON D'ANTHROPŌN IDEN,
of the serious questions whereto civilized men, as distinct from prig, pimp or nitwit, will give serious answers.

Of the Books that a man would read. The books that I shall, I hope, reread, with more diligence, and a deeper comprehension.

Homer, Ovid, or Golding's and Marlowe's versions of the *Changes* and the *Amores*, Gavin Douglas with reference to the latin original, at any time Shakespeare's Histories, *Pericles, Hamlet, The Tempest.*

Ronald Storrs is a civilized man and a brother to any man, whatever his politics; he at least reads the *Odyssey*, the *Divina Commedia* and something or other of Shakespeare once every year in the original. If every other provincial governor did as much the British Empire wd. stink notably less in the world's nostril. It might even be clean.

I still think one shd. hear the total of Mozart's violin sonatas once yearly. Palotai with perhaps larger musical learning thinks once in every two or three years wd. be enough. That merely means that he wd. cover a larger field.

Nobody, in 1938, knows anything of Vivaldi. A few (less than six) scholars have approximately respectable ideas of his compositions. Not one of them has even read through all of his composition. You cd. probably read most of it in Turin and Dresden. For Boccherini the job is more difficult. I don't even know where his work is. And I doubt if anyone else does.

Civilized man (1938) has an approximate idea of the inadequacy of Larousse; of the so called *Encyclopœdia Britannica*, and of the *Encyclopédie de Musique et Dictionnaire du Conservatoire.* Though the french works are commendable.

23. THE NEW LEARNING: PART TWO

I was about to write: "HELL!! A new learning imposes itself!" A new learning is necessary, is demanded by every one of the few hundred sufferers who have a respectable decent and clean curiosity.

The Forschungsinstitut in Frankfurt, thanks largely to Leo Frobenius, drives *toward* a new learning. Bilingual texts of the classics cd. be turned out in a few years. At least in the form of drafts, with blanks left for their editor's own lacunae, and no dishonour.

The microphotographic edition of music shd. NOT be delayed. It OUGHT, in a decent world, to be WELL under weigh before this present booklet gets to the print shop. Neither of these campaigns puts anyone out of a job. Microphoto strips in the margin in no way exclude the necessity of proper engraved or photo-engraved editions, critical editions, repristinations, fittings of the stuff to modern convenience.

If Fr. Di Milano and Besard for their own delight and that of their hearers chiselled down Dowland's and Janequin's choral works to something they cd. play on the lute, Münch has an equal right, and is equally laudable in settling the same eternal beauty in fiddle part. If the piano obscures the fiddle, I have a perfect right to

THE NEW LEARNING

HEAR Janequin's intervals, his melodic conjunctions from the violin solo.

"I made it out of a mouthful of air"

wrote Bill Yeats in his heyday. The *forma*, the immortal *concetto*, the concept, the dynamic form which is like the rose pattern driven into the dead iron-filings by the magnet, not by material contact with the magnet itself, but separate from the magnet. Cut off by the layer of glass, the dust and filings rise and spring into order. Thus the *forma*, the concept rises from death

> The bust outlasts the throne
> The coin Tiberius.

Janequin's concept takes a third life in our time, for catgut or patent silver, its first was choral, its second on the wires of Francesco Milano's lute. And its ancestry I think goes back to Arnaut Daniel and to god knows what "hidden antiquity".

The Persian hunting scene, the Arabian ribibi. Here, that is, in Janequin we find ground for one of the basic dissociations of music. If I have said it ten times in one way or another, nothing wd. excuse me for omitting restatement.

As from the floral background in Pisanello's Este portrait (The Louvre), from the representation of visible things in Pietro di Borgo (della Francesca), there is a change to pattern and arabesque, there is an end to the Mediaeval Anschauung, the mediaeval predisposition.

In music there is representation of the sole matter wherein music can be "literally" representative, namely sound. Thus the violinist reading Janequin's music transposed said: a lot of birds, not one bird alone.

Down on through Vivaldi and Couperin there is this kind of music, music of representative outline.

And in distinction to it is music of structure, as J. S. Bach in fugue or keyboard toccata, or Hindemith today in his Schwannendreher.

Not contradictory, not hostile one to the other, but two blessed categories, each for a particular excellence. As exclusive, to take a simile on one line only, not as simile of kind or of a like sort of difference, but a simile focussed on mutual exclusivity as indicating its *degree*— as exclusive "as Velasquez and Ambrogio Praedis".

I have heard Bach described as barocco, and in a sense this indicates profound apperception. Bach builds up from the bottom, as distinctly as Wren did. In Bach's case the result is magnificent.

Infinitely preferable to romantic draping and flaccid suspension.

Materially speaking St Hilaire is as much built up from the ground as St Pauls.

This fable teaches the danger of metaphorical expressions in criticism of art.

There is no doubt that Bach's spirit is in great part that of a robust material world. Vivaldi moves, in his adagios, in the spheres of the Paradiso (Dante's Paradise)

and then suddenly thinking of that parallel one finds that the musicians are playing Bach, not Vivaldi. Old Johannes has got there.

THE NEW LEARNING

One's speculation as to whether any man who wasn't both spoiled priest and operatic impresario could have contained Vivaldi's adagios, the long sailing melody, the gaiety, the pre-Mozart; one's speculation is hurled topsyturvy.

Net result one (the present explorer) had at least one taste in common with Johann Sebastian. Bach approved and the present writer approves of Vivaldi.

As to the relation of Bach and Vivaldi, of Italian and German music, I am ready to throw all the reference books into the scrap-heap, with all their copy-book mottoes.

Berenson and co. may know a little about the italianate Flemings and vice versa, Memling, Cosimo Tura etc. and how the nordic brought his eye south, where who taught which next man. When it comes to melody, which is after all what I (a damned poet anyhow) care about, I back the Italians.

Perhaps no Italian cd. ever carry as many melodic lines in his head at once and make so firm a total "structure", namely lateral movement, in time space as cd. Johann Sebastian? Mr Porpora's German editor has touched up Mr Porpora? (David, Hochschule der Violin.)

And in a sense it doesn't matter a damn. In another, enormously.

I suspect up to the hilt that the infant Mozart did not enflame all Italy, because THEN Italy knew so much more, more that is, about that kind of beauty in music, than it does today in the back slosh of Mascagni and Puccini. . . .

and to give hell its due, Puccini knows how to write for the bawlers. I mean he KNOWS how. If that's what you like, be damned to you for liking it, but I take off my hat (along with your own beastly bowler) to the artifex.

After having listened to that mouthing and yowling I understand why it is difficult to raise an audience to listen to the singing of better poetry than Puccini had ever heard of (except in a library catalogue).

Lawes and Campion will not gather 10,000 groundlings. Not in our time.

Repeating from a forgotten article: after working in the Vatican library and comparing the civility, in the high fine sense of the word, of that ambience, I said to Wm. Yeats: Anticlericalism is no good (it being known between us fairly well what we did and did not believe). I said: I can see a time when we may all of us have to join together, that is everyone possessed of any degree of civilization. We will have to join the Monsignori against Babbitt.

"But CONfound it!" said the propagator of the Celtic Twilight, "In my country the Church IS Babbitt."

For the duration of this essay Babbitt is Sinclair Lewis as well as Sinc's affable and superficial caricature of American nullity. Babbitt is the state of mind which tolerates the existence of England and America as we have known those countries. It is the state of mind which can see without boiling, a circumjacence, that tolerates Mellon and Mellonism, the filth of american govt. through the reigns of Wilson, Harding, Coolidge and the supremely uncultivated, uneducated gross Hoover, the England that swelters through the same period and the France of that period, and every man who has held high office in these countries without LOATHING the concessions made to foetor and without lifting hand against them, and against the ignorance wherein such mental squalor is possible.

If there is anybody who disagrees more strongly with some of the details of contemporary Italian and German views and proposed laws on conjugality than I do, I am unaware of that man's existence. But at least the italian editorial writer last under my eye, did have the sense to speak of spiritual union, and to recognize the difficulty of striking a practical average (for making a law) between the state and the individual.

The dirty childishness of the English and American mind, and in especial their editorial writing in our time, does not face ANYTHING with courage.

For years one has diagnosed the blither of American discussion as in part an ignoring of the demarcation between state and individual.

In the last lustrum a rare few ang/saxs may have recognized the problem, or some problem along this frontier.

The mysteries will never be legal, in the sense that one will never be able to legislate them into an average, or a rule of thumb, for the multitude. The law should keep from them.

Until the power of hell which is usura, which is the power of hogging the harvest, is broken, that is to say until clean economic conditions exist and the abundance is divided in just and adequate parts among all men, legal enforcements and interjections of the legal finger in relations between man and woman, will be deformation and evil, and no lawgiver will be able to cure the bone disease of society by bits of sticking plaster and paint.

I reviewed P. B.'s novel, which she thought psychological. Every character, whether psychiatrist or patient, in the insane asylum there depicted was driven off the norm by economic pressure of one sort or another. An enthusiast for health and the open air, Calvert, is driven (current issue *Open Road*) into advocacy of abortion, which is the last crime any normal and healthy woman wd. commit SAVE UNDER ECONOMIC PRESSURE. The punishment is, I agree, sufficient without the law's interference. The law for two centuries has been pimp for the usurer. By the same post we have a british slave-owner preaching morality, not from love of God, order or beauty, but because lorry girls diminish the utility to him of his hirelings.

A civil society is one where Strength comes with enjoyment. I am not trespassing into politics with this statement. A democracy run by clean men, decent men, honest men cd. or shd. attain Kraft durch Freude quite as well as a "dictatorship". Naturally a foetid and sham democracy doesn't. This is due to foetor, not to its —ocracy.

For a millenium the Roman Church did next to nothing to educate Spain.

The catholic rump and rubble have paid in blood.

THE NEW LEARNING

Democracies have for a century failed lamentably to educate the people and keep the people aware of the absolutely rudimentary necessities of democracy. The first being monetary literacy. They pay in the festering hell of England's degraded areas.

Padre José's name was enough to get me a photo of the Cavalcanti ms. in the Escorial (that was before Spain started killing off Spaniards with foreign assistance). Similar degree of civilization does NOT inhere in Cornell University.

Russia is not a civilized nation. Russia was a nation with a few cultivated persons perched near its apex. Ditto Spain. A few chaps in Madrid read Rémy de Gourmont. These litterati were neither numerous enough, vigorous enough nor sufficiently "all round" men to "save Spain". "Spain, a rabbit," says E. Gimenez Caballero, quite recently.

24. EXAMPLES OF CIVILIZATION

The Tempio Malatestiano is both an apex and in verbal sense a monumental failure. It is perhaps the apex of what one man has embodied in the last 1000 years of the occident. A cultural "high" is marked.

In a Europe not YET rotted by usury, but outside the then system, and pretty much against the power that was, and in any case without great material resources, Sigismundo cut his notch. He registered a state of mind, of sensibility, of all-roundness and awareness.

He had a little of the best there in Rimini. He had perhaps Zuan Bellin's best bit of painting. He had all he cd. get of Pier della Francesca. Federigo Urbino was his Amy Lowell, Federigo with more wealth got the seconds. The Tempio was stopped by a fluke? or Sigismundo had the flair when to stop it? You get civilization in the seals. I mean it was carried down and out into details. The little wafer of wax between the sheets of letter paper in Modena is, culturally, level with the Medallions. The Young Salustio is there in the wax as Isotta and Sigismundo in the bronze discs of Pisanello. Intaglio existed. Painting existed. The medal has never been higher. All that a single man could, Malatesta managed *against* the current of power.

You can contrast it with St Hilaire. You can contrast

it with ANY great summit done WITH the current of power.

If ever Browning had ready an emphasis for his "reach and grasp" line it was waiting for him in Rimini. And the Malatesta had his high sense of justice, for I think Gemisto wd. be even more forgotten without Sigismundo's piety.

Here is indeed a very pretty field for speculation and research. Gemisto's conversation at Ferrara.

You can get some very nice dinner scenes.

Cunizza at Cavalcanti the elder's.

Gemisto during the conference of the Eastern and Western churches. Gemisto commenting on Xenophon. Trying to work out the genealogy of the Gods. Ficino, by comparison, merely a valedictorian? But brought up by Cosimo, endowed by Cosimo to Cosimo's credit.

Valla hammering on terminology, upsetting the donation of Constantine because Constantine COULDN'T have written it, any more than Valla could have written a Ford model T advertisement. Valla ending up as Papal secretary, because the Papacy needed a latinist, and was still sufficiently intelligent to KNOW that the Papacy needed a latinist.

Pico Mirandola comes out a poor fifth in such company. Not that one need disparage Pico or even Mr Pater's conception of Pico (with Mirandola's prize paragraph nicely lifted from its multifarious context).

Pater infinitely more civil than Addington Symonds because he is less DULL. In fact he is not dull in the least. He is adolescent reading, and very excellent bait.

EXAMPLES OF CIVILIZATION

The supreme crime in a critic is dullness. The supreme evil committable by a critic is to turn men away from the bright and the living. The ignominious failure of ANY critic (however low) is to fail to find something to arouse the appetite of his audience, to read, to see, to experience.

It is the critic's BUSINESS *adescare* to lure the reader. Caviar, vodka, any hodge-podge of oddities that arouses hunger or thirst is pardonable to the critic.

He is not there to satiate. A desire on his part to point out his own superiority over Homer, Dante, Catullus and Velasquez, is simple proof that he has missed his vocation. Any ass knows that Dante was not a better racing driver than Barney Oldfield, and that he knew less of gramophones than the late Mr Edison.

25. BOOKS "ABOUT"

Reading books about Shxpeare wd. never become a favourite pastime with me, nevertheless I do, loosely speaking, agree with most of those I have looked at, this is, I take it, because no one is likely at this date to write a book on the subject and manage to get it published unless he has thought more about some factor or detail than does the average reader, or given it more attention than one usually does in casual perusal. No one is writing about W. S. in the hope of boosting Shakespeare's sales, of forcing him on the public for sake of getting him fed. No one can hope to corner the topic. It is equally true that I can not now recall any criticism of Shakespeare save what I heard in college and a little by Wyndham Lewis (author of *Tarr* and of *Cantleman's Spring Mate*). Plus one attempt at "attribution" which wd. have implied that Rutland or someone began writing the plays at the age of 12, and produced 'em at the rate of twins yearly (approx.) until premature demise.

The boredom by Baconians occurs, I take it, because these suburbanites are hell bent on distracting attention from the text and its meaning.

The study of savages has in our time come to be regarded as almost the sole guide to anglo-saxon psychology. If we reflect on African and oriental vagueness as to time, if we reflect on what is often called "feminine" lack of punctuality among our more irritating acquaintance, it shd. not unduly astonish us that the idea of a MEASURE of value has taken shape slowly in human consciousness. Savages or small boys swapping jack-knives ... Mischung von Totemismus ... Papua-Sprachen . . . die Idee eines Wertmessers noch nicht scharf ausgepragt (Helmut Petri, *Die Geldformen der Sudsee*). The idea of a measure of value not yet sharply defined. (Auspragen also monetize or coin.)

The degeneracy of the very coin as an object to look at, sets in early in Europe. Greek money is still ornamental. The medal emerges again with Pisanello and co.

The real use of gold? false teeth (diminishing), spectacle frames (largely superseded but still valid), ornament ... partially superseded by platinum. Reburial of gold is not a sign of trust but of MIStrust, a vote of nonconfidence in man and more especially in the honesty of a government, or at best an assertion of the supposed damnability and vileness of one's national neighbours still justified in both cases though not immeasurably.

An England without .... wd. or shd. less impel other nations to hoarding. A few usurers in the grand reptilian line make any nation a peril.

A few "financiers" unjailed are enough in a few generations to pervert the whole press of a nation and to discolour its education (for Regius professoriate ... vide Hollis' *Two Nations*).

No adequate study yet exists of the effect of Law-worship as pervertive. It wd., I think, be impossible wholly to segregate racial tropism in such a study. The near-eastern races that have evolved code-worship in lieu of truth worship, form, or could be categoried as a group to themselves—to be treated either re tropism pure, or as examples of arrested development.

When a code ceases to be regarded as an approximate expression of principles, or of a principle, and is exalted to the rank of something holy in itself, perversion ineluctably sets in. The attempt to square nature with the code, leads perforce to perverted thinking. The Mohammedans killed off their own civilization, or at least truncated and maimed it out of 90% of its vitality. All through an exaltation of conformity and orthodoxy.

Code-worship appertains properly to tribes arrested at nomad level.

I can not over-emphasize the assertion that the Catholic Church rotted when its hierarchy ceased to believe its own dogma. Cavour was the best XIXth century friend of the Church. The Church rises with the rise of civilization around it. There is an infinite gulf between the Italian church in our time and what was in Cardinal Antonelli's. Shaw made at least one valid assertion in saying: conversion of savage to Xtianity = conversion of Xtianity to the savage.

Civilized Christianity has never stood higher than in Erigena's "Authority comes from right reason". That is Xtianity which Leibniz cd. have accepted. Bossuet was no nearer the human level of decency than numerous leader writers in our day. A tumid rhetorical parasite, hardly better than some University Presidents.

And, as I said to the Reverendo the day before yesterday, "Not that I want to prove Aquinas wrong. I merely think him unsound."

The shallow mind that wants to blur or obliterate the distinction between faith (intuition) and reason.

M. Descartes . . . as usual.

Mlle X. "Mais, moi, M. Descartes, qui ne pense pas?"

You may assert in vindication of values registered in idiom itself that the man who "isn't all there" has only a partial existence. But we are by that time playing with language? as valuable as playing tennis to keep oneself limber.

Even Erigena's dictum can be examined. Authority can in material or savage world come from accumulated prestige based on intuition. We have trust in a man because we have come to regard him (in his entirety) as sapient and well-balanced. We play his hunch. We make an act of faith. But this is not what Erigena meant, and in any case it does not act in contradiction to his statement, but only as an extension of it.

Shakespeare gets TO the far orientals because he does not shut his meaning into egg-shells. Or at least . . . picked up I can't remember where . . . the memory of an oriental viva voce defending Shakespeare's formlessness on the ground that he reached out and merged into nature.

One is here on very dangerous ground. The ideogram

is in some way so much more definite, despite its root filaments, than a shell-case definition.

I pointed out in *Noh* that we err very often in supposing that our system of categories is the only possible kind. A persian rug-maker can have colour categories finer than ours. You must see what the other fellow is using as demarcation before assuming him vague or muddled.

I am, in these paragraphs, doing no better than any other DAMNED writer of general statements. I am too far from concrete and particular objects to write any better than Bertie Russell or any other flat-chested highbrow.

I take it ROSSONI gets more DONE than all the rest of us economists because he does NOT allow himself to be too far distracted from the particular and material realities of his grain, his wool, his Ersatz wool made out of cow's milk.

He saw the point of stamp-scrip in ten minutes and started to think out how it wd. FIT into the corporate system. NO! the state couldn't issue it. The *corporazioni* could. The state wd. *fare il suo affare*, on the sale of the stamps. In six weeks Por had two articles out, one in Rossoni's *La Stirpe* and the other in, I think, *Regime Corporativo*.

The superiority of these Corporate State fellows over Gesellites and Doug/ites is that they are not the least afraid to discuss other ideas. At present date of writing 16th March 1937, the economic sectaries are all drying on the stalk from ortodossia praecox. They have been hit by the disease prematurely.

BOOKS "ABOUT"

"*Moneta*" in Rossoni's lexicon meant gold. *La vera moneta è oro. Moneta* in Italian therefore equalling COIN in English.

I was free to talk stamp-scrip if I wanted to call it medium of exchange. If I talked about it too easily, and especially if I tried to explain it to men of inadequate comprehension, they wd. merely think me a lunatic.

All of which was perfectly true. And at the time of this conversation I didn't carry an ADEQUATE definition of money in my hip pocket. For the purpose of that conversation "medium of exchange" had to serve.

Instead of his Seven Heretics ("Tomorrow's Money"), Butchart should have . . .? No I withdraw. Butch did a good job, a bit of necessary clearing of British underbrush. The NEXT juxtaposition of views shd. comprise

The Canonist doctrine of the just price,

Gesell,

Douglas, both brought up to date and into focus, and

The actual achievements of the totalitarian states which won't stay still and will not be, at the date of publication six months or a year hence, what they are today, March 16th anno XV Era Fascista. With Por's announcement of what he expects to print in six weeks time, lying before me.

Date line: 16th March 1937. Civilization having attained Rossoni's *amassi*, the *bonifica* etc. That is, the grain-pools, grain and wool assembled, middlemen's extortion and the wiles of monopolists knocked out, and profit over pre-calculation to be returned to the farmers.

BOOKS "ABOUT"

Possibility of eliminating the superstition of taxes, a total change in the how, envisaged. The state able to USE these materials as it needs them without other taxation for that end. The VOU club in Tokio, the Vegh, Palotai, Halmos, Koromzay quartet, Münch-Rudge musical research. A couple of new reviews, one extant or hoped for.

Mr Egon Heath affably notes that in an earlier essay I recommended no original works by Russian, German or English poets. But that it (the vol) was admirably calculated to mould the reader's mind to a Sino-Latin pattern of culture.

My Japanese colleagues thought a normal reader wd. not go astray on my *A B C* as they had already read Shakespeare. Mr Heath is speaking of an earlier sketch.

I shdn't. try to teach a duck to swim. I assume the English reader has already to his sorrow or whatever (usually muddle) a "mind" unformed in the English manner, hereditarily unformed, and that the blithering pea-soup of russianness wd. worsen it.

NO form ever yet having come out of Russia that hadn't first been taken in there from elsewhere (vide De Schloezer's *Strawinsky*).

A german component exists, but it wd. be difficult to find "form" originating in English or German poetry after the Seafarer (ang. sax) and the Minnesingers.

Chaucer's form is from the Mediterranean basin.

26. ON ANSWERING CRITICS

The idea that one shd. not, is sound in 99% of cases where a work of art is concerned. Not re criticism. If one has written a poem or painted a picture one's critic is either right or wrong. If right in blaming a fault, it is up to the artist to correct it, or do his next work without it. If wrong, the critic is possibly an ass, in any case the work outlasts him, and he is not worth a reply.

Exception: attacks by the very young and honest, where a reply can educate at least a morsel of the next generation. My private belief is that the form of such reply shd. be as caustic as possible. The bare fact that an infant mewl is noticed indicates benevolence on the part of an elder.

Let the critic or essay-writer disabuse himself of the idea that he has made or is making anything. He is, if decent, fighting for certain ideas or attempting demarcations. If any serious critic makes a point, if he raises any objection whatsoever that can lead to more exact definition, the criticized is in order when answering, and his duty to answer depends only on time disposable and his energy. The being too proud to answer is usually fake, and in any case leads to Butlerism, the little Nicky Flunkies hiding their heads in their plush britches.

If no other method serve to get it into the head of

169

professors, I shd. recommend burning it into their backside with an iron. University LIFE was such and at its apogee when the professor was expected to answer an opponent. Abelard went to Paris and defeated his precursor. Degradation can go no lower than when (as has occurred in our time) a hired professor mis-states the theorem of his opponent in a periodical closed to replies. There shd. by now be no need of my naming the more flagrant cases, one in particular of a man with a changed name holding seat and being paid by a british "university".

George H. Tinkham has aptly branded the technique of some of the tyrants and bleeders as cinema technique: "gives 'em something new to think of before they have understood it"—"it" being the preceding wheeze.

"Supreme Court or Abdication, or before the war, national ownership of coal-mines."

These irrelevancies are the camouflage of tyrants used via the hired press to keep mankind's attention off truth, off the root issues, off the modus bene vivendi.

The earth belongs to the living.

Goods are of varying durabilities.

Services are ephemeral.

The performing musician cuts his form in the air and in the time flow. He writes it as in less stable water.

The usurers' system is nowhere more crass than in its marring of players. After all, if I write a distich, the immediate public and all editors can go to hell and be damned. The bust outlasts the throne. The written line stands on paper or parchment or, if good enough, even in the oral tradition. But the sonata is played and must next time be replayed. The composer exists in a sejunct world. His composition does stand on the page. But the performer's "work" is transient. Only a slight residue remains to him as prestige.

In the usury system or the corporate or the new wriggling, every thousand men shd. maintain a musician. That is a performer. At present $\frac{4}{5}$ of the remuneration goes to railways and hotels, and barely $\frac{1}{5}$ to the performers. Each town shd. maintain a few players—up to the grade that they can pay. And those performers shd. draw to them the few pre-eminent. The "star" system has obscured music and musical values. A whole pseudo-aesthetics has grown up about performers. They themselves in many cases have ceased to think about music, have ceased (if they ever began) to think of any hierarchy of values in the total known of music.

There is the theory of wooing the audience. There is a vast blither and abysm of unconsciousness. There is a vast crooners' commerce, replete and complete with press agents, trainers etc. The recipient of vast cheques maintains a whole stud farm and can not be expected to attend to anything outside her or his business (such as knowledge not immediately applicable to Gershwin and Puccini). Far be it from me to deny the vast resources of technique used and available and necessary in such a career. As Fernand L. says "*c'est autre chose*".

Just as materialist philosophy comes out wrong when

it gets down to details of conduct, so this ballyhoo comes out wrong or inadequate.

Mud does not account for mind. Kant, Hegel, Marx come out in OGPU. Something was lacking. The anthropomorphic expression (not to be confused with anthropomorphic belief, such as God an old man with a beard) comes nearer truth than does a merely arithmetical cosmogony.

That is not to deny the pleasure of pure contemplation of sound waves, or of making mental diagrams of them. I recur to mention of Leibniz because his monad was organic, quasi protoplasmic. Christianity in so far as there is cosmological thought at all in the New Testament is based on ONE principle: attraction, which implies attractivity. This is not inherent in number as such.

When a Catholic critic "makes allowance for" my love of Confucius, I wish I cd. think he had thought it down and out to this point.

If I *could* think that, I wd. *then* suggest he go further into the analogies between New Testament thought and that everywhere diffused through the *Analects* and the *Ta Hio.*

Suburban minds and sectarians fritter about with differences. They ignore convergences and differences of appearances, which latter differences MUST exist whenever two men see the same congeries of objects from different positions (bar cases of absolute symmetry which do not occur in history and economics).

Perhaps the first scholarly effort of New Economy

in England in our decades was Butchart's collection on "Money", in his second effort he put together Seven Men none of whom took the trouble to understand any of the other six. The book is valuable for two pages by Soddy and for lighting up a few pages of Douglas.

The FOUR active domains, or the four expanses of thought that the truly curious reader shd. look into are Gesell, Douglas, the Canonist doctrine of economics, wherein interest is treated under the general head of just price, AND the actual practice and achievement in the corporate states of our time.

This latter is a practice inapplicable in countries which have no corporate institutions, it might be unnecessary in any democracy that had the sense to learn money.

But NO extant democracy can afford to ignore the lesson of corporate practice. The individual "economist" who attempts to do so is either a fool, knave, or ignoramus.

Obvious and archi-obvious and triple obvious: parliaments as now run (Parliament, U.S. House of Representatives and Senate) are as obsolete as the Witenagemot. It is marvellous that the jaw-house has survived into the press age. Unbelievable that it CAN continue into the age of radio UNLESS it avail itself of just that. I.E. unless the people have guts enough to insist that their representatives go on the air so that swine, pimp, juggums and booglum be HEARD and their insufferable nullity be known to their constituents, and that men of good will and some brains be attracted to the Congress or the Parliament as a post where they can efficiently serve a true cause.

If the proponents and conservatives of representative institutions can't understand this, those institutions are obsolescent and represent only the velleity of a few imbeciles.

They have, since let us say 1865, served the gombeen men almost exclusively.

PART IV

Section VII

27. MAXIMS OF PRUDENCE

Consult a small man or a fussy man or an idle man, if collaborating perforce with such. With a large man or a busy man, consult as little as possible. Present the fait accompli. He will prefer an error on your part to a waste of his own time, or a sign that you cannot make a decision.

Am I yet old enough, or have I yet known even the above long enough to advise juniors even in so limited a domain?

Has Eliot or have I wasted the greater number of hours, he by attending to fools and/or humouring them, and I by alienating imbeciles suddenly?

28. HUMAN WISHES

The Etchells-Macdonald reprint of Dr Johnson's *London* is a manifesto of civilization. Mr Eliot's preface is full of urbanity. My own slap-dash is eminently thereby rebuked.

> "To be original with the *minimum* [for once italic'd] of alteration, is sometimes more distinguished than to be original with the *maximum* [italics his] of alteration."

This was Anatole France's conscious process raised into a system. If I remember rightly Arthur Symons said a finer thing when he praised Whistler for that he "sought neither to follow a model nor to avoid one".

> See nations slowly wise, and meanly just
> To buried merit raise the tardy bust . . .
>
> Where wasted nations raise a single name
> And mortgag'd states their grandsires wreathes
>   regret
> From age to age in everlasting debt.

One wonders, at the first passage, why *The Vanity of Human Wishes* is a rare reprint, and why Gautier's name stirs a glow brighter than Johnson's among lovers of poetry. Even if one has knocked about and read Bernard (gentil) or enough forgotten 18th century french verse to know how much of Gautier did not need to be new coined.

I offer two comments, one that I have used long and always with diffidence. "The bust outlasts the throne. The coin Tiberius," is the positive (the poeic, the making). Pope and Johnson are mainly a negative statement.[1] Their positive implication is the value of intelligence, the right to be impatient with fools, the value of being undazzled.

Even Elegiac poetry at its best is not mere senile blubber or the pleasure of crabbing something, it is an "And yet . . ."

The day before yesterday Pius XI was boosting La Sainte Foi Catholique as the bulwark of personality and individual freedom. Thus circumjacence civilizes even an old institution.

I have put in that sentence to keep me from closing the paragraph too tight.

Looking at Johnson's *The Vanity*, where it is most typical of its mode, and where it most brilliantly illustrates and attains the apogee and top notch of that mode, being "as good as Pope with a touch of Saml. J. into the bargain", its triumph is of the perfectly weighed and placed word. Its general statements, slickingly epigrammatic, give the reader what he himself brings to the text.

The "*slowly* wise, and *meanly* just" summarize long observation. They are verse for the man of fifty, who has

---

[1] Pope's imitation of Chaucer is early and a positive image; wd. indeed have been admirable propaganda in 1911.

a right to metrical pleasures perhaps as much as his juniors. Yet the whole poem is, as the intervening century plus has judged it by relative neglect, couched in style of "senate's thanks and gazette's pompous tale".

You are never for an instant permitted to forget that the thought is in full dress uniform. Johnson has enough thought to carry the uniform *to a reader searching* for the thought and the technique of its expression. Almost nothing suffers by being excerpted, line, distich or four lines at a time.

The cadence comes to an almost dead end so frequently that one doesn't know the poem is going on.

Gongorism was excess attention to high-coloured detail. The 18th century English verse from this angle is a very superior kind of intellectual gongorism, if you compare it with *Madame Bovary*. Or with the aesthetic of W. Carlos Williams, manifested this spring by Kitasono.

In a highly superior and accomplished way the WHOLE of 18th century literature was a cliché. The live thought was burrowing along in Pietro Leopoldo's cabinet in Tuscany, and its effects were about to be obliterated (for an age or so) by the French outburst.

Given these restrictions, one must endorse Mr Eliot's introd. to Saml. Johnson, a piece of work considerably superior, I believe, to that of his notes on Jonson (without the h), yet taking it by and large the poem is buncombe. Human wishes are not vain in the least.

The total statement is buncombe. The details acute and sagacious. Metastasio knew more.

Just as, jumping several small hurdles, the Whistler

show in 1910 contained more real wisdom than that of Blake's fanatic designs. Neither monopolizing the truth nor exhausting it.

The "whole of the 18th century" was a cliché which the Romantics broke up, in disorderly and amateur manner. The distressing Rousseau etc. . . . ending with Whitman.

Johnson's verse is not as good prose as that often found in Tom Jefferson's letters. There is probably no couplet in the two reprinted poems that has the quality of Jefferson's.

"No man has a natural right to be a money-lender save him who has money to lend." Or any other of the citations on p. 116 and following of my Jefferson and/or Mussolini.

It is all very well for Leone Vivante to claim that the word is component of the thought and that thought may be very often incomplete or unachieved until the word puts a shell on it. But the "often thought yet ne'er so well express't" angle very often means that the idea is NOT thought at all by the expressor during or preceding the moment of expression. It is picked up and varnished, or, at best, picked up and rubbed, polished etc.

Hence ultimately a greater trust in rough speech than in eloquence.

No, it's no good. I intended to praise both the poems and their introducer, but the poems are facile, they are not really thought at all, or are thought only in reflection (using the term as of a reflection in a mirror), thought remembered in a moment of lassitude.

HUMAN WISHES

I am looking even at:

His bonds of debt and mortgages of lands

which ought to melt a credit-crank if anything cd., and soften his judgement.

The age was decadent. It was going bust. Curiosity couldn't have attained a 1930 disinvoltura and ease as in: *Perche vuol mettere le sue idee in ordine?* (Why do you want to set your ideas in order?)

Gli indifferenti non hanno mai fatto la storia. The on-looker may SEE more of the game, but he does NOT understand it.

Not only is the truth of a given idea measured by the degree and celerity wherewith it goes into action, but a very distinct component of truth remains ungrasped by the non-participant in the action.

And this statement is at diametric remove from a gross pragmatism that cheapens ideas or accepts the "pragmatic pig of a world".

Mencken writes me (his letter dated March 1st). "Certainly the fact that a professional politician makes a mess of something is no proof that it is intrinsically unsound. Nevertheless, I believe that all schemes of monetary reform collide inevitably with the nature of man in the mass. He can't be convinced in anything less than a geological epoch."

Above statement does not invalidate geological process.

29. GUIDE TO KULCHUR

Ridiculous title, stunt piece. Challenge? Guide, ought to mean help other fellow to get there. Ought one turn up one's nose? Trial shots. 18th century *in the main*, cliché. 19th mainly MESS.

Man ought to be able to look at that poem of Sam Johnson's and see how nicely weighted the adjectives. Ought to "appreciate" . . . and yet not be blindfolded by whatever high accomplishment.

Oughtn't to think Haydn's melodic line up to Mozart's. Even if a Haydn quartette can be so advantageously sandwiched between two Bartoks as to serve as perfect segment (engine-cooler or whatever) in a concert.

Ideogram of this "culture"/division between the Best, the 95 % and upward, and the second division of writing, painting, sculpture, cooking or any other damn process.

"And pause a while from letters to be wise"

(rhyming with "turn thine eyes"). Saml. quite right if this means that the culture (damned word if there ever was one) ought NOT to be a blighted haystack of knowledge so heavy it crushes or smothers.

"Deign on a passing world to turn thine eyes."

Nope! That poem is highly accomplished but it is NOT
up to the level of prose writing which is touched time
and again in Tom Jefferson's letters or in John Adams'.
Stendhal was quite right in objecting to a medium where
you had to

"Deign on a passing world" etc.

And you can't very well dodge it in rhymed couplet, any
more than you can get the Saml. J. or Alex Pope neat-
ness and slickness into Byronic slap dash *and keep* the
quality that made *Don Juan.*

Any sort of understanding of civilization needs com-
prehension of incompatibles. You can't Goya and Am-
brogio Praedis at the same time, using those names as
verbs.

The Johnson is, or ought to be, a "mine" or ready-
remedy-case for quotations. Comfort to have the poem
decently printed. Abomination of desolation and may
hell rot the whole political ruck of the 19th century as
lasting on into our time in the infamy which controls
English and U.S. finances and has made printing a mid-
den, a filth, a mere smear, bolted down by the bank
racket, which impedes the use of skill and implements
for the making of proper books or of healthy popula-
tions. The first step toward a new Paideuma is a clear-
ance of every prelate or minister who blocks, by diseased
will or sodden inertia, a cleaning of the monetary system.
There is no mediaeval description of hell which exceeds
the inner filth of these mentalities.

The violent language of theologians during the scission is justified . . . they saw. And the elimination from protestant Europe, England and America of any sense of mental corruption and of any need to describe states of decaying mind by the analagous states of material rot and corruption, is the justification of the theological hate. It is the extenuation of misguided attempts to cure heretics and heresiarchs by material fire.

All of which paragraph is not to be taken as a plea for setting up the inquisition again 115 years after the last burning for heresy.

As I have said before: A church or prelate believing its or his own dogma wd. not run to such excess. A sincere man might suffer great mental torture in trying to devise a means of preventing contagion. I have NOT found among the educated English in my time ANY sense whatever of mental corruption.

The puritan is a pervert, the whole of his sense of mental corruption is squirted down a single groove of sex. The scale and proportion of evil, as delimited in Dante's hell (or the catholic hell) was obliterated by the Calvinist and Lutheran churches. I don't mean to say that these heretics cut off their ideas of damnation all at once, suddenly or consciously, I mean that the effect of Protestantism has been semiticly to obliterate values, to efface grades and graduations.

Pius' last encyclical (against communism) is on the track of this. The term corporate has some significance. The liver and heart in a healthy body do NOT try or tend to reduce each other to a common level of protoplasm. The endocrines participate, they do not seek a common level.

The genius of Mussolini was to see and repeatedly to affirm that there was a crisis not IN but OF the system. I mean he got "onto that fact" early. Plenty of us see it now.

The imbecility of America from 1900 onward, was loss of all sense of borderline between public and private affairs.

English law in our time has been supremely immoral. It has made crime. Its divorce laws are an infamy, the King's proctor an obscenity. The libel laws such as only criminals cd. have devised, a shelter of iniquity, a premium to blackmailers. The purpose of law is to eliminate crime not to incubate it and cause it to pullulate. Naturally the Prohibition amendment in the U.S. was the fine flower of legal bestiality, a record so far as publicity went, but in real degradation not lower or viler than less advertised british statutes.

The British have a talent for servility, sycophancy, bootlicking, we Americans for irrelevance, simple imbecility and insouciant inconsequence. If we are not more enslaved than the English, it is possibly because we haven't enough mental coherence to remember the orders from Wall St long enough to black the stock exchange's boots. I mean we wouldn't remember to do it regularly every morning until it became a habit and was gradually invested with an aroma of sanctity, picturesque custom, etc.

Nous avons le génie pour la mauvaise organisation, said

a French woman, as we had to pass three desks, exchange two sets of coupons, pay tax in small change in order to use a free ticket to a première performance at I suppose the what's-its-name theatre, with a square front near the Arc de Triomphe.

The kow-tows and genuflections of savages to a witch charm are NOT more idiotic than caucasian snootings at " *papiers* ".

And (on the other foot) as fast as a clean man builds up a sane social consciousness, or the state spends a few million on beautifying the highroads and their borders, some foetid spawn of the pit puts up a 30 foot wooden advertisement of synthetic citronade to defile man's art in road-making and the natural pulchritude of the vegetation. Commerce, mother of the arts AND *una* "*scroada*", das heisst Schweineri, scroferia!

30. THE PROOF OF THE PUDDING

Ideas are true as they go into action. I am not resurrecting a pragmatic sanction, but trying to light up pragmatic PROOF. The thread going through the holes in the coin . . . is a necessary part of a thought system.

The moment man realizes that the guinea stamp, not the metal, is the essential component of the coin, he has broken with all materialist philosophies.

Communism does not attract one to Russia. Spaniards like bull-fights. When the *Lusitania* was sunk, one deemed (and correctly) that Germany had lost that war.

This entirely apart from the almost certainty that the boat carried munitions to kill Germans. But the sense of measure was lost. A winning Germany wd. not have sunk the liner.

One might however strike a medal to Chas. Ricketts' ejaculation: "Oh Yeats, what a pity they can't ALL of them be beaten!"

That was an artist's invocation, and true in effect. They all were beaten. Even the Morgan ideology is sinking. That is to say it is loathed by all clean and knowing men.

The loss of a sense of measure is unlucky. The component of error in an idea shows in its working out.

And before that demonstration occurs, note that when

an idea does not go into action, this is because of some inherent defect in the idea (vide the whole story of cranks from the dawn of all human records).

When Isaac Singer invented his sewing machine they had it one evening almost in order, it worked but didn't take up the slack thread. This was easy to remedy. The thinking man does not insist on conserving the first plan of an engine or an invention. Cranks do. Cf. the general incompetence of economic theorists.

There is no use blaming the mass of humanity. A vague and general notion may or may not be able to "get going". But it is not *true* until it is.

I repeat: this view repudiates materialism. It is volitionism. It inheres and adheres in and to certain kinds of thinking, certain systems of values.

The Catholic Church rises and sinks with civilization circumvolving it. Again I repeat: I cd. be quite a "good catholic" IF they wd. let me pick my own saints and theologians.

And if (perhaps in addition) they wd. get down to brass tacks in applying their doctrine of the just price and show more vigour in teaching it. My Canadian enquirer asks "why are all Catholic Churches mortgaged?" Pius XI has wiped off a good deal of soot left in Rome by Pio Nono and his cronies. Perhaps another ten years will see further enlightenment. I have yet to find any prohibition of enlightenment in the better "fathers".

The worship of the supreme intelligence of the universe is neither an inhuman nor bigoted action. Art is, religiously, an emphasis, a segregation of some component of that intelligence for the sake of making it more perceptible.

The work of art (religiously) is a door or a lift permitting a man to enter, or hoisting him mentally into, a zone of activity, and out of fugg and inertia.

L'art religieux est mort? Gourmont's reportage was correct in respect to time and place, Paris 1890. The art of a particular sect dies. Religious art comes to life periodically. M. told me Surrealism was not an art movement but a moral discipline.

I am not confirming this view or contradicting it. I register the fact that young M. cd. make such an assertion with considerable fervour.

The state exists for the individual, but in our time the individual who does not deem his own acts and thought in certain ways and degrees up and down as to their use to the state (that is the universitas, the congeries of humans grouped in the state) is an inferior individual.

The lack of such a scale and ambition, ends up in the gang now ruling England. The "best of England" having gone out and got shot in the first months of the 1914 war.

As Lady L. said, "All they can do is to stand up and be killed." That state of mental inertia was attained after two centuries of social malady, in the credit tract.

Registering the fact that if H. J. was shocked at the lack of manners and morals he encountered in Europe, the present writer was at least surprised at the analphabetism and rabbity ignorance of letters which quite well dressed English folk offered to his young enquiries, 1908 to '11.

A live religion can not be maintained by scripture. It has got to go into effect repeatedly in the persons of the participants.

I wd. set up the statue of Aphrodite again over Terracina. I doubt, to a reasonable extent, whether you can attain a living catholicism save after a greek pagan revival. That again is why Christianity is tolerable in Italy and an offence in England, France and most of America.

Civilized man will not stand a savage religion. He can fake it, or ignore it. It can mean nothing vital to him. B. M. has with usual aptness remarked that fanatical hate, odium theologicum, occurs during the decadence of a cult.

● ● ● ●

Communism as revolt against the hoggers of harvest was an admirable tendency. As revolutionary I refuse a pretended revolution that tries to stand still or move backward.

Communism as theory is not only against the best human instincts, it is not even practised by the higher mammals. It suits monkeys more or less, and wild dogs are said to collaborate.

A movement, against capital, that cannot distinguish between capital and property is a blind movement. Capital is a claim against others which is not of necessity extinguished even by continual payment at 5% or at 50%.

THE PROOF OF THE PUDDING

The plough is NOT the same kind of thing or "instrument" as a mortgage. Homo even half sapiens ought to perceive a distinction.

There is a borderline between public and private things. Sanity bids us observe it.

A system which becomes in practice merely another hidden and irresponsible tyranny is no better than any other gang of instigators to theft and oppression.

Men not yet at sufficiently high mental level to consider soberly the requirements of a monetary system are unfit to administer even a lavatory or a chicken run.

● ● ● ●

The sentence: "Shakespeare never repeats" stands as praise of a particular writer's fecundity. Whether it wd. be as impressive if used of Lope de Vega or Vivaldi (even if true) I am not prepared to vouch. With implication of categoric, imperative or universal prohibition it is invalid. At least it is invalid for criticism and philosophy, and its application even to all art is unproved.

Brancusi's "*Toutes mes choses datent de quinze ans*" is worth equal consideration. After 50 a great deal of a man's statement may rightly be reaffirmation of what he has tried repeatedly and found good, a persisting mode of selection, or of maintaining his scale of values.

Much that seems over-harsh in my criticism wd. not seem so if men wd. reconcile themselves to recognizing the varying durabilities both of goods and of works of art, and of books in especial.

THE PROOF OF THE PUDDING

I have not diminished one iota of Eliot's praise of Sam Johnson. The two brief poems are not as serious as Lucretius on Nature. No one has, in all probability, ever asserted they were.

Dull as I believe Lucretius' poem to be, one can respect the author's sober intention to go over, to state clearly, a philosophy. I doubt if Roman prose is better as verbal manifest than Lucretius' verse. Just as I am inclined to deny that Johnson's verbal manifest in iambic penta-meter (so called) is as resilient a registration of thought as are many passages in Tom Jefferson's letters—even if the Johnson is above the general level of the "poésie" that Stendhal attacked, with its fustian "à la Louis XIV".

Justice inheres in the universe and in human affairs at least to this degree, namely that honest work has its reward in the arts if no other where. The merits of the lexicographer are there in *The Vanity of Human Wishes*, the fine weighing and placing of the epithet (as Mr Eliot notices).

A third or second rate sculptor tried to fake, tired of faking, did a year's honest work and it showed in his carving (teste scriptore). Binyon's translation of the *Inferno* is a notable monument to the honest labours both of translator and original author.

Whatever gods are mocked, neither Apollo nor Min-erva suffers deception. Magic, rabbit-out-of-hat-trick, if you like, but valid magic, and honest hat-trick pre-sented as hat-trick, not the cheating of small boys out of pennies.

31. CANTI

There is no mystery about the Cantos, they are the tale of the tribe—give Rudyard credit for his use of the phrase. No one has claimed that the Malatesta cantos are obscure. They are openly volitionist, establishing, I think clearly, the effect of the factive personality, Sigismundo, an entire man. The founding of the Monte dei Paschi as the second episode has its importance. There we find the discovery, or at any rate the establishment, of the true bases of credit, to wit the abundance of nature and the responsibility of the whole people.

As history becomes better understood I think this emphasis will become steadily more intelligible to the general reader.

PURITANS

The word puritan has become a term of reproach, made so by the "stinking puritan" who is a pseudo. Comstockery is a variant on the failure to distinguish between public and private affairs. The stinking pseudo fusses about the private lives of others, as distinct from and often as an avoidance of trying to ameliorate public affairs, such as monetary abuses.

For the hundredth time, the Church of England is

mostly an ally of mammon. To the point that a colonial parson (who can't be unique in his conviction) writes me privately in such a manner that I can't print what he says without danger of libel.

Gli indifferenti non hanno mai fatto la storia. I am not satisfied with my own journalism. I suspect it of being coloured by my convictions. The indifferent or "cold" historian may leave a more accurate account of what happens, but he will never understand WHY it happens.

I have seen the nitchevo journalists missing the mainspring, almost always missing the mainsprings.

A complete laissez-faire, a conviction of universal vanity, a disgust with the métier itself, a belief in their own impotence, an attribution of similar lack of motivation, of constructivity, of volition to all other men, leaves them on the outside.

NOVUM TESTAMENTUM

The Gospels are somewhat anti-semitic in tendency. I might paraphrase Dr Rouse: This is the story of a man who set out to reform Jewry from the inside, and they did not like it.

"Culture: what is left after a man has forgotten all he set out to learn"?

Cf. Gourmont's "instinct" as result of countless acts of intellection, something after and not before reason.

All the aphorist can do is to attempt to establish axes of reference.

In the historic process: a continuous infiltration of

attempts to set up power based NOT on right reason, not on being right, not on attempting justice. Attempts to establish secret and irresponsible power, unchecked by any ethos, and sheltered from observation.

In our time, the curse is monetary illiteracy, just as inability to read plain print was the curse of earlier centuries.

Every morning a fresh tidal wave of obscurantism and slop poured over the world's mind by the news sheets. Cui prodest. The U.S. precedes England at least in insisting on a half-yearly publication of ownership of periodicals and daily press.

No man knows the meaning of ANYTHING in any paper until he knows what interests control it. Curiosity in this domain is limited to an élite. It is almost unenglish to mention any such topic.

The stink of non-conformist sects has been in their losing the sense of all obscenity save that related to sex.

A stupidity which effaces the scale and grade of evil can give nothing to civilization.

You can perhaps define fanaticism as loss of the sense of gradations. Protestant sects are largely without a scale of values.

Naturally all bureaucracies are against truth and light, even though museums have a limited use. The setting of the museum above the temple is a perversion. Setting preservation of dead art above the living creation is a perversion. The avoidance of past work because a living present exploiter of past discovery fears comparison with past mastery is obscene, it is *vigliaccheria* or jackal's cowardice.

The iconoclast, the mob that destroys a work of art is mob because it fails to dissociate the work from a separable significance.

Nevertheless the breaking of the concrete symbol may be necessary tocsin.

Winston's nephew wd. possibly have accelerated English reform more actively by peppering Winston's hippopotamic rear with a little bird shot, than by going out to shoot Spanish apothecaries, though I doubt if anything cd. make Winston think straight, or turn his attention to any real problem.

TIME, AGAIN

On the eve of his 21st birthday Gerhart M. packed a suit-case and silently left the parental mansion. His father had spoken of the nuances of Bach. The timing of the departure indicated determination to separate. It also indicated sensibility and conviction.

A few days before his 30th birthday the younger Münch said: Now my father wd. know that at once. Meaning wd. know the exact pace of playing indicated by the metronome signature, 80, 84, etc.

This I took as the first sign of middle age. I said so. I said you have admitted yr. father knows something.

I was also pleased at further confirmation of my own theory or belief in "great-bass". The really fine musician has this sense of time-division and/or duration. An alteration of it inadvisedly or needlessly, for any cause not inherent in the composer's pattern, is bad music, bad playing.

It ultimately reduces all composition to slush if not checked in season.

The theory of pleasing the audience, of wooing the audience, the theory that the audience really hears the performer not the composer, and that there can be no absolute rendering of the composer's design, ultimately destroys all composition, it undermines all values, all hierarchy of values.

The sweeter the poison, the more necessary the defence. If the composer doesn't know how to write down what he wants, that is his fault, not the performer's.

There is an enormous leeway even in the best graph, BUT it is a leeway of intensity, not of duration. It is a leeway in graduations of force and of quality, not of duration, or in the lapse of very small time intervals between the beginnings of notes.

Between a legato and a marked staccato, there are graduations, which do not mean that there is leeway about starting the notes.

Rubato, is compensated. In the direction for "*rubato*" the composer *could* indicate the limits wherein he intends the compensation to occur. Strictly speaking this is supposed to be inside the bar.

There is no doubt that lots of mediocre music is badly graphed, and a great deal *is* mediocre BECAUSE the bad graphing indicates very loose conception on the part of the composer.

CANTI

We NEVER know enough. The good artist (I dare say even Strawinsky) is oppressed by his own ignorance —ignorance of simple fundamentals of his craft, even when he knows more than anyone else dead or living.

This doesn't mean that they have no pleasures. A man may enjoy playing his best in a game, and losing.

The simplicity of the arts is mystery and inviolable. I know two highbrow composers who agonized for months on a problem that the café-tango composer B. solves apparently without effort, whether from having been through a conservatory or playing jazz, I have not discovered. Mozart also wrote a great many notes between one bar line and another. OF course. "The trained never think." Like the school teacher in Frobenius' anecdote, they are scandalized when a pupil stops at a fundamental. It is so OBvious that if you use 64th notes or 32nds you can make more "funny shapes" than you can with $\frac{1}{2}$s and $\frac{1}{4}$s, and still keep an even bar measure. Tell it to little children.

I strongly suspect that Rummel and I in 1910, following other students who were supposed then to know more than we did, failed to recognize what might have been supposed to be a ms. indication. I suggest that the next digger try to interpret troubadour tune on the hypothesis that the line (of verse) is the bar and can be graphed to best advantage as a (that is one single) bar.

32. THE NOVEL AND SO FORTH

To distinguish between communication (of knowledge, transmission of wisdom, stimulation of perception) and the production of reading matter?

Stevenson had learned that: A man who can't forgive any mortal thing is a green hand at life.

Turgenev that "the heart of another is a dark forest", and "Nothing but death is irrevocable".

They had also learned the technique, more or less, of the novel. Kipling got off a good one on "the traffic and all that it implies". Government was to be applied to that and to nothing else. His generation balked at the money problem, without which the traffic does NOT flow.

"Comedy for presenting the individual character and tragedy for emotion", the comedie des mœurs is already there in Plato's dialogues, as for example the old colonel who gets annoyed with logic. Serious dialogue unreadable. If man hasn't worked an idea out to his own satisfaction, very difficult for him to hold reader's attention while shifting about from one snap at it, to another. Idem paradox. Lazy man's humour, range finding. Of very limited use. I suspect that all these devices were already catalogued when Quintilian began writing on rhetoric, and that their relative positions in the art of writing are about as important as our vague recollection of grammarians' lists.

The ignorance of such synthetic product of the intellectual lackey system comes to pimple-head when some post-graduate student attributes the use of oxymoron in one writer (the present one) to oxymoron used in a somewhat younger author.

Whether perception of such naiveté can be used to foster a more orderly approach to literary criticism I know not. Neither am I going to be bullied into wasting compositor's time by perpetually transforming that antient and strong construction into the currently weaker "I do not know". One can go too far in humouring pedants and fanatics for colloquial speech when printing one's thought.

Between America where "they" know nothing and continually discover the moon, and Germany "where they know everything and make no distinction between anything and anything else" one might aspire toward

Klabund's translations reach me only now, I will not say by accident, if that is to mean that they haven't reached me by normal process as reward for leading the kind of life I do lead, on the other hand they might perfectly well not have reached me in another 25 years.

THE NOVEL AND SO FORTH

I believe they are wholly independent of Fenollosa. A current from China has gone on in steady trickle, from Voltaire's time (Pauthier, Judith Gautier etc.). There is no need of passing on my Cathay to Germany, nor of taking Klabund's (I believe subsequent) translations to England. All that the latter seem to lack is a sense of hierarchy. In the first eagerness for new prospect both Klabund and I have lost hold on the technique of von Morungen, Vogelweide and Hans Sachs.

Gut Gesang haben wir hie notirt /
Das in vier Stimm gesungen wird /
Tenor / Discant / Alt und der Bass /
Mit schön höfflichen Text dermass /
So lieblich zusammen concordirt /
Und also ubersüss sonirt /
Dass sich ein Hertz erhebt darvon /
Das Gesang erfund Amphion.

Die Geigen wir gar kunstlich ziehen
Dass all Schwermütigkeit muss fliehn /
Wie sie erklingen kunstlich gantz
An einem Adelichen Tantz /
Mit leisen tritten höfflichen prangen /
Hertzlieb sein Hertzlieb thut umbfangen
Das Hertz und Gemut sich freuwen muss /
Und tantzen mit geringem Fuss.

Gut Lauten hab ich lang gemacht
Aus Tannenholtz / gut und geschlacht.

THE NOVEL AND SO FORTH

It is very hard to stop quoting Das Standebuch. I don't think the verse is, technically, up to that of the best earlier Minnelied, the von Morungen alba, the translation of the Canticles. But I can't see now, any more than I have been able to see at any other time during the past 30 years, that German tonkunst in poetry has advanced or maintained the earlier verse-art.

On the African front the German donation is indisputable. Before "lifting" large chunks of the Congo collection from the Musée du Trocadéro, Guillaume Apollinaire had called Frobenius "father".

I suppose, for all that, the rest of the world took up African art as a Paris fad.

Once a cultural vortex breaks it is slow work starting another. The weaker the dying vortex the more difficult it seems to get anything into it (therein lies I presume the imperfection of the term vortex as simile).

Electric magnet pulls steel and not wood, or at least the action is more obvious.

There are clearly some things that you can get INTO a dying capital more quickly than others but we have no clear criteria of their relativity.

Does the diseased centre draw medicine, or only palliatives—the book trade and the live thought pulling in different directions not necessarily diametrically opposite one to the other.

Waves of bad taste as well, and active currents. Obviously we judge countries (and generations) by their anthologies. If their own critics and advocates can't arouse a scintilla of interest, the general critic, or student of Weltliteratur can hardly be expected to do so.

As in English there is the god awful slump into boiled cabbage and badly cooked vegetables after, say, Rochester, who is already on the way down, so in German after, say, Hans Sachs. And you do NOT get out of such slumps by a Tennyson or a Rilke.

Without a rigorous technique, NO renaissance. I don't say technique is enough, or that a Bartok's struggles to renew a technique are enough, but without rigorous overhauling of technique and rigorous demands laid on technique, no renaissance.

There is a limited gamut of what will come over from Chinese verse WITHOUT the rigours of Chinese technique—acoustic technique, over and above the universal technique of matter and of visual suggestivity. There is a limited gamut of what will come over from primitive poetry. After that, it is: just more of the same.

The Lioness warning her cubs (vide infra) is new, and I think unkillable. Cosmology we have ever with us.

> Qui dira les torts de la platitude
> Et qui dira ses droits?

CONFUCII CHI-KING

SIVE

LIBER CARMINUM

Who, for that matter, will say something solvent and

THE NOVEL AND SO FORTH

elucidative as to the Penelope web of European aware-
ness?

P. Lacharme ex soc. Jesu. A very learned man most
skilled in Chinese and Tartar languages, of whose life no
trace remains save this notable work, begun in 1733
and not really finished when he left off about 1752. 71
sheets once belonged to a certain Delisle, later handed on
to the ministry of marine, then to the society of Astron-
omers, Paris. Chinese words written in Portuguese style.
Julius Mohl wrote 'em out in French style when prepar-
ing his edition in Paris, 1829, printed or published
Stuttgart and Tubingen sumptibus D. G. Cotta, 1830.

Ad montes orientales iter fecimus, et diu est ex quo inde
reverti non licuit, jam ab oriente venimus et coelo tenebrose
decidit pluvia, interea, cum ab orientali regione maxime
velimus abire, animus noster occidentalem regionem cogi-
tans dolore conficitur. Quid autem aliud possumus quam
vestes paremus. Jam exercitus apparatum omittamus. En
insectum Chou dictum rure, in arbore moro, silens et soli-
tarium jacet, ecce etiam adest sub curru.

The weariness and fact of war already there in the
Songs of Tsao, *Odes* I. 15

Kong lieu etc. had this kingdom of Tcheou 670 years
before the Tcheou came to Empire, and so forth.

The translation lay 80 years in ms. and I suppose
Mohl's edition missed the boat. Latin having by 1830
ceased to be the lingua franca of western culture.

Now we WANT the ideograms, even where Lacharme
is clear reading.

THE NOVEL AND SO FORTH

At any rate 3000 years ago the Chinese poets were aware of the unutterable dullness of warfare. The fine edge of chivalry is something utterly different from the weariness of plugging along in the mud, season after season.

33. PRECEDENTS

As to earlier guides to Kulchur or Culture? I take it
Plato and Plutarch cd. serve, that Herodotus set a pre-
cedent, that Montaigne certainly provided such a guide
in his essays, as did Rabelais also, and that even Bran-
tôme might be set down as a guide to gusto. Every critic
however anti-paterine ought to want to accomplish
something of the sort that Pater indubitably did with
his *Renaissance*. Pater made his limited circle of
readers want to know more of a period. I think I owe
him Valla, I can pardon his inflation of Pico della Miran-
dola. I suspect McKail is a paterine product, and one
can read McKail's *Latin Literature*. Whether Lionel
Johnson's *Post Liminium* shd. be added to such a list I
am unsure. It proves that Lionel was well read. At this
date I remember nothing else of it save that proof.

Fontenelle and Landor tried consciously, I think, to
make summaries. Neither Bayle's *Dictionnaire* nor Vol-
taire's quite serve as a summary. I can only pose this as
problem.

They obviously do NOT exaggerate their own know-
ledge. They are unpretentious in so far as they don't ask
you to suppose that they know it all, and yet from Mon-
taigne or Rabelais you would, I believe, acquire curiosity
by contagion, and in a more mellow form than from the

PRECEDENTS

18th century collectors of heteroclite items laid out all of 'em from the same point of view, all dealt with by an identical process, whereas Montaigne and Rabelais are handling them with a more general curiosity.

You do NOT know all about any substance merely by testing it with litmus paper.

I am, I trust patently, in this book doing something different from what I attempted in *How to Read* or in the *A B C of Reading*. There I was avowedly trying to establish a series or set of measures, standards, voltometers, here I am dealing with a heteroclite set of impressions, I trust human, without their being too bleatingly human.

In travelling one marks certain maxima, and tries not to appropriate everything. The charm of nine "sights" out of ten is in sense of discovery, a moderate temporary ownership, that ought to be left to the next man.

For ten years I never named Pitigliano. I now leave it open. Find it. No one has been there in the interim and set up a bill-board for wumplets (at least let us pray that they have not). There are still undiscovered cities *in* Italy.

34. ON ARRIVING AND NOT ARRIVING

Culture is not due to forgetfulness. Culture starts when you can DO the thing without strain. The violonist, agonizing over the tone, has not arrived. The violonist lost in the melodic line or rather concentrated effortlessly on reproduction of it has arrived.

There is no faking in the arts. No artist can present what he hasn't got. Edgar Wallace triumphed by modesty. One can learn from that if from nothing else in his craft.

Eckart v. Sydow's admirable anthology *Dichtungen der Naturvölker* (Phaidon Verlag, Wien) (HAUSSA, SUDAN).

THE LIONESS WARNS HER CUBS

Ware of one with sharp weapons
Who carries a tiger-tail tuft
Ware of one who comes with white dogs,
O son of the shorthaired lioness,
Thou my child with short ears,
Son of the lion, that I feed on raw meat,
Carnivore,
Son of the lioness whose nostrils are red with bloody-
    booty,

ON ARRIVING AND NOT ARRIVING

Thou with the bloodred nostrils,
Son of the lioness who drinkest swampwater,
Water-lapper my son.

R. Prietze,
Haussa Sprichwörte und Lieder, 1904

35. PRAISE SONG OF THE BUCK-HARE

I am the buck-hare, I am,
The shore is my playground
Green underwood is my feeding.

I am the buck-hare, I am,
What's that damn man got wrong with him?
Skin with no hair on, that's his trouble.

I am the buck-hare, I am,
Mountaintop is my playing field
Red heather my feeding.

I am the buck-hare, I am,
What's wrong with that fellow there with his eye on a
        girl?
I say, is his face red!

I am the buck-hare, I am,
Got my eyes out ahead
You don't lose me on a dark night, you don't.

I am the buck-hare, I am,
What's wrong with that bloke with a poor coat?
Lice, that's what he's got, fair crawlin' he is.

PRAISE SONG OF THE BUCK-HARE

I am the buck-hare, I am,
I got buck teeth.
Buck-hare never gets thin.

I am the BUCK-HARE, I am,
What's that fool got the matter with him?
Can't find the road! Ain't got no road he CAN find.

I am the buck-hare, I am,
I got my wood-road,
I got my form.

I am the buck-hare, I am,
What ails that fool man anyhow?
Got a brain, won't let him set quiet.

I am the buck-hare, I am,
I live in the big plain,
There's where I got my corral.

I am the buck-hare, I said so.
What's wrong with that loafer?
He's been to sleep in a bad place, he has.

I am the buck-hare,
I live in the bush, I do,
That's my road over yonder.

I am the buck-hare, I said so,
Women that don't get up in the morning,
I know how they look by the chimney.

PRAISE SONG OF THE BUCK-HARE

I am the buck-hare, I said it,
I can tell any dumb loafer
Lying along by the hedge there.

I am the buck-hare,
Women don't love their men?
I can tell by what their cows look like.

Von Sydow gives note to effect that this is in **Wm.**
Radloff's *Proben der Volksliteratur*, 1866. Teleuten,
Sibirien.

36. TIME-LAG

Here again is the time-lag. Van Buren's autobiography was written in 1861, and unpublished till 1920. Are we to assume that Radloff buried a very few lively poems in a mass of dullness? Are we to assume general incuriosity, while faddists and university infants carded out again the overcombed wool of a limited set of "classics". Did Père Lacharme's latin arouse NO curiosity whatsoever. We must assume Lacharme's latin as a basis. Who saw it before Mohl? and after Mohl's edition where did it lie doggo for 107 years?

Regio quam alluit amnis Fen dictus humida est, et depressa juxta amnem herba Mou decerpitur. Hic vir formosus quidem, sed caret prudentia; praeclara est specie; sed nullo consilio; a regis auriga multum abludit (et regis currum regendo ineptus est).

Surely there is the bite of Catullian irony in the *formosus quidem, sed* and in the *multum abludit.*

Even from the latin one cd. get

A low damp kingdom, by the river which they call Fen
and they mow Mou grass along the river bank.
This man is handsome, my word! and lacking in pru-
  dence,
marvellous in appearance, and null in advising,

TIME-LAG

a bit off key for a charioteer
and useless for driving king's wagons.

By the river Fen in a bend
They harvest the mulberry leaves.
Handsome is this man, my word!
He is bright as a flower. In fact you wd. think that he
was one, rather than a King's wagoner.
But the king's wagoner expresses himself very badly.
They call it the bend of the Fen river where they mow
Sin grass. This man is bright like a bit of jewelry. He
is handsome, he is beautiful like a gem.

Next lines I do not understand. Whether printer or
translator is cause of the muddle, or whether Lacharme
meant to leave the grammatical muddle as indicative
of difference between Chinese idiom and latin I don't
make out.

What puzzles me is that the latin has led nobody to
dig down into the original during a hundred years. The
English translation before me (pub. 1891) is an infamy.

I admit that I have owned the Lacharme for 15 or 20
years, but I can account for at least part of my time
during that interval.

The yoke of the universities has been heavy.

O mus ingens, ingens mus, noli milium meum comedere.

Whether the nucleus of it is there in Prof. MacD's
"And besides, Mr Pound, we shd. have to do so much
work ourselves to verify your results"?

Dated U. of Penn. 1906 when I suggested doing a

thesis on some reading matter OUTSIDE the list of classic authors included in the curriculum, and despite the fact that Fellowships are given for research and that a thesis for Doctorate is supposed to contain original *research*.

Even if results were wrong, or vague, or contained, like all other verbal manifestations, a component of error? even IF the student wd. be surer of not wasting his time etc. etc. safety first, read only what ten generations have approved of without reading. . . .

Nulli curae tibi fuerunt res meae.

I will go into better lands? Happy the land where I can live my life in quiet.

There is at least enough in Lacharme's latin to give one an understanding of why Kung fu Tseu told his pupils to READ the Odes.

Dust on my head, that I trod the earth 50 years and have not read them in the original. But no reason for leaving others unwarned.

37. THE CULTURE OF AN AGE

                    is what you can
pick up and/or get in touch with, by talk with the
most intelligent men of the period?

I said to Frobenius: "I shd. like you to drift round to an
opera by my compatriot A." "Ah!" said the Geheimrat,
"that will interest my wife, she is the musical member of
. . ." I said: Damn your wife, or polite words to that ef-
fect, allowing for the lady's probable charm and intelli-
gence etc. In my broken German I said: "NO! it is your
opinion I want, I wish you to judge between die zwei
Barbarismus" (as ever in doubt as to german gender of
anything).

I take it he will try anything once. "Not satiric,
naive," said the Geheimrat. "Wrong to use royal instru-
ments for proletarian music. I have a friend who has
invented a mechanism etc. . . ."

Ito, as I have remarked, opened up. There were no
barriers of race or distance after he had seen Umewaka
Minoru's photo on my mantle shelf.

A German, sufficiently civilized to prefer Bach, Lubek,
Tielmann, The Stammbuch, Minnelied . . . says "they
(the English in C . . .) are all like that, now a German
might be DUMB, but wd. at least try to understand.

They all (all the English) try to slide off it." The specimen present having been a familiar object of cognizance for two decades, I naturally noticed nothing. The foreign eye is half-way house to Burns' wish for a mirror showing to oneself what others see easily.

Section IX

38. EDUCATION OR INFORMATION

The general belief current during my youth in American beaneries was that one shd. go to Germany for systematized information . . . plus a long elegy on what German Universities were not. I take it that one must still go to Germany for information, catalogues etc.

I wasted time starting a study of Lope in Madrid, if it is valid to believe that a thesis on the Gracioso (Sancho Panzas etc.) in Lope's plays was the main aim. The ang/ sax. world shd start that sort of thing in the Brit. Museum or in some subsequent American what-not. But it wd. be erroneous to suppose that the Brit. Mus. is a place for research into European history or that its post-war activities keep up with European thought. It wd. be a waste of time trying to learn about Italy under the gloomy dome. Paris has no book-shops worth mentioning. The French book trade caters to news-stand public. The German book trade is said to be organized. Whether their annual supplements to the universal catalogue etc. etc. are as efficient as claimed, I leave to the next sufferer.

France shd. be commemorated in Elias Lowe's story of the Parisian biologist who had written on crocodiles all his life. After the monumental and definitive work on

219

the subject he visited Africa to look at a crocodile. One advanced toward him. He climbed a tree. The crocodile then reared up and proceeded to follow him.

"Mais non! Mais NON!" ejaculated the scientist, "Les crocodiles ne montent PAS les arbres."

In like manner I remarked in the Bibliothèque Nationale that their book catalogue was a scandal. The idea was new to them. They fizzed, quite vigorously and effervescently, but finally seeing that I meant it, trailed off into elegy on the larger appropriations made to keep up that in the Brit. Mus. Their mss. room is quite pleasant and serviceable.

When Oxford ceased to vaunt its learning, one was told that the town still contained "characters" more or less quaint and crusted. This product I believe exists in greater variety and mellowness in our peninsula. There are as many libraries and archives as there are librarians and archivisti.

And with the rarest exceptions they are an augment to the pleasure of study. No one who has spent less time than I have in these odd corners can have an adequate idea of the unmined treasure lying about more or less ordered in Italy. Microphotography (ut dicta) shd. open up vast reaches of music. When one thinks of the number of old buffers ready to copy anything for a couple of lire, and apparently able to read the most crabbed script with ease, there is also a vista of possibility in typewritten copies of documents done with four or five carbons, one say for the local record, one Rome, and Milan etc.

Naturally there is nothing duller than the results of

such digging, UNLESS the searcher have some concept to work to. Not the document but the significance of the document.

That is, perhaps, where XIXth century philology went astray. It aimed at burying the young student in "research" before he knew what he was after. He was to dig it out (blind, ham-strung, as blacks in a diamond mine).

I know only too well from the state of stupidity induced by detailed research when doing my Cavalcanti, how low the intelligence can be dragged by work on minutiae after a man has passed 40. But that aint the 'arft of it . . . to prove which you can, if yr. stomach is strong enough, contemplate the wreckage, the overwhelming in platitude of men who were shoved down a similar tunnel in youth and have never come up again.

Rough parallel wd. be to imagine Edison setting out NOT to invent the electric-light bulb but just to invent, at large, anything that happened in the course of his twiddling with this that and the other.

The opposite, going not to seed but to confusion, is manifest in those who set out to find PROOF of something or other. Even this mania, this one-trackness occasionally ploughs up more truth than mere lack of direction. Luigi Valli's *Linguaggio Segreto* oughtn't to mislead any reader of judgement. The lack of proof in his arguments, the non sequiturs and failures to see other alternatives might even serve as a lesson to cranks and faddists. Some kind of line to hang one's facts on is better than no line at all.

39. NEO-PLATONICKS ETC.

Alongside or rather a long way from alongside of factual study, for 2000 or more years has run the celestial tradition, the caeruleum coelum, the augustum coelum, etc.

"The heaven which is above the heavens (etc.) no earthly poet (etc.) has sung or ever will sing in a worthy manner."

"The colourless formless and intangible essence is visible to the mind which is the only lord of the soul. Circling around this in the region above the heavens is the place of true knowledge." ET cetera.

This kind of thing from the Phaedrus, or wherever it comes from, undoubtedly excites certain temperaments, or perhaps almost anyone if caught at the right state of adolescence or in certain humours.

For the Western world Plato is the father of this sort of prose rhapsody. And deleterious students can, I suspect, net vast tracts of the same sort of thing in the orient, even (and/or especially) in non-Confucian China.

This sort of thing bumped into hebrew tradition. It overflowed the Church fathers.

It annoys Mr Eliot. At least I assume that it is this sort of writing which causes Mr Eliot to break out against Plato Inc. (or rather not incorporated in any but the "société anonyme" sense).

NEO-PLATONICKS ETC.

Man drunk with god, man inebriated with infinity, on the one hand, and man with a millimetric measure and microscope on the other. I labour and relabour the discipline of real theology or of any verbal combat or athletics that forces or induces him to define his terms clearly.

And this can NOT be limited to mere definition of abstract concepts. There is no doubt whatsoever that human beings are subject to emotion and that they attain to very fine, enjoyable and dynamic emotional states, which cause them to emit what to careful chartered accountants may seem intemperate language, as Iamblichus on the fire of the gods, *tou ton theon pyros*, etc. which comes down into a man and produces superior ecstasies, feelings of regained youth, super-youth and so forth, not to be surpassed by the first glass of absinthe (never to be regained by the second or 50th imbibition).

Two mystic states can be dissociated: the ecstatic-beneficent-and-benevolent, contemplation of the divine love, the divine splendour with goodwill toward others.

And the bestial, namely the fanatical, the man on fire with God and anxious to stick his snotty nose into other men's business or reprove his neighbour for having a set of tropisms different from that of the fanatic's, or for having the courage to live more greatly and openly.

The second set of mystic states is manifest in scarcity economists, in repressors etc.

The first state is a dynamism. It has, time and again, driven men to great living, it has given them courage to go on for decades in the face of public stupidity. It is

paradisical and a reward in itself seeking naught fur-
ther . . . perhaps because a feeling of certitude inheres in
the state of feeling itself. The glory of life exists without
further proof for this mystic.

Assuming that the early Catholic tradition has been
broken (for the general public) or, for sake of brevity
skipping the controversies of Byzantium and of the de-
clining Roman empire in Italy . . . for the sake of start-
ing somewhere or other, so as to have a treatable field
of reference or a field wherein there is tolerable visi-
bility:

Gemistus Plethon brought over a species of Platonism
to Italy in the 1430s. I take it he is more known by his
sarcophagus in Rimini than by his writings. There is a
ms. of his greek in the Laurenziana in Firenze, a Ger-
man named Schulze (or something of that sort) included
him in a study of philosophy, I think Gemisto gets a
whole vol. whereof a copy lies in the Marciana (Venice).
A bit of him was translated early into latin and printed
in the back pages of an early edtn. of Xenophon, but
left out of the reprints. I think it is the edtn. of 1496.
And they say Gemisto found no one to talk to, or more
generally he did the talking. He was not a proper poly-
theist, in this sense: His gods come from Neptune, so
that there is a single source of being, aquatic (udor,
Thales etc. as you like, or what is the difference). And
Gemisto had distinct aims, regeneration of greek people
so they wd. keep out the new wave of Barbarism (Turk-
ish) etc.

At any rate he had a nailed boot for Aristotle, and his

conversation must have been lively. Hence (at a guess) Ficino's sinecure, at old Cosimo's expense, trained to translate the greek neoplatonists. Porphyry, Psellos, Iamblichus, Hermes Trismegistus....

Whence I suppose what's-his-name and the English mystics with reference to greek originals sometimes (John Heydon etc.).

What remains, and remains undeniable to and by the most hardened objectivist, is that a great number of men have had certain kinds of emotion and, *magari*, of ecstasy.

They have left indelible records of ideas born of, or conjoined with, this ecstasy.

Se non è vero è ben trovato. No one has complained that this kind of joy is fallacious, that it leads to excess, that its enjoyers have need of detoxication. It has done no man any harm. I doubt if it has even distracted men from useful social efforts.

I shd. be inclined to give fairly heavy odds to the contrary. An inner harmony seldom leads to active perturbing of public affairs. Grant that the concentrated man is irritable if suddenly distracted, I doubt if this irritation is greater even among testy mystics than among any other species of concentrator.

"Old Krore" (G. R. S. Mead) never did any harm. He is even mentioned with respect by various continental editors of mystical snippets, tracts, volumes, etc. He used to say: There is something beyond that. Mme Blavatsky said: Now Mead, when you get to the North Pole you think that the earth is a ball, but you know, Mead, it isn't, when you get there you will find another sphere. . . .

(mental picture is, I think, a species of dumb-bell or figure 8 solid).

Mead years after was looking for a meaning and did not suspect the old lady of pulling his leg. Nevertheless he had a sense of humour, as in "I know so many people who were Mary Queen of Scots. And when I consider what wonderful people they used to be in their earlier incarnations, I ask WHAT they can have been at in the interim to have arrived where they are."

40. LOSSES

I suspect that England after Waterloo, or say from 1800 onward, suffered a particular and special darkness due to interruption of normal communication with the Continent. No more Voltaires came over to admire la Grande Nation and study English authors. From the appearance of Gautier's *Albertus*, or say from 1830 down to 1917, FRANCE was European civilization. Any man with a mind, during that period, whether Turgenev or James or Whistler or Picasso, had to know Paris, had to know the French mind?

This statement is too general and sweeping. Browning? Camillo Cavour? Browning carried on from Landor. Cavour worked in circumstance, various need to use a Parliamentary system. Cavour taught it to Lombardy. Let us revise the opening paragraph and say every man *born* after 1830 had to know French writing.

Note, when I got to London the men who were old *enough* were all right. Col. Jackson, Luke Ionides represented something hearty, pre-Victorian, they had something that Palmerston might have recognized as appertaining to men. It   as Gosse's generation that was contemptible, mingy, they were carrots not animals. Born under the Victorian fugg, insularity, a meagreness, a dwindling.

LOSSES

The British mind in 1909 was decadent. I said so, and I got the languid reply: "But surely other empires have decayed, why shouldn't we?"

Never in all my 12 years in Gomorrah on Thames did I find any Englishman who knew anything, save those who had come back from the edges of Empire where the effect of the central decay was showing, where the strain of the great lies and rascalities was beginning to tell.

Douglas had been in India. Nobody wanted to hear about THAT. Another bloke whom I met at a tea fight had, for years, been pointing out that ONE cruiser of an enemy power cd. interrupt all the Indian trade. They told him to keep quiet. He had the melancholy joy of observing the *Goeben* accomplish the predicted disruption.

Once I thought I had met an exception to my hypothesis. His passport fell open on the table, and I read "born in Pekin".

For the 300th time I repeat that it is quite useless telling these things to people who do NOT want to hear them. The Lancashireman from S. America said yesterday, "the men in my club, there'll be seven about a table and six will get up and go away, and I ask the seventh: why? And he says: They don't like your ideas."

The "ideas" of these returning Britons are more often mere facts, detached observations, with no theoretic bias.

Living in England I felt at least a guest's loyalty to his host. Even now, having escaped from the froust, I still insist that the mere collapse and deliquescence of an

LOSSES

Empire can't in itself do any good, or "help civilization".

I have the Italian view as I heard it from Carlo Delcroix in his office, at the beginning of the Abyssinian acquisition: But we don't want to do any harm to their empire.

As in my letter to Muir: I believe in an economic truth and I believe that at least four men or four groups of men have approached that truth, and that there are common bases in KNOWN economic fact, whereon to erect a science.

A science *enters* an art, e.g. the known chemistry of pigment can serve a painter, either when he mixes his colours or when he gets them from a trusted manufacturer who does not violate known chemical laws.

To recapitulate, I take it from my ex-Russian ex-General that the fall of Alexander's empire was a disaster. I suspect the cutting off of English mental life after 1800 was a disaster. I am dead certain that when latin went into desuetude, there was an as yet uncalculated but very great loss to higher culture in Europe, whatever concurrent gains occurred in the lower reaches.

Till 1850, latin, I think, was the language of learning in Turin university. Leo XIII still wrote it for pleasure.

I am not advocating an excessive conservatism or weeping over spilt milk. I am indicating that a great mass of interesting printed matter has been EXCESSIVELY neglected by the educational higher bureaucracy in our time.

LOSSES

Latin translations of greek, the Lacharme version of the ODES, Salmasius' *De Modo Usurarum*. Somebody's british school book in 1830 or 1820 still showed the old culture. I have seen a french edtn. of Fracastorius dated 1796. That may have been due to an interest in pornography only. Not that the poem amounts to much in that line. I merely give the date as last edtn. I have chanced on, illustrating the duration of the vogue of third rate Renaissance latin writers.

Leibniz wrote latin because in his day German did NOT serve as means of correspondence with the intelligent men with whom Leibniz wanted to keep in touch. 1646/1716. Bach 1685/1750, Handel (the dull) 1686/1759, Vivaldi the, at moments, celestial, possibly 1675 to probably 1743.

Leibniz's life, in the heavy era? An intelligent prince, who dies, the dead suet following, the Hanoverian substitution of a sense of royal duty for an interest in the life of the mind. What a life!

The Bourbons were garbage. The French court was punk. Civilization did exist in Italian cities in the Quattrocento. The nuclei of 18th century mental life were already present. The dispersal toward the north meant dilution.

I know no handy analysis of the teutonic paideuma of the Leibniz-Bach episode. Good long episode, 1660 (Leibniz wd. have begun to think at 14) to 1750. Goethe born 1749. Beethoven 1770. And in the Kreuzer the nuclei of all that slipped and slopped down into the XIXth century messiness, blurr, soup.

LOSSES

Take Germany's best 90 years. 1660 to 1750 with retrospect to verse technique in von Morungen etc.?

1653 Wm. Young's sonatas printed in Innsbruck.

Did the slither of Stuartism, the boom in Usury in England, the puritanical illiteracy and general disorder throw the centre of Europe's mental life into Germany at that time?

Just as the kaiser's filth and the European bank-botching in 1914 threw the centre of English publication for a few, all too few alas, years, into New York?

Historians have no curiosity? Very few have any accuracy. Those who verify dates almost never try to carry their inquisitiveness down into causes.

41. ODES: RISKS

CONFUCIAN pedagogy in the home seems to have consisted in C's asking his son whether he had read a couple of books, one, the Book of the Odes, the other the Rites. (As recorded at the end of the XVIth chapter of the *Lun Yu*, second part of the Conversations.) Tching-kang asked Pe-yu (C's son) whether he had heard "extraordinary things" or anything his father "don't tell the rest of us". Pe-yu replied in the negative, and said: "He is usually by himself. Once when he was alone and I was hurrying through his room, he said: Have you studied the Odes? I said: not yet. And he told me that if I didn't I wd. be unable to take part in conversation. Another time he said: Have you studied the Rites?"

Our general notion of Confucius (Kung) has perhaps failed to include a great sensibility. The Conversations are the record of a great sensibility.

42. GREAT BASS: PART TWO

The wobbling about by deficient musicians, the attempt to give life to a piece by abundant rallentandos and speedings up, results in reduction of all music to one doughy mass and all compositions to the one statement of the performing executant, said wobbly time is due to their NOT divining the real pace of the segment.

The 60, 72, or 84, or 120 per minute is a BASS, or basis. It is the bottom note of the harmony.

If the ear isn't true in its sense of this time-division the whole playing is bound to be molten, and doughy.

The sense of high order and clarity is not due to sense

pitch as between

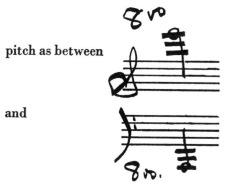

and

alone

but to the sense of proportion between all time divisions from 10 to the minute or era up to top harmonic 8vo an 32mo above treble stave.

233

GREAT BASS

Failing to hit the proper great bass, the deficient musician fumbles about OFF the gt. bass key as a poor singer fumbles about a little flat or a $\frac{1}{4}$ tone too high.

Mr. W. Lewis, calling me in one place a revolutionary simpleton, makes honourable amend, calling himself a chronological idiot in another. Music is the least of his troubles, or interests, yet I wdn't go so far in a censure. On the only occasion I can remember his being present during the execution of some English music in the prevalent manner, he said that he knew nowt about it, but thought such things should not happen. There is more hope for such an illiterate than for the graduates of what corresponds in music to the London School of " Economics ".

43. TONE

Everyone feels something about it. Plenty of players will admit in theory that there is a right speed for a piece or movement, but "they let it go at that". There is probably a stricter sense sic: just as there is silence or dullness of sound produced by interference of sound waves in the middle stave, so there is an aid, reinforcement or interference from the great bass, according as the speed is right or not.

Listening to the Bach A minor Concerto I have wondered whether the violin part is intended to flow through it as colourless water. Impossible to *know* from hearing piano reduction of the orchestra. One wd. have to listen to a number of performances with orchestra to *know*. It wd. have been a legitimate and highly distinguished intention on the composer's part to make the binding-force of so great a composition almost imperceptible (locally).

Certainly in all work for strings the speed is of more importance than generally understood. (Lie down, Towser, "everyone knows" that the tempo has *some* importance. I am talking of its having *more* importance.)

A minuscule excess of speed is less emollient than a lack, as a singer singing sharp is less soupy and porridge-like than one singing flat.

TONE

The nastiest true thing ever said against Germany was said I believe by A. Waley, who encountered a German historian of art who spoke of certain values being merely aesthetic values and not pertaining to his subject.

On the other hand my country has produced jews and aryans who slither on with talk about "influences" regardless of whether the pieces of writing "influenced" were composed and/or published years before the work alleged to have formed the author's style.

POLLON D'ANTHRŌPON IDEN
The Odes
The Homeric Epos
Metamorphoses
Divina Commedia
The Plays

That is a fairly solid pentagon. And to the Odes collected by Kung, add the *Ta Hio*, *The Unwavering in the Middle*, the *Analects*. By Plays, I mean (and I trust even the lowest reader will not fail to gather the meaning) those of Shakespeare (Shxper, Jacquespère with no regard to the spelling).

Cocteau alone in our time has put life into Greek drama.

I cannot believe that a list like the preceding in any way circumscribes one's curiosity. The mere act of such isolation (or compression) at once causes the mind to leap out with: "and Montaigne? and etc. etc. etc.??"

TONE

With 309 concerti of Vivaldi unplayed, lying in Turin as I write this, it is as useless as it wd. be idiotic to write of musical culture in Europe.

All you can talk of with regard to actuality is the chaos of musical scholarship, the corruption of musical publication as of everything else by the profit impulse, and the concentration of the power to endow institutions in the hands of vulgarians and incult bellies (e.g. the paralysis of scholarship at Y . . . by men who donate money for buildings without donating money for their upkeep, thereby incurring an expenditure on masonry and repairs to the detriment of learning).

The kind intentions of some endowers having for centuries blinded mankind to the fact that almost every endowment is a bond on labour, an entail of work on a great number of people for the sake of utility to a few.

Palliatives better than nothing, but a sane humanity wd. keep sharper eye on causation.

How far, for example, has Venetian life been endowed out of existence, by men with most uplifted intentions?

The basis of credit is the abundance of nature, plus, for administrative purposes, the responsibility of the whole people.

The Carnegie Peace endowment does not mean peace. It means a tax of half a million dollars a year on the American producing public, for the benefit of one of the most useless, null and generally despicable secretariats ever allowed to infect the planet. Not but what Andy Carnegie meant well.

He either did not foresee or he acted ill. Not that any

normal human being cd. be expected to foresee the totality of Nic Butler. . . .

Certain names of this present era will stink to posterity wherever kindly oblivion fails to efface them.

Certain poetic beauties are a sort of recurring decimal. I am as certain as one can be of anything that my lines are not due to Lacharme's:

Sol oriens, venusta scilicet puella domi meae degit, domi meae degit, et vestigiis meis insistens venit. *Odes* I. 8. 4.

PART V

Section X

44. GOVERNMENT

GOVERNMENT has been based on fact, fancy, superstition, folk-ways, habits, ideas, ideologies.

Fact, sheer physical strength, working through armies.

Fancy condottieri hankering for armament as pictured in Valturio's treatise.

Superstitions merging into ideas, ideas cloaked or camouflaged as ideologies. And with the latter the *witan*, the assembly, the assembly of delegates from smaller local assemblies. Wherewith government by the hand-press, by newspaper, by radio.

Reformers, monetary reformers who haven't even yet arrived at the concept of linotype government, can not expect to rule in a radio age. To reiterate: Lenin won by Radio, Roosevelt used it. Coughlin used it as minority weapon.

Representative ("democratic") government cannot survive unless the jaw-house is put on the air. If people "elect" weasels and speechless apes who cannot stand the test of radio-diffusion, naturally they (the people) will continue to be bled, starved and kept in rotten

GOVERNMENT

h.uses by A . . . s, B . . . s, C . . . s, D . . . s, and the dither of bank-pimps now reigning.

The best govt. is (naturally?) that which draws the best of the nation's intelligence into use. Roosevelt's alleged aim was O.K. But the small town professor and other objects professionally labelled "brain", "intelligence", do not necessarily fill the bill. Much as I admire the achievements of the Fascist Quindecennio in Italy, their tax system is still primitive and monetary knowledge rudimentary.[1] Enlightened by comparison with the bloody and barbarous English methods, than which no greater proof of degradation personal and national cd. exist.

The habits of servility, of cap-touching are so strong in England 1938, that only a very small élite yet recognize that the topper and morning coat may cover something more degraded than the jackal and less ethical or intelligent than a newt. The red Herring, the recurring decimal, etc.

I spend 8 years demanding a proper English edtn. of Frobenius. K. Kitasono has an article on Paideuma in *VOU* within the minimum time after receiving the volume (Feb. issue 1937). The red herring is scoundrel's device and usurer's stand-by. Supreme Court, Nationalization of mines or whatever. Race prejudice is red herring. The tool of the man defeated intellectually, and of the cheap politician. No one will deny that the jews have

[1] 1938 shows notable Italian advance on 1937 when the above was written.

racial characteristics, better and worse ones. "Every Polish nobleman had his jew."

The use, and more than use, the NEED of Frobenius' dissociations shows at this juncture. Whatever one think of his lists of symptoms, Hammite, Shemite, etc. he rhymes with Dante "che'l giudeo fra voi di voi non ride". It is nonsense for the anglo-saxon to revile the jew for beating him at his own game. The nomad in search of cattle, the romantic tradition. Happy is the man who inherits a rich field and a strong house and can take up a classic "Anschauung" with no inconvenience (to himself).

"All things that move, move by reason of some imperfection in themselves"?

Obviously the need of nutriment indicates incompleteness in the moving animal. It is not self-sustaining, it is not completely autonomous.

The tree picks up its roots and turns them inward to walk. How convenient to stick one's foot into the earth and be nourished? At sacrifice of the freedom to be nomadic?

Frobenius' lists of characteristics of races leave one with inability to accept, for oneself unconditionally, either a patriarchal or a matriarchal disposition. I prefer a lex Germanica to a lex Salica. My predisposition (at least in youth) being nomadic. It is not for me to rebuke brother semite for similar disposition. Happy the man born to rich acres, a saecular vine bearing good grapes, olive trees spreading with years.

The question whether I believe Frobenius right or

wrong in any given point seems to me frivolous. He cd. be wrong in 40 points and still bear gifts above price.

That a man find the car of Persephone in a German burrow is already a mental property. That one's roots are not a disease but parts of a vital organism is worth feeling.

The tenderness of the shepherd is subject for analysis. Whether the cow has need of a cow-herd I leave to ethical specialists.

I doubt if man deserves freedom until he can get along without being cow-herded.

"The art", says my venerable colleague once Vorticist W. Lewis, "of being ruled"! The art of not being exploited begins with "Ch'ing Ming"! and persists invictis, uncrushable on into Gourmont's *Dissociation d'idées*. If the affable reader (or delegate to an international economic conference from the U.S. of A.) cannot distinguish between his armchair and a bailiff's order, permitting the bailiff to sequestrate that armchair, life will offer him two alternatives: to be exploited or to be the more or less pampered pimp of exploiters until it becomes his turn to be bled.

The bailiff's order may be openly such, or it may be a bailiff's order heavily camouflaged, but homo not completely a sap-head will smell, divine or see clearly the difference between his roof and a mortgage.

In one recent period of British public life many laws were passed so ambiguous in wording that lawyers knew not how to interpret them. In the same period a law was put through which led

244

to overbuilding some of the ground still left open in London.

The London ground rents and entail, lease system etc. have defiled English building. A man will be very hesitant to build permanent beauty if he knows that someone else can bag it at the end of 9 or 99 years. As "B. H. Dias" I spent my odd time for several months observing the decadence of wood-carving, fanlights over London doors.

Economics is NOT a cold subject. Any more than the study of spirochetes was without bearing on human happiness.

Nothing has been viler in our time than the sloth and hypocrisy of pacifist careerists who have pimped for the obscurantists.

If I can't go quite as far as my Viennese café conspirator and believe that *all* pacifism is a diabolic and conscious device engineered by the war-makers as a definite part of their mechanism, I can at least believe that vigorous serpents have instinct, and that men resolved to live by human blood, unconsciously and/or semiconsciously, favour and finance obscurantings.

There is a body of sane writing in our time and/or a body of writing by enlightened men, some perceiving more, some not so much of the verity. Larrañaga, McNair Wilson, Christopher Hollis, all outside the strict sects of reformers. You will I think get nothing clearer on the monetary system than Soddy's

"Preposterous that banks . . . shd. by trick usurp

function of Parliament . . . and make forced levies on the community's wealth."

And, I reiterate, until America at least makes the intelligence of her founders available in print, we may expect all forms of idiocy, as usual, in that mind-swamp. Swamp = mud plus stagnant water.

All extant systems are due to the brute and sodden ignorance of the taxed.

At date of this writing (or up till a few days ago) Douglas himself was still being bull-headed about Gesell, and the rest of the sectaries all blind or half-blind re the knowledge current in other camps. Odon Por has kept a level head, being in Rome and keeping tab on international knowledge. Hollis continues to learn and, more than most men, maintains a contact with official and unofficial, financial and honest worlds.

If I have said it ten times in other books and not yet in this book it shd. be repeated here and in all books for a decade UNTIL it enter the popular mind:

Economic light in our time has not come from the HIRED, it has not come from preconditioned bureaucrats (governmental, universitaire and/or ecclesiastic). It has come from free men, an engineer (Douglas), a man of commerce (Gesell), Soddy, a prof. of physics, NOT of hired economy, Larrañaga a builder of roads, a technician, Rossoni, Por, McN. Wilson—NONE of them in harness. Orage, an editor who had the intelligence to quit a rusty and inefficient set of theories. Coughlin, H. Fack, a country physician, Vincent Vickers—voilà l'estat divers d'entre eux!

GOVERNMENT

Men stirred by the infamy of the bleeders and the abject sloth and pusillanimity of the hirelings.

The gross pig-like materialism fostered during the Victorian deadness has so deromanticized the occident that even the "column of infamy" has gone out of fashion. The thought that IF remembered at all, posterity will consider them as dungheaps and worms crawling in dungheaps is no deterrent whatever to 98% of government job-holders and ministers or holders of university sinecures. The truth is not honoured.

All that a G. G. or A. G. or an Al Capone (to take a more picturesque type than usually gets into a Cabinet) care for is security. Farley's ink that fades into invisibility is a bit of celestial irony, if it be not intentional.

America (the U.S.) has not paid its debt even in thought to the men who kept the U.S. OUT of the League at Geneva. If we have Susan B. Anthony in the rogues' gallery recently shoved onto our postage stamps, we shd. think up something better, some really honorific memento, say a monument really well sculpted, for Lodge, Knox, Borah and George Holden Tinkham, for having kept our fatherland out of at least one stinking imbroglio.

The League of Two Measures. The recurring decimal as in my title? The recurring decimals of infamy have among them and in high place, the *Captans annonam*, all forms of hogging the harvest, as one evil, and the false measure in its myriad kinds, as another.

Usura falls under the main consideration of unjust

price. Mankind's fog concerning it comes from NOT defining one's terms.

First the clear definition, then the clear articulation. Münch comes back from Capri "out of practice", having spent his time orchestrating and composing, his playing is greatly improved. (That rhymes with Dolmetsch's pedagogy for training children.) The muscles follow the mind. Tho' that precept can no more be carried to excess than I cd. become a great pianist by devoting myself to musical composition for three years on end.

Franchetti's comment "someone who hasn't become completely imbecile from playing the piano", ought to be written in letters of gold. "He plays like a composer", as compliment (but "He sings like a composer", may gods and angels defend us!).

45. THE RECURRING DECIMAL

Gavin Douglas re-created us Virgil, or rather we forget Virgil in reading Gavin's *Aeneids* and know only the tempest, Acheron, and the eternal elements that Virgil for most men glazes over.

Golding made a new Ovid. Chun-Tchi found the Odes to be so full of virtue; deemed them so valuable as an instrument of government, that he ordered a tartar version, and in his preface, translated, we find: Cum igitur ex hoc libro tanta utilitas exoriatur; eumdem volui encomiis exornare meis, et haec praefationem scribere.

(Eleventh year of the reign of Chun-Tchi, the emperor A.D. 1655).

Lacharme found the tartar version very useful when he wanted to make definite translation of the Odes.

Mussolini has told his people that poetry is a necessity *to the state*, and Carlo Delcroix is convinced that poets ought to "occupy themselves with these matters", namely credit, the nature of money, monetary issue etc.

These two facts indicate a higher state of civilization in Rome than in London or Washington. From this angle London is a mere bog or clog in the world's sub-sewage.

THE RECURRING DECIMAL

No british minister, let alone chief bleeder or Chancellor of Exchequer, wd. have the moral courage to pass half an hour in my company discussing, even in parliamentary language, the nature of money, or the infamy of starving the people.

Roosevelt's cabinet, with the exception of Ickes, has not the necessary acumen to consider these questions with the seriousness you wd. find in any european seminar outside of England.

I have no doubt that the reader will think this expression violent, and I shd. think so myself if I had not seen in the flesh a British Colonel, a man who was recently standing in the very public eye as champion of a cause most unpopular in England, shrink from a sheet of paper carrying my 8 Volitionist questions as if it had been an asp or a red-hot iron.

I shoved it into the pocket of his dinner jacket but doubt if he has ever had the moral courage to look at it. "Les hommes ont je ne sais quel peur étrange de la beauté" and that ain't the 'arf ov it dearie.

The kakotropic urge in economics is beyond anything a normal man can believe without long experience. They fear the light as no bed-bug ever feared it.

Some men will only sustain an "unpopular cause" when they have an intimate circle of admirers keeping them at it.

Civilization becomes admirable when people begin to prefer a little of the best to a great deal of the pasty. One of the rights of masterwork is the right of rebirth and recurrence. Janequin's Birds, out of Arnaut (possibly), out of immemorial and unknown, takes a new life on Francesco da Milano's lute. The Rapallo music is more than justified when Münch's Janequin is followed by his reduction of Vivaldi's Sol minore Concerto.

After Strawinsky's Pulcinella, there wd. be "no sense" in continuing certain forms of mediocrity and wateriness in our handling of early Italian masters.

The piffle offered performers in many editions of Vivaldi shows neglect of Bach's intelligence when faced with same problem. Bach had a perfect right to reset Vivaldi for his organ. He wanted a USABLE version of magnificent compositions. Münch is, to date, his most serious successor in the recurring decimal of good Vivaldi presentation.

"You may be able to do it with a few instruments," said Maestro Piccardi apropos of an unorthodox project. Idem with the Vivaldi Concerti, put a soloist with a dull conductor and the best qualities of concerti disappear; or at least so much of the fine carving is blunted that one's rage outweighs one's pleasure.

Any and every experiment and attempt to display old music is justified *as experiment*. Respighi shows us a wrong way in his attempts to set chamber music for large orchestra.

Without having heard Casella's resetting of the Chaconne for orchestra, I wd. defend even that *on principle*. Bach's Chaconne is a stunt piece. He had, magnificently, the right to investigate the maximum that one fiddle cd. carry; do it justice.

Four fiddles OUGHT to be able to make the reader

hear phases of Bach's thought that are usually (not ineluctably) obscured in performance of this composition.

The rights of experiment include the right to be unsatisfactory. Erlich's 605 experiments were useful. Errors, i.e. wanderings in search of truth have their rights.

The reductions of concerti for piano and fiddle, or for smaller groups of instruments, have their rights. It is sheer superstition, and academic superstition at that, to condemn them unheard.

They have been mostly BAD. Editors have given the first fiddle the soprano line, without double stopping, and chucked the rest of the parts onto the piano, with small or no sense of quality and orchestral effect. They have neglected the lower register of the fiddle (note that Honegger doesn't in his own fiddle sonata).

They have used soupy chords instead of contrapuntal dechifrage of figured basses and in short behaved as if neither Strawinsky NOR Johann Sebastian had ever existed.

I hereby express an appreciation of Münch's progress from his first setting of Janequin to his Vivaldi 1936.

Nothing cd. be more inconsidered than the superstition that because I have in the past discovered or log-rolled for violent and disruptive work (of high merit) I am forever bound by some law of consistency to discover nothing having merits of antipodal variety.

We have not an unlimited number of executants having sensibility such as that possessed by Olga Rudge and by Münch himself. We have indeed an wholly in-

THE RECURRING DECIMAL

adequate number of executants who can understand the most high qualities in music. We have a whole swill-pail and swamp of vulgarian virtuosi who can take the quality OUT of Mozart, Boccherini, Porpora or Caldara and substitute barber's hair oil.

If by the first anthology *Des Imagistes* I was able to start a process partially to desuetize (de-suet-ize i.e. take the cold fat out of) current poetry, I see no reason why I shdn't in time delouse the presentation of 17th and 18th (and 15th for that matter) century music or even a little contemporary composition, by analogous process, at least under favourable or exceptional conditions (say in the town hall of Rapallo, if powerless to affect the more bulbous fatty and opulent festivals).

46. DECLINE OF THE ADAMSES

The tax system is an infamy, based on crass ignorance of the nature of money. Actions of public utility shd. not be taxed. And even heavy taxes have never proved a deterrent to bestiality in all its forms.

The tragedy of the U.S.A. over 160 years is the decline of Adamses. More and more we cd., if we examined events, see that John Adams had the corrective for Jefferson.

In Italy the trouble is not too much statal authority but too little.

Liberalism is a running sore, and its surviving proponents are vile beyond printable descriptions. They have betrayed the "*Droits de l'homme*", they are more dastardly than Judas. The definition of liberty, on the Aurillac monument, is the "right to do what harms not others".

In our time the liberal has asked for almost no freedom save freedom to commit acts contrary to the general good.

The Italian state spends millions in beautifying its roadsides. And the minute Corrado Ricci is dead and the Duce's attention turned for a fortnight in some other direction, a scrofula of advertising signs breaks out on the via Aurelia. As usual in advertising, it is largely for synthetic products. Good food needs no smeary hoardings.

Jefferson never saw a roadside bill-board, he never foresaw modern advertising, and if he had he wd. have loathed the underlying diseases.

● ● ● ●

What ultimately counts is the level of civilization. No decent man tortures prisoners. No clean man wd. tolerate the advertising atrocities between here and Genova. No man free of mental lice wd. tolerate the bank racket or the taxing system.

These statements belong to a higher phase of civilization than that yet existing in the majority mind or in the rattling and buggy skulls of most cabinet ministers.

The function of music is to present an example of order, or a less muddied congeries and proportion than we have yet about us in daily life. Hence the emphasis in Pythagoras and Confucius.

The "record of Confucius is the record of a very great sensibility", the history of western philosophers is preponderantly the record of defective sensibilities, hence the normal man's boredom at the very mention of "philosophy" in the west. T. Beecham: "*That* is a critic. Cdn't. you tell it by looking at him?" Repeat and multiply re majority of writers on philosophy in our time or in 2000 years of Europe. General topics, "*i massimi problemi*" treated by men who had no particulars, no personal experience of the facts. Geo. Moore: "Tell us about yr. love affairs, Teddy!" (G. M.'s apostrophe to the first Roosevelt.)

Putting usury on a pedestal, in order to set avarice on high, the protestant centuries twisted all morality out of shape. "Moral" was narrowed down to application to carnal relations. Thus acting as usurer's red herring. The hogger of harvest has always set up a red-herring system. The gerarchy, the proportion of venal and mortal sins is always confused in his official code.

It seems unlikely that any man of cabinet rank in England or the U.S.A. has, during the past 20 years, committed any act that cd. in any way however slight or remote conduce to support or fostering of art or letters. We have been governed by boors, we have been governed by pot-bellied vulgarians, and the bourgeois mass has not attained a level of civilization sufficiently high to resent it.

47. ROYALTY AND ALL THAT

Plenty of people were ready to blame Edward, and none of them paused to consider ethical training. There is no use in a man's mugging up historic events as listed in encyclopediae if he be unable to see what goes on around him.

Having seen three empires and two monarchies "fall" or "do belly flops", the historian of my generation cannot be expected to regard such institutions as adamantine and perdurable.

You can measure their stability and the degree of their importance by the attitude of typical writers and men. Egidio Colonna wrote for the Instruction of Princes. Machiavelli wrote for eye of a sovereign. So do we not.

My Tory friend explodes "The King OUGHT to be a stuffed rabbit". My progressive acquaintance says that really he has never been able to think of royalty counting at all. When, in 1916, some left-wing and/or socialistic or liberal gang in London started talking about republic and eliminating the King, Orage thought it "funny to bother about".

A socialist wrote a rather good political poem with refrain "The King costs 20 million pounds a year", i.e. King regarded as detail in general problem of state expenditure.

ROYALTY AND ALL THAT

The real government having long since slipped from jaw-house to press controlled by interests, and by 1918 entering the radio phase.

There is no use in expecting children to remember history, or adults to read it, if it be merely retrospective. All they can do is to like as much as is offered as Märchen (fairy tale, or escape). The Church of England has been carefully depicted by Trollope. It is a local and rather unpleasant issue. Said Church since Trollope has not had the energy to revive. Items: curate came to me in London as to a confessor. Did I despise him for being one? He had no other means of livelihood. Considering the foetid state of economic system, what else *could* the poor blighter do? I absolved him.

Idealist enters church of Eng. because he sees a huge machine that *ought* to function. To anyone outside, the English Church is a bureaucracy, a mass of sinecures, an organ of retrogression, of rancid hypocrisy. The office of King's proctor England's leading obscenity.[1]

On the other hand the Church of Rome has undergone a very great change, a revival, uncommented and never cataclysmic enough to cause comment. Involuntary as far as its worse elements were concerned. Unavowed because the foetor of the first half of the XIXth century, or the era 1820 to 1870 was never avowed, and in the nature of things could not be avowed. The Church today is a far different affair from what it was in the days when Pio IX slithered down and Cardinal Antonelli was the chief power. An institution which has survived the

[1] Mild reform has occurred since I wrote this.

picturesqueness of the Borgias, the picaresqueness of the Renaissance, and produced Pauthier, Lacharme and Don Bosco, has an inherent resilience.

I, who write this, remember the RRivrinnd CCava-llliere DDDottoRRRRe AlexaNNdeRRRR RRrrrr-berrrrtson with a scotch accent as tthickk as three tweeds and a tartan. And evverrry sunday, under the shadow of the old Campanile, and while the new was building, he poured out his admiration of Paolo Sarrrrrpi and told the unwary travelllor how the banditti were in pay of the ppppope. This wuz in the Sc'tch kiRRRRk in Venice, as was. I also remember after "the" war that the international gombeen were so strong there was propaganda: "Souscrivez à l'empreunte papale!"

The real revolution *continua*, it goes on, propaganda or no propaganda. The historian or he who introduces his reader to the study of history must at least *know of* this process.

History that omits economics is mere bunk, it is shadow show, no more comprehensible than magic lantern to savage who does not know what causes the image. Magic as the gramophone or the telephone to the Bedouin at first hearing.

From sheer force, physical prowess, craft, jaw-house, money-pull, press to radio, government has undergone revolutions of modus and instrument.

Ideologies float over this process. Emotions, appetites, are focussed into political forces.

When any set of functionaries (such as kings or legis-lators) ceases to be held in confront with ethics, that set of participants declines. It either rots in itself, or goes into desuetude. The low cultural level of governors in our time wd. or shd. have aroused the amused or indignant contempt of participants in high civilizations.

Edward VIIth's reading matter wd. have been taken as a joke by Lorenzo Medici. The late Senator Cutting in correspondence with me over Catullus etc. answered my enquiry: How many literate senators are there?

He sent nine names, ending "and I suppose Dwight L. Morrow". Another legislator commenting on his colleagues used the phrase "Know what its all about!" He thought there was an infinitesimal number of 'em who had *any idea* of this. Curiously enough he thought Cal. Coolidge had had an inkling. And he counted this as partial explanation of Coolidge's public success as above duller and more animal members.

There is no use in trying to "understand" history as a mere haphazard list of events arranged chronologically. At least not as in extant tables. You can on the other hand read almost any biography with some interest if you have some sort of provisory scaffold, hat-rack or something to work from.

Of extant "monuments", if you have a passion for system, you can try the picture of Mœurs Contemporaines in Homer, the various early scriptures, Herodotus, you can get it firmly in mind that Demosthenes was onto most forms of business swindle, let us say all of them that are not due specifically to material mechanisms invented since 1600. We are beginning to piece together a little true Roman history, such as difference in rates of mortgage interest in more or less orderly Rome, and in more or less disorderly conquisted provinces.

We have one Mohammedan fact that will take a head-line in future histories. One of the early kalifs did pay a national dividend. He ran with an empty treasury no national debt and a share-out. Conquest in his day was far less productive than the 20th century industrial system.

Whig historians have not emphasized feudal distributism. British bores tried to study history from historians, being, for the most part, pompous and prosy asses they were incapable of reading verse (though Macaulay wrote it).

The praise of *largesse* in the troubadours is a fact in history. The attempt of Frederic II of Sicily to enlighten Europe both culturally and economically was a MAJOR event.

Feudal dues have been stressed and the feudal duties (noblesse oblige) have been overshadowed. The french decadence, the use of fine words when fine actions had ceased, left a bad taste in the popular mind.

S. Malatesta gave away a lot of castles on, or shortly after, his accession. Such acts have a meaning and a social significance. Madox Ford used to talk very vehemently, but not very coherently, of the damage done in England by commutation of duty of overlords to their people into mere money payments.

The black darkness of Europe occurred not in the "dark ages", hitherto so called, but in the ages of usury. By that I mean ages when usury was subterranean, unnoticed, undenounced, camouflaged under thrift propaganda, mercantilist tosh, down to the filth of Manchester and the slop of Victoria's time.

This is not rabid prejudice against Mrs Albert Memorial. I hold (naturally) that the pseudo-gothic and the taste of the period was the result of causes.

Just as the respect paid to Vicky was of causes. Vicky was an advance on her Belgian Uncle. In a time when most royal persons were disreputable, in the decade of enthroned rastaquouires, when half the kings in Europe had no more ethic than Alfonso XIII. When half of 'em were mere Wall St touts or the equivalent, shady speculators, Vic and Albert were at least above minor dishonesty in matters of money. One might hold that from firm conviction they were (indubitably) reactionary. One might argue that in their eagerness to hold off Napoleon III, they even committed technical high treason. Certainly they put spokes in Palmerston's wheels when Pam was the government. But the view of government in the 1840s and 50s was not as it now is.

Nevertheless England cd. in those dim and bewhiskered days point with pride to her Royalty *on a comparative basis* with what other kingdoms had. (Bomba for instance, of the french rucklings.)

There is no doubt that in any international light of the 1930s Russell and Gladstone are, personally, comics, but given the proportion of their own time they were serious matters. No civilized age will take 'em for models. Their clothing and their general attitude to life were ridiculous. But Gladstone did not like Bomba's treatment of political prisoners.

All these attenuating and complicating details can be got into some kind of focus by infinite labour.

Civilization went on. I reiterate that the cultural level is the determinant. Civilization had been in Italy. It had hung on in Provence and the Exarchate after Romulus Augustulus.

A conspiracy of intelligence outlasted the hash of the political map. Avicenna, Scotus Erigena in Provence, Grosseteste in Lincoln, the Sorbonne, fat faced Frankie Petrarch, Gemisto, the splendour of the XVth century, Valla, the over-boomed Pico, the florentine collectors and conservers . . . even if mere Serendipity hunters. In politics this enlightenment mattered. Varchi wanted the facts.

The real history went on. 1760 to 1790 in Tuscany with the work of Pietro Leopoldo and Ferdinand III of Habsbourg-Lorraine, wiped out by the Napoleonic flurry and the name Habsburg defiled and become a synonym for reaction and—Gregorian obscurantism. Nevertheless Tuscany carried on. Glory mislaid in Italy itself because Cavour and his melodramatic confrères took the spotlight, and there has been no stop since. Only a breather between 1870 and the New Era. During that breather Italy lived on its immediate past. Every town had its (usually incompetent) monument to Garibaldi, Mazzini, Vittorio Emanuele and most of 'em at least a plaque to Cavour. Venice to Daniele Manin.

ROYALTY AND ALL THAT

London had monuments mainly to soldiers, as I recall it. Italy did not give enough credit to Ricasoli.

Shallow minds have been in a measure right in their lust for "secret history". I mean they have been dead right to want it, but shallow in their conception of what it was. Secret history is at least twofold. One part consists in the secret corruptions, the personal lusts, avarices etc. that scoundrels keep hidden, another part is the "plus", the constructive urges, a *secretum* because it passes unnoticed or because no human effort can force it on public attention.

The real history of France during the age of infamy was Flaubert and co. The intellectual struggle against French political pimpery, frumpery, and finance. The history of French literature during the XIXth century is worth knowing. French public history of that time is for a faecal analysis only. No one wants to preserve it save as pathology. La Tour du Pin did at least write against it.

The history of the United States was ill recorded. It now begins to emerge in historians already mentioned. Not only our American history but our literature in the correspondence of J. Adams, Jefferson, J. Q. Adams, Van Buren.

We had on the whole something to be proud of, at least as main effort, up till the Grant administration. Thereafter we mainly slumped into bog and sewage.

An as yet unadvertised dramatist, Wm. Mahl has got Jim Fisk into readable drama.

Our serious historians of 30 years ago were still groping. This is not to sniff at their efforts. Take 'em as blind but patient writers of monographs and one cd. speak with esteem of the lot of 'em. I mean, I don't think they were deliberately rotten, or that they committed deliberate fakings and forgeries. It is only when a set of ideas is dying that you get deliberate forgers, and that men, astute at short range, deliberately blind themselves for the sake of emoluments and to hang onto their jobs. Such a phase of ideological dying we have recently lived in.

The most astute rascals have pursued a cunctative policy, they have been "slow to admit". They have hung onto forgeries and falsifications until truth cd. be presented as "sound opinion". Great is their reward in hell. A future enlightened public will give them their just sentence and their name will be slime for posterity.

Dr. etc. with several titles, ex-rector of the Q. University, said "The error of my generation was that we underestimated Marx". There is a confession at 70. The error of the left in the next three decades was that they wanted to use Marx as Koran. I suppose that real appreciation, that is, the real attempt to weigh Marx's veritable merit began with Gesell and with Gesell's statement that Marx never questioned money. He just accepted it as he found it.

Only in March 1937 had I got a man on the American communist fringe (not a party member, but a Marxist) to notice that Quincy Adams was communist (of a sort). And this man is one of a few dozen Americans who live twenty years ahead of their time. Gli uomini vivono in pochi.

I took that from Machiavelli and put it on the front page of my "Gaudier".

When the vortices of power and the vortices of culture coincide, you have an era of brilliance. It took the *Manchester Guardian* or froustery six months to discover that *BLAST* was satirical. 24 years have not been enough to teach 'em that Vorticism was constructive. In fact, it has passed as a small local movement, and I myself do not care a hoot whether the name remains pasted to it. Kung fu Tseu was a vorticist. Happy is the man who can start where he is, and *do* something.

John Cournos deserves the credit for being the first to see what Gaudier had got *into* his *VORTEX* (vide p. 64, *The whole history of sculpture*). If that phrase be in some senses an exaggeration it exaggerates in the right way. It prods the hearer into getting down into the meaning of a highly delectable document.

The piffling nature of the age can be measured by the time that it took a few people to learn the real Gaudier, and the speed with which a faked Gaudier was (two decades later) accepted.

Section XI

48. ARABIA DESERTA

Doughty's volume is a bore, but one ought to read it until we discover some better and quicker antidote to exaggerating both the hell of mercantilist industrialism, left us by the rotten XIXth century, and the disadvantages of life in the open, Bedouin romance etc. The book at least shows something of what goes on before, and/or without, the inconveniences still bound up with mechanical civilization.

K. Carl's book on the Chinese court (vide ante p. 81) portrays a high culture. Wu Yung[1] gives us perspective (*The Flight of an Empress*).

His clear eye and pellucid style are contemporary with all men in: "Money is easy to collect. If you are willing, we will help you. At that time the banks in different places were glad to do business of this kind. They wd. choose a man who was anxious for promotion and lend him large sums at high interest. . . . They wd.

---

[1] Wu Yung's editors seem to ignore that their frontispiece, the portrait of the Empress Tz'u Hsi, is from the painting by my compatriot Katharine Carl.

have lent me 10 or 20 thousand taels without the slightest hesitation. Some of the bankers came personally to me to persuade me."

So much for the simple life among mandarins, and among chinese governors of a province.

Beyond this we have several points wherefrom to measure.

I. General Grant's diamond-headed cane went to Li Hung Chang finally. Wu Yung has forgotten which american president it was who received, and whose widow transmitted the cane. Fortunately for his sense of beauty he is not led to speculate on the probable sources of what paid for the cane. It being unlikely that Grant had any decent friends when he started round the world, though there may have been several Americans who regretted his fall.

II. The general reflection on the contrasts in Wu's China, might be: A high civilization in decadence. A few people highly cultured, the probability of these people having constituted a very small percentage of the chinese population? (That is an open question. No one who writes in English has tried to sort out the varying levels of chinese civilization in our time.)

III. We have the spectacle of disorders, very like the Boxer disorders, in Russia and Spain, where the civilized segment of the population was a mere handful and the number of semi-savages enormous.

IV. Contemporary with Wu's remarks on banks, Mr Cullis sends me this morning the following excerpts.

"At the same time [viz. 89 B.C.] the debtors & the creditors at Rome had a quarrel, for the money-lenders used to lend at interest, while an old law distinctly declared that Usury was forbidden, & that the offender against this law was liable to penalties. For the ancient Romans seem to have objected, like the Greeks, to usury, regarding it as mean, & hard on the poor, & provocative of strife and enmity, just as the Persians regard borrowing as deceitful & conducive to fraud [A. seems to be mixing up two things here?]. But now that long-standing usage had established the practice of receiving interest the creditors began to demand it, relying on this usage, but the debtors wished to defer payment owing to the [Social] wars & the disturbances, whilst some even began to threaten to enforce the penalty against the money-lenders. Then the praetor Asellio, who by virtue of his office had charge of such questions, when he had failed in his attempts to bring about a reconciliation, gave leave to bring actions, pointing out to the jury the discrepancy between the law & general practice. But the usurers, enraged at this revival, had him murdered . . . in the middle of the forum . . . whilst he was carrying out the sacred rites & wearing the priestly insignia. . . . Yet no-one declared the names (of his murderers) for the usurers kept the matter secret."

(Appian, *Bellum Civile* I 54.)

"Although it is illegal to recover money at all that has been lent to provincial communities, my predecessor allowed Brutus to exact the usual rate of interest at

12%: when the Slaminians were unable to pay this, he got Scaptius the money-lender thru whom he was working to secure a troop of horse from the governor & invest the town. When they were still unable to pay, he took the 5 leading citizens & had them starved to death. And now that I am governor he is demanding 48% from them. . . ."

(Cicero to Atticus; 51 B.C.)

By comparison with Salmasius, Mr C's first excerpt seems a bit vague, as indeed he himself recognizes, but the fact of the excerpts being made at all shows that our young men are getting back to a sane state of curiosity. They do read classics in search of living material and of real notes *pour servir à l'histoire*, as did Salmasius.

Given enough of this it shd. within a few decades be impossible for us to have secretaries of the Treasury and infamous Chancellors of Exchequers who dare not and/or cannot define money, credit, or property.

Sovereignty rests in money. The United States Constitution is the greatest state document yet written, because it alone of them all, clearly recognizes this power and places it in the hand of congress. If Roosevelt's attack on the Supreme Court is nothing but una manovra politica, it places him with Baruch and Farley: flimflam. The change proposed in the court was unnecessary. The law gave him power for the needed regulation.

The basis of a state is its economic justice. It exists by texture. Communism with its dictatorship of the proletariat is merely barbarous and Hebrew, and it is on a level with primitive theocracies. Its god is baal; that is irresponsible power regardless of intelligence or justice.

No people ignorant of the nature of money can now maintain its rights, let alone attaining or holding to sovereignty. We have in our time two parties: the infamous, which tries to sabotage economic knowledge; the intelligent, which demands full light on the issue of coin, paper means of immediate exchange, and of credit.

Credit, from this angle, becomes the privilege of delaying compensation.

In this sense the man or entity having credit is one who is privileged to delay compensation for something recd.

49. KUNG

Knowledge is seldom lacking in the degree that will is lacking. Kung's life appears to be in conformity with the best modern views. I suspect that a minority has always held these views. Kung's first public job was a Douglasite assessment of the productivity of the province set for his inspection.

Naturally he was the mover.

He believed that travel broadens the mind, and that knowledge of local conditions is good antidote for theorists. He visited the best musician he had heard of. While interested in increasing agricultural production (as Cavour or Rossoni) he was by analogy against the Bedaux and Stakhanov sweating and speeding-up systems. He did not bother to give advice on how to produce more to a minister whose sole aim was to push up the amount of tribute sweatable from the peasantry.

Tuan Szetsun remarked that he found nothing unusual in the classics.

Kung is modern in his interest in folk-lore. All this Frazer-Frobenius research is Confucian. Ovid had an interest in these matters, but nothing shows that it was as sober. Ovid, I keep repeating from one decade to another, is one of the most interesting of all enigmas—if you grant that he was an enigma at all.

仁者以財發身，不

仁者以身發財

KUNG

Of living men, Edmondo Rossoni, with his agricultural experts and his care for crops, is nearest the Confucian model. Nothing cd. be more false than the idea that Kung was preoccupied with the dead. He was concerned with the living. Cemeteries shd. be on high ground, hills least use for cultivation.

Our Congressional investigations and Farinacci's demand for the condemnation of Toeplitz innovate nothing. The trial and condemnation of Chao-tcheng-mao a week after Kung accepted the Sse-keou (chief magistracy in Lou) still serves as paradigm for reformers. It was the one condition Kung made before he wd. accept the office. C. T. Mao was the Mellon-Norman plus of the time.

Next a fight with the meat-trust—one individual monopolist, who got off by restitution of what he had made by violation of just price. Violation due to monopoly.

THE LESSON of Chinese history? As I can have no pretence to "potting" it here, might nevertheless be of two kinds. By implication, we might more despise and suspect the kind of education which we (my generation) received, and we might acquire some balance in NOT mistaking recurrence for innovation.

My generation was left ham ignorant, and with the exception of a few, mostly tongue-tied and inarticulate, specialists the whole occident still ignores 3000 years of great history.

We have not even heard of Tai Tsoung or of Tchin Tsoung. The America of our immediate forebears considered ideogram as a laundry check.

KUNG

Our history has been parochial, not that there is any harm in studying the history of one's own parish if one knows what one is at. But to call a book "General History", and omit the great emperors, is as stupid as to omit Constantine or Justinian—unless it be clearly stated that one is concerned solely with men and events that have been entwined in the development of occidental institutions—the lex Romana being here pertinent to us in a way that no tale of public events, wars, shiftings of borders ever can be.

The specific lesson (1938) might be to recognize the U.S. Constitution as an innovation, and to hesitate for a very long time before scrapping it in favour of expedients and experiments oft tried and oft proved ineffective.

Fads and excesses are never new. One might note that Wu Yung in the recent Boxer times and Kung B.C. found beheading prevalent. Nevertheless the Chinese chronicle records "abolition of capital punishment". It records a law that the Emperor shd. reflect three days in a sort of retreat, no jazz and only necessary food for three days, before pronouncing a death sentence. (Ordinance of Tai Tsoung 627/649.)

Tai cut down taxes. Tai remobilized the teaching of Kung fu Tseu. At his death the Tartar princes demanded the privilege of immolating themselves in order to serve their Lord in the next world.

That might give one perspective, datum for a custom and a conviction that stretched from the Pacific to the Mediterranean. These Tartars were prevented from observing this antient custom only because Tai had fore-seen that they wd. ask to do so, and forbidden it. 1013 *de notre ère* Tchin Tcoung brought out a new edition of the classics *and* ordered their distribution.

Before thinking that old-age pensions, medical relief, educational endowments etc. etc. etc. are news, one shd. at least glance at a summary of the chinese story.

To separate what is Chinese and what Japanese needs more knowledge than I yet have or am ever likely to come by. Harakiri for high nobles is pre-Confucian. No more a Jap invention than belief in Paradise was patented by our local theologians.

The idea that orientals are men lacking emotion is more idiotic than almost any other.

We might come nearer to understanding them if we considered their admiration of impassivity to be admira-tion of something attained *per aspera*.

In any case we are in a thick fog of ignorance. Daimio, Samurai, a new Generation. Earlier Japanese poets imitating Chinese as Europeans in the seicento wrote latin.

We can blame our ignorance on no one man and on no single professor. The cutting off of England from Europe from the time of Napoleon, and the damnable stinking and pusillanimous subservience of American poor fish to second-rate and tenth-rate English opinion do not wholly excuse us.

Though their lamentable effects enter an explana-tion.

We have had 150 or 200 years of Chinese scholarship

printed in French and/or latin and we COULD have got on with it faster.

Serious history revives, bit by bit, in our own time. There is no serious history without study of social texture wherein IS the money factor. Book-fools (blessed be the ideogram for that word), understanding nothing of their present, naturally do NOT pick the live details from past chronicle.

Kung went for the big bad boss. Instant trial ended in seven days. He went for the meat monopoly. Tai Tsoung reduced taxes. Pietro Leopoldo and Ferdinando III cut down taxes. Taxes are infamy.

Date/Italian Senate March 18th, 1937. Rossoni perceives possibility of complete change in the taxing system.

The present tax system can be continued only by ignorant men or by scoundrels. Taxes were lowered before Gesell saw how to focus all or a reasonable part of them on the medium of exchange. The state serves in creating a MEASURE of exchange. A tax that can never fall on any man save one who has a hundred times the amount of the tax in his pocket AT THE MOMENT the tax falls due, is the least nocive of taxes. It must ultimately supersede taxes designed merely to oppress the people and to sabotage all sorts of effort which conduce to the general good or well-being.

The enemies of mankind are those who petrify thought, that is KILL it, as the Marxists have tried to in our time, and as countless other fools and fanatics have tried to in all times, since the Mohammedan decadence and before then.

MAKE IT NEW

Naturally, the more a man knows, the more he will be able to get out of Aristotle or any other great writer. Aristotle did not save the world economically. It is even doubted whether he wanted to save it. No man is blameable for what others fail to learn from him or for their distortions or misproportions in derivation. Aristotle did not implant a clear concept of money in the general western mind. He saw that money was a measure.

The pregnant phrase is that wherein he says it is called NOMISMA because it exists not by nature but by custom *and can therefore be altered or rendered useless at will.*

KUNG

If we put this "be rendered comparatively useless" we shall have got the juice out of "altered and rendered". The rendering more or less useful or useless is now part of the bank wheeze.

The second paragraph selected by Mr Butchart is not quite tight in its phrasing. "Guarantee of future exchange" is thoughtful.

As working hypothesis say that Kung is superior to Aristotle by totalitarian instinct. His thought is never something scaled off the surface of facts. It is root volition branching out, the ethical weight is present in every phrase.

The chief justice had to think more soberly than the tutor and lecturer.

Give the greek points on explanatory elaborations. The explicitness, that is literally the unfoldedness, may be registered better in the greek syntax, but the loss must be counted.

There is nothing exclusively Christian in Aesop's contention that we are "all sons of Zeus". It affirms moderate kinship without excessive equality.

50. CHAUCER WAS FRAMED?

That he was slayne, lernynge philosophie,
Right in that citee, nat but for envye.

Legende of Good Women, l. 1899.

How civilized *was* Geof. Chaucer? His narrative sense is
or is not lower than that of the best Northern ballad
writers?

"Adam Bell, Clym of the Clough and Wm. Cloudesley"
the gangster films of their day. Relative civilization of
Stevenson, Kipling and Henry James?

What are we to make of the "de raptu meo" suit
against Chaucer. Did government officials, London Port
authorities etc. in "them days" indulge in a bit of kid-
napping on the side, and why were three of 'em in it?

If Prof. Pollard really wanted to prove Chaucer's
respectability, why not posit that he was "framed"?
Young girl in the train case, lady loose in the park.
Chaucer the first really Victorian public official? Got
away with being twice held up and relieved of road-
worker's wages within 24 hours?

Married a Court Lady, went abroad on a couple of
Embassies, we are a bit vague as to what position he
held in the delegations? interpreter? clerk able to write
and read? Or as indication that Fourteenth Century
England held poesy in high esteem?

Chaucer's real civilization was three hundred years

old. It inheres in his sense of verbal melody, in the tonal leading of words meant to be sung, or in sense of song modes worn smooth in the mind, so that the words take the quality for singing.

The culture of Crestien de Troyes and of Beroul, plus his own humour. Pollard doubts if he knew the *Decameron*. Italian anecdote preceded the *Decameron*.

Turning abruptly to the blood and thunder of the ballads. Libri gialli. And to the general decadence of ethics and the angle of tolerance, note a preface dated 1842

"and care has been taken, by the omission of all objectionable passages, to prevent the liability to charges which may be brought against more extended collections" (of the Ballads).

Not only do barbarians (meaning especially the English) tolerate murder in books where they are squeamish of bawdiness, but they prefer blood to a natural openness or even refinement. Usury is contra naturam. It is not merely in opposition to nature's increase, it is antithetic to discrimination by the senses. Discrimination by the senses is dangerous to avarice. It is dangerous because any perception or any high development of the perceptive faculties may lead to knowledge. The money-changer only thrives on ignorance.

He thrives on all sorts of insensitivity and non-perception. An instant sense of proportion imperils financiers.

You can, by contrast, always get financial backing for debauchery. Any form of "entertainment" that debases perception, anything that profanes the mysteries or tends to obscure discrimination, goes hand in hand with drives toward money profit.

It might not be too much to say that the whole of protestant morals, intertwined with usury-tolerance, has for centuries tended to obscure perception of degrees, to debase the word moral to a single groove, to degrade all moral perceptions outside the relation of the sexes, and to vulgarize the sex relation itself.

Against this Miltonism, only the Romantic rebellion strove. That rebellion was itself finally degraded to luxury-trade advertisements, Nature still finding an advocate where none was consciously intended. The kill-joy is an enemy.

Both jocundity and *gentilezza* are implicit in nature. There is plenty of propaganda for exuberance, plenty of support for Rabelais and Brantôme. But that does not by any means exhaust the unquenchable splendour and indestructible delicacy of nature.

You have two millennia of history wherein we see usury opposed to the arts, usury at the antipodes of melody, of melodic invention, of design. Usury always trying to supplant the arts and set up the luxury trades, to beat down design which costs nothing materially and which can come only from intelligence, and to set up richness as a criterion. Short curves etc. "opulence" without hierarchy.

If a man starts noticing ANYthing, there is no telling what he mayn't notice next. Hence the blurb reviews in the daily wypers.

CHAUCER WAS FRAMED?

Against which Grosseteste (I suppose the one who wrote on the nature of light)

> The virtu of the harpe, thurgh skyle and right
> Wyll destrye the fendys myghte,
> And to the cros, by gode skylle
> Is the harpe lykened weyl.
>
> Robt. de Brunne, trans.

I have never writ anything more to the point than:

The truth about a field is one thing to an impressionist painter wanting to paint it, another to the farmer who means to plant something and make it grow.

The magic of music is in its effect on volition. A sudden clearing of the mind of rubbish and the re-establishment of a sense of proportion.

51. HAPPY DAYS

From the time of Queen Anne the prevailing tone of the better British observers has been one of disgust. The violence of Pope's enemies as example. The general trail of acidity, of defensiveness or, at worst, of plaintiveness among gentler victims is amazing if one, in the face of a clear sea and before the serenity or storm of the Italian hills, look back on it. Hardy quotes ole sheepy Wordsworth almost with an edge: such readers may suppose

"that by the act of writing in verse an author makes a formal engagement that he will gratify certain known habits of association; that he not only thus apprises the reader that certain classes of ideas and expressions will be found in his book, but that others will be carefully excluded".

One might almost say that Wordsworth's remarks about what people expected of verse in the time of his Lyrical Ballads had been extended to prose volumes in the present era of wrath and abomination.

Hardy was equally on the defensive in the *Apology* (1922), and moreover felt, with perfect right, that it was an outrage that he shd. be on the defensive at all.

It requires now, as it wd. then, a great effort of imagination even to sketch out why Hardy shd. have been put on the defensive or what variety of tick or parasitical insect might have censored him.

A conscientious critic might be hard put to it to find just praise for Hardy's poems. When a writer's matter is stated with such entirety and with such clarity there is no place left for the explaining critic. When the matter is of so stark a nature and so clamped to reality, the eulogist looks an ass. At any rate he looks an ass the moment he essays the customary phrasings of enthusiasm. It is not life grim. It is not life *plus* ANY adjective the would-be eulogist can (at least in the present case) find.

Τάδ' ὧδ' ἔχει.

NOT with an "air" of tragedy greek or other.

No one was hurried to read it. If any one did read it (apart from Madox Ford, who started the *English Review*, was it? because a poem of Hardy's lay there to be printed) nothing glib presented itself to "be done about it".

A critical document that ought to be better known appeared in Harriet's *Home Gazette* about 1912 or '13, it afterwards appeared as preface. It gave Ford's specifications as to what a poem shd. be. Given those specifications, poem after poem of Hardy's leaves one with nowt more to say.

Expression coterminous with the matter. Nothing for disciples' exploitation. When we, if we live long enough, come to estimate the "poetry of the period", against Hardy's 600 pages we will put what?

1898 to 1922, roughly a quarter of a century, plus the

retrospect and the early pieces. A vain regret that one couldn't have written novels for thirty years or whatever before courting the muses?

All right. It, Hardy's verse, is full of Browning. Browning being "the only poet younger than himself" who had aroused Beddoes' interest. And Beddoes' editor omits Landor from the list of poets writing english after the death of Shelley. My god what an England!

In this England Hardy was of the great English line . . . the life he records is English, it was not a life any civilized man wd. have immigrated into. It was, unmistakably, all right for Hardy to live it.

If I have, a few pages back, set a measure for music, I set another for poetry. No man can read Hardy's poems collected but that his own life, and forgotten moments of it, will come back to him, a flash here and an hour there. Have you a better test of true poetry?

When I say that the *work* is more criticism than any talk around and about a work, that also flashes in reading Hardy. In the clean wording. No thoughtful writer can read this book of Hardy's without throwing his own work (in imagination) into the test-tube and hunting it for fustian, for the foolish word, for the word upholstered.

Here also are poems that his French contemporaries, and those older a bit than he was—the best of them—could have respected. There is a flood of life caught in this crystal. Landor, who was quick to see Browning's prying inquisitiveness, wd. have been quick to give credit for the clarity in Hardy's portrayal.

Sero sero te amavi, pulchritudo tam antiqua, quam nova. There is a clarity like Hardy's in the best English sporting prints, in stray watercolours, anonymous of the period.

"One never sees" placed together the names, or "it wd. seem fantastic to place together" Hardy, Swinburne, H. James, the pre-Raphaelites, yet on one alignment they stand together, that is in disgust with the social estimates of their era, in rebellion against the sordid matrimonial customs of England. And between 'em they bred a generation that, at least in its minded section, carried their disbelief into action, without however evolving a new code.

The answer to experiment is not relapse into the intolerable. Though that is the weak man's answer and the "swing of the pendulum" tendency.

Hardy stood for the joie de vivre (Ralph Blossom). He declined (persistently) a stage-set joie de vivre. He declined (persistently) to blink anything or to take sand for sugar or to go through any of the polite motions implicit in accepting sand in one's tea.

HAPPY DAYS

"who will not see
What life's ingrained conditions are."
The ironic choosing of breezy sire rather than foresight-
ful son for companion. But neither he nor James ignored
the undertow. James definitely isolated it in the pos-
thumous *Ivory Tower*. If Hardy did not isolate it, put
it that Hardy did NOT accept the code of his time. Put
it that he did in the main choose sex tangles that do not
depend directly on the money factor, and that wd. usu-
ally remain after it had been settled, as James took his
scene mainly above the level of monetary pressure, thus
both gt. writers sought a permanent subject matter, a
permanent *enredo*. But put it also that no sane and
clear code can be formulated until and unless all tangled
relations between men and women have been analysed
and set in two categories: those due to money and those
that are independent of it.

Marriage has scarcely ever been lifted outside this
zone. Neither have irregular relations.

Blessed Romance exists beyond it, or romantic fiction
ignores the pressure or sets it in an allegory with
dragons and shining armour. At any rate there is no new
code evolvable until the preliminary economic under-
brush has been cleared (ref. once again my note on P.
Bottome's *Private Worlds*, a novel about a Mad-house,
where every case was due to money, and where the doc-
tors and rest of the entourage were all enmeshed and
conditioned by it). Any real portrayal of modern life
must deal with situations which are 80% monetary,
though halfwitted writers may be ignorant even of this

basic fact affecting their fictions. Clichés, "money won't settle it all", "money won't do everything".

Reply being that until BOTH parties are free from money pressure, any "solution" is impossible. Five varieties of Roman marriage, possibly the most serious attempt on record to devise a code taking COUNT OF monetary pressure.

The code of Hardy's time, and Hardy's plots all imply monetary pressure. When you have isolated the situations wherein it does not enter from those where it does, you will at least have two categories of situation, and can talk with augmented clarity of t'other or which, instead of confounding them together.

52. THE PROMISED LAND

It ought sometime to be said, though no one will be paid for the printing, that the serious Victorians, from Hardy to Swinburne, did NOT accept the current code of morality and that they had a contempt for that church which, in the words of my great uncle Albert, interfered "neither with a man's politics or his religion".

Only Rudyard Kipling, who had a most British mind regarding women, put up some sort of episcopal frontage, because he was distinctly cautious when it came to matters of thought, outside his given limits, limits wherein thought was mainly a sort of technical and courageous ingenuity. Hence the romantic female colossus who spat out to me "Narrsty little wrratt!" at mention of Rud K's much public name.

Hardy, who lived on after the era, came to his final "Surview". Cogitavi vias meas. "That the greatest of things is Charity." But out of the lot of them only Browning had a revivalist spirit.[1] Whether as an artistic device to rouse pity and terror, or as defence mechanism, flaunted in writing because it did not work in their private lives, the others wrote as non-interveners.

Whether from truly deep instinct, whether because intuition showed them the hopelessness of staving off a

[1] ? and Swinburne.

great and unguessed war. . . . I do not make out—and I protest again, in season, out of season, against the pretended omniscience of critics (journalistic convention, Kipling being the wise-guy etc.).

In any case they bred a generation of experimenters, my generation, which was unable to work out a code for action. We believed and disbelieved "everything", or to put it another way we believed in the individual case.

The best of us accepted every conceivable "dogma" as a truth for *a* situation, as the truth for a particular crux, crisis or temperament.

And a few serious survivors of war grew into tolerance of the "new synthesis", saw finally a need for a "general average" in law. There was, in this, perhaps no positive gain save that, again, a few saw a dissociation of personal crises and cruces, that exist above or outside economic pressure, and those which arise directly from it, or are so encumbered by, and entangled in, the root problems of money, that any pretended ethical or philosophical dealing with them is sheer bunk UNTIL they be disentangled.

All of which is not to deny the permanent susceptibility to tragedy, the enduring tangles, situations etc. that depend wholly on free emotion, emotion conditioned only by hungers, appetites, affinities, and durabilities of attachment.

A refusal to recognize two categories leads, in novel writing, to tosh, unmitigated and blithering tosh. The only professional writing worth the name has been, for years, Crime Club, and that, I take it, is, again, instinctive. The whole people having an intuition of a crime somewhere, down under the Bank of England and the greasy-mugged regents, but accepting an escape mechanism of murder, burglars, and jewel-thefts.

When you get out of the hell of money there remains the undiscussable Paradiso. And any reach into it is almost a barrier to literary success.

> Sì vid' io ben piu di mille splendori
> Trarsi ver noi, ed in ciascun s'udia
> "Ecco chi crescera li nostri amori".

There is nothing in modern critical mechanism to deal with, and I doubt if there is anything handy in our poetic vocabulary even to translate, the matter of this and the following Cantos.

> Vedeasi l'ombra piena di letizia
> Nel fulgor chiaro che da lei uscia.

Sober minds have agreed that the arcanum is the arcanum. No man can provide his neighbour with a Cook's ticket thereto.

Bosschère remarks rather bitterly that this is perhaps the only indelible indication of justice vouchsafed to us.

> And at dead of night I call;
> > Though to no prophets list I;
> Which hath understood at all?
> > Yea: Quem elegisti."

It is almost a breach of taste to quote Hardy's final poems in a book of yatter such as the present is.

THE PROMISED LAND

As to novel writing, I have nothing to add to James' prefaces. As to narrative writing you can however take bearings, sic: Chaucer, "the ballads", say for example Clym of the Clough and Wm. Cloudesley; Hardy's dramatic short poems, the situation as in *Conversation at Dawn*. After novel writing he wrote verse narrative. No 40 or 200 page versifications, but something shorter. Turn to *Erectheus*, any one wd. perhaps suppose 1906 to '16 a better time for poesy than the 1870s had been.

And I say this despite all the rocks anyone can throw at Hardy for romance and sentiment. Whether in a communist age we can, or will in our time be able to, concede such emphasis to the individual elegy and the personal sadness, I doubt. And if not? the transition may have been from literary to rhetorical.

But a craft that occupies itself solely with imitating Gerard Hopkins or in any other metrical experiment is a craft misdirected. We engage in technical exercise faute de mieux, a necessary defensive activity. Out of these sentences you may omit neither the "solely" nor the "necessary" without destroying their meaning.

20 novels form as good a gradus ad Parnassum as does metrical exercise, I dare say they form a better if the gods have granted light by that route. Hardy is Gautier's successor as Swinburne cd. not be.

Is one however permitted to detect a damned lack of sociability in late Victorian writers?

> Pastime and good company
> I love and shall until I dye.

THE PROMISED LAND

Henry VIIIth's mind was as good as, as good for a time as, Hardy's. Wd. it be correct to say that both of them or that neither of them believed in polygamy? And if they disagreed on the subject, which was it from whither?

A gain in narrative sense from 1600 to 1900, but the tones that went out of English verse? The truth having been Eleusis? and a modern Eleusis being possible in the wilds of a man's mind only?

The requirements being far beyond those of merely an intelligent literary circle (which doesn't in any case exist). We lack not only the means but the candidates. Think of any modern waiting five years to know anything! Or wanting to know! If ever anything but a fanaticism could? A collection of misfits? Not the flower of a civilization. Was it ever possible save with conviction and a simplicity beyond modern reach? now that knowledge is a drug on the market, said knowledge being a job lot of odds and ends having no order, but being abundant, superhumanly abundant.

A divine parsimony of ideas? Or an ultimate sophistication? Sophistication is not, emphatically is not, enough. The overcoming of personal jealousies possible only in the high light of belief or the oblivions of pure curiosity. Says Valli, all these poets were Ghibelline. That seems to be provable assertion, while the rest of his, Valli's, wanderings in search of a secret language (for Dante, Guido and the rest of them) are, at mildest estimate, unconvincing. "Something" behind it? Certainly "something" behind it or beyond it. Which the police called "Manichean" knowing nothing either of Manes or of anything else.

"I wish" yodeleld Lord Byron "that he wd. explain his explanation." That was in another country and a different connection, but I admit that the foregoing pp. are as obscure as anything in my poetry. I mean or imply that certain truth exists. Certain colours exist in nature though great painters have striven vainly, and though the colour film is not yet perfected. Truth is not untrue'd by reason of our failing to fix it on paper. Certain objects are communicable to a man or woman only "with proper lighting", they are perceptible in our own minds only with proper "lighting", fitfully and by instants.

PART VI

Section XII

53. STUDY OF PHYSIOGNOMY

I offer for Mr Eliot's reflection the thesis that our time
has overshadowed the mysteries by an overemphasis
on the individual. R. L. Stevenson, whom no mystic has,
so far as I know, ever mentioned, had more emotional
wisdom than most men. (*Virginibus Puerisque.*) Eleusis
did not distort truth by exaggerating the individual,
neither could it have violated the individual spirit. Only
in the high air and the great clarity can there be a just
estimation of values. Romantic poetry, on the other
hand, almost requires the concept of reincarnation as
part of its mechanism. No apter metaphor having been
found for certain emotional colours. I assert that the
Gods exist.

And this very simple sentence leaves Mr Eliot just
as much in the dark as he was before asking: What Mr
P. believes?

Will he be any happier in his nest of frousty and in-
sular parsons if I say: I assert that a great treasure of
verity exists for mankind in Ovid and in the subject
matter of Ovid's long poem, and that only in this form
could it be registered.

That assertion in no way conflicts with a belief that

STUDY OF PHYSIOGNOMY

European knowledge increased from the fall of the Roman empire onward. And that many respectable minds collaborated in mediaeval theology. I don't in the least wish that I had missed a Xtian education in childhood, even though I shd. be hard put to remember a word of it, and though the Old Testament is most certainly in the main a record of revolting barbarism and turgid poesy. The New, they tell me, is written in most disreputable greek (misprints occurring every time I endeavour to quote that language must give infinite pleasure to those students who know (professionally) enough of it to be sure that I don't).

I am now aged enough to see nothing ridiculous in 19th century french maçons and free thinkers having had their offspring Christianly (that is catholicly) educated.

A culture persisted. Only in basicly pagan Italy has Christianity escaped becoming a nuisance. Only there has it escaped the dastardly fanaticisms which grow into it in barbarous climates.

CAMPANOLATRY

As note in very small print (because it is explanatory and not in the main line of the text). In order that the serious reader (one in every 900) can calculate the personal distortion in my writing. I was brought up in American school and sunday school. Took the stuff for granted, and at one time with great seriousness. Questionings aroused by the truly filthy racket imposed on denizens of Kensington, W.8 by a particular parson. It appeared to me impossible that any clean form of teaching cd. lead a man, or group, to cause that damnable and hideous noise and inflict it on helpless humanity in the vicinage. Followed this through Trollope and in the porcine physiognomy of other parsons. Vigorous anticlerical phase ensued.

STUDY OF PHYSIOGNOMY

NOT based on noise itself but on the states of mind necessary to induce that gross and piglike tolerance of infamous sound. Plenty of evidence forthcoming as to corruption of british mind, ecclesiastical bureaucracy etc. The effect of a "trifle" like the noise wd. have been effaced had I found any contrary evidence, i.e. of any health or cleanliness in British religion. But for the noise I shd. not have been started investigating. What I *found* was disgusting. Idea that there could be clean and beneficent Christianity restarted in Tempio Malatestiano. Country priest not the least disturbed that I shd. be making my farewells *solo ai elefanti*. Namely that I had come for friendly word with the stone elephants and not for altar furniture. Still further sign of enlightenment from old nun in hospital: E. P. not catholic. No, thank heaven! NOT protestant, not jew, but accepted greek deities. "Zè tutta un religione." Oh well it's all a religion.

I am writing about civilization. England's reputation for hypocrisy is certainly not new. I remember hearing an active sermon, I believe in that funny church with a round front and a spike near Oxford Circus. That wd. have been about 1909. Add about 30 years, and the impression I record, that most protestant and nearly all anglican parsons are uncivilized, many are pigs, some have made a tolerable compromise, i.e. are doing certain things they don't quite believe, as a compromise (Blougram's Apology etc.). They think the end justifies etc. or that things wd. be worse if they didn't administer. No intellectual curiosity in any anglican publication. Church Assembly a year ago did touch problem of work and employment (the latter defined as sale of work usually under econ. pressure). *Thoughts after Lambeth* one of Eliot's most creditable essays. I wonder who suggested it? But J. H.'s criticism "lot of dead cod about a dead god" quite just as describing a good deal of T. S. E.'s activity.

STUDY OF PHYSIOGNOMY

Coughlin has effected a good deal of rough very popular education.

You turn to Hardy's preface and find, I think, that he had bet a goblet of hope on the Eng. ch. because he had first bet a bucket on New Catholicism and seen it spilt. It was a faute de mieux, if hope weren't there, he (from Max Gate) cdn't. see where it was likely to exist.

That anyone "believes" seems now doubtful. Washington quite sanely cd. mention "the benign influence". The benign influence of Dickens' fiction can also be maintained as existent. I believe in the benign influence of litterae humaniores. And there is no doubt that in the more or less 2000 years of Xtn Europe there have been Christian humane compositions.

When Wm. Baxter sold his king and his church, he lacked certain moral sensibility.

All very well to define man as laughing animal, political animal etc. De Gourmont doing it rather better: reproducteur, electoral, contribuable.

I doubt if Zaharoff knew much of what he was doing. I come back repeatedly to the sow and the truffles. Useless to expect the sow to perceive anything outside her own field of reference.

Presidents, bankers, prime ministers need not be supposed to possess a field of ethical reference much above that of pigs. In fact it is difficult to explain the history of the past centuries if one postulates such an equipment for them.

An advance wd. imply either in public mind or in the spirit of controlling oligarchies a preference for human rulers, and an intolerance of having lower animals "at the helm".

The study of physiognomy shd. be encouraged.

AND TENDING TOWARD A CONCLUSION.

54. AND THEREFORE TENDING

Having put down one's ideogram of culture, or say one's road map intended to aid the next man to a few of the summits, with less fatigue than one's own, one has almost a duty to attempt rectification, i.e. to compare one's outline with some gt. book against which one may be prejudiced or at least wherewith one supposes one's self to be not in accord.

When I started this brochure nothing was further from my mind than the *Novum Organum*. It will not serve my purpose, for, taking it by sheer chance from a dusty shelf, I find I have marked certain passages, therefore I must have read it or read at it. A number of my "most outrageous" remarks might have been taken from it (not I think from marked passages). Bacon found Aristotle unsatisfactory.

As against "Arry", F. B. and I are of one party (more or less). One's measuring book shd. not be of an author in whom one has specialized, that wd. mean a fixed attitude, possibly an unconscious feeling of proprietorship in the work. I can't at this day Ap. 16, '37 have any sense of proprietorship in the Nichomachean Ethics. Ease might tempt me to use a Chinese philosopher recently edited. I have 40 pages of notes on him hanging at my right. A man's hand is stained in the clay he works with. I have in those 40 pages branded X. as a guide to counterfeiters. I see no excuse for filling the reader's mind, even a little, with refutation of X.'s doctrine. My most enjoyable moment of perusal was when I found his introducer saying that "only the most rigid Confucians" had resisted the persuasiveness of X. The treatise for (or notes taken by) Nichomachus offers a better tavola rasa.

Here at least we have a summary of Paideuma, as built up by gk. civilization to the year 300 and whatever ante Christum. Wide enough to serve as card-index for the essentials of the good life.

A set of cubby holes whereinto one can sort one's values and make them into a schema.

I take oath of impartiality. Mr Swabey said I had been a bit hard on Arry, so I got out Mr Rackham's edtn. of the N.E. Up till page xxii of R's introduction I was quite ready to believe that my general mossy impression of the Stagirite was wrong, and that he might be a safe guide to the young. I was already thinking of Mr Rackham as standing "as near wisdom as any man is likely to come in our time in Europe". I was ready to test his most admirable introduction by the text following after it, and if necessary sing palinode to my impertinence as on pp. 46 of this volume. He had stated so many admirable things to inhere in his author.

The gent. reader is warned that I shall now devote several pages to an analysis (of a sort) of the Nichomachean treatise. Those in search of daisies and scintillations had better skip the next pages.

AND THEREFORE TENDING

It must however be admitted that I had not read half a page of the text of the N.E. before I had again the old feeling to wit (as on reading Aquinas) that the author of the words there shown was not a wise man, and that we have here a second-rate book. (I speak specifically of the text of Rackham's edtn. apart from all questions of authorship, or alibis as to whether Aristotle intended this as final form, whether it were mere notes for lectures or notes taken by students *at* lectures. As strand in the European cultural story, the early latin translations wd. equally serve. "Moerbeke's" or whoever's.)

I have not got through 4 pages before my gorge rises. Here indeed have we a swine and a forger. (Ref. Schopenhauer's admirable essay on style, and how you tell the true man from a false one.) Aristotle's hedging, backing and filling, if you compare it with a true work like the *Ta Hio*, is a give away. This bloke, were he alive today, wd. be writing crap for the "Utilities". He has lasted because "like to like". He is not a man with the truth in him. Rackham has attained considerable beauty in his apologia, but it won't hold up for four pages of his translation.

Four or six years ago I was scandalized at reading that the University of Paris had prohibited in 1313 or whenever the teaching of Aristotle. By p. 11 of the Ethics I am ready to say "and a damn good thing too", i.e. the exclusion of him from curricula intended to guide the young. This is not by any means an opinion I had this morning expected to write down this evening (16 Ap. 1937).

AND THEREFORE TENDING

BUT SUPPOSE that Aristotle knew something, suppose that the old (or middle-aged or whatever he was) bastard had "got hold of something" from Plato, from Plato's gossip of Socrates. A word almost an ideogram. This treatise was not written, these notes of his not given or taken after Darwin and Huxley (*and* Ball, prolonged and protracted researches of).

εὐδαιμονεῖν

This is not "well-being" in any ordinary sense, or well-doing or doing well, or happiness as in any current use of the word. This was spoken a bit after Socrates had been told to drink hemlock. This is rooted in all Socrates' trances, it is not even "to be in good spirits". There is no ready made current English for it. It is not to be among good angels. It is to be possessed of one's good DAEMON. It is aperient, in the sense that it lets in all the Arabian commentators, and gives a clue as to why mediaeval theologians took up Aristotle, with their angel-ology, and their ouranology, or demonology = good-daemon-ology. With this word (almost an ideogram) we are down through the blither and yatter, the *Spectator-New-Statesman-Villard-Webbite* weekly choinulism, down onto the pre-Socratic paideuma, into folk-lore. Damn the dictionaries. The bleating lexicographers have not looked at the roots of the ideogram. This word is out of thaumaturgy not out of a print shop. It don't prove that Arry was anything but a Bloomsbury simp, but he used it.

And the journalist's bleat cannot be cut off from the

tradition of Socrates or from the fact that the bleaters were kicked out of Rome, because their logic chopping was a public nuisance, found bad for the morale of the -verts (con- or per-). Consules decretum etc. as Prof. Q. writes to L. V. (illegibly) furono cacciati da Roma nel 161 senatus consultum. As is told by Suetonius. C. F. Strabo and Valerius Messala were the consuls (appunto 161 a.c.). Quod erat factum ut de philosophis et rhetores de ea re ita censerunt ut M. Pomponius praetor . . . plus accompanying note from the distinguished L. V. writer on philosophy et uxore, neither of whom can decipher Prof. Q.'s handwriting, but enough appears legible to confirm Fiorentino ut Romae ne essent (with a ref. that appears to be Gallus 15, 11, I.).

We are indebted to Rackham for the hint that Aristotle's text is a mass of notes. If we accept Schopenhauer's acid test for writers, the work is bad. It is heteroclite, a hodge-podge of astute comment and utter bosh, material for a sottisier, but above all subversive, morally bad. Safe for an old bloke of 50 (like myself) if he be constantly on the watch for trickery, or let us say not even trickery, but mis-fire, sentences that are so, or half so, but in total effect obscurantist as often as aperient.

Rackham has given us a clue to the evil in the last sentences of p. xxii of his introduction, but I am trying (against great odds) to keep that incision for termination and summary. That is to say I want to KNOW whether the evil which shows through Rackham's sentence is his, Rackham's invention, or if it really subsists in the Aristotelian text itself.

AND THEREFORE TENDING

Not that there is nothing in pages succeeding the first use of EUDAIMONIA and EUDAIMONEIN to indicate that Arry knew he had hold of a word with a past.

Greece rotted. The story of gk. civilization as we have it, is the record of a decadence. Language had already got down to *Times* leader and *D. Telegraph* level. Arry wd. have succeeded in the most louche modern milieux.

Certain books do no evil, I do not mean weak books but books of the strongest kind. The just critic must discriminate them from books where we find as it were poison mixed in sweet cake, which a strong stomach can digest, or an alert mind read with nothing more damaging than irritation. But these latter are not for curricula.

This does not imply acceptance of Arry's statement that the young "shd. not study moral philosophy", even though the use of that phrase may have implied a perception on Arry's part that *his* lectures weren't suitable pabulum for the inexperienced.

My point being that they are definitely the compost, intelligent enough to serve counterfeiters by providing them means toward the confusion and obfuscation of others.

I wd. even go further and state in parenthesis, with the date Ap. 16 anno XV, that the things still needing to be remedied in the Italian State are due to an Aristotelic residuum left in Mussolini's own mind.

Despite all he has sloughed off in evolving his totalitarian formulae.

As another species of footnote Sadakichi Hartmann sends me a sort of helter-skelter table, which has perhaps one value, or two, its sincerity and the impossibility of its becoming academic.

There has been certainly no collusion, and Aristotle is among the "near great" on his list. I mention this because Sadakichi has lived. Has so lived that if one hadn't been oneself it wd. have been worth while to have been Sadakichi.[1] This is a tribute I can pay to few men (even to those listed in his table of glories).

The European reader may need still further note introducing the above mentioned author, whose dramas have not had a wide European circulation, and whose poems are scattered in lost periodicals. When after seventy years of life he finally appeared before the, in the full sense, public, not one in a million knew him as the Chinese magician in Fairbank's *Thief of Bagdad*.

RE THE NICHOMACHEAN NOTES

BOOK I

I wd. not give this First bk. of the Ethics to a young man, as I think it tends to confuse rather than to enlighten. I say this, after weighing even the fact that the author does pull out into the open, xiii, 2. with "the true statesman seems to be one who has made a special study of goodness".

One cd. sift the text into three categories of items. Stuff fit definitely for a sottisier, a list, that is, of imbecilities; second, the bulk of the book, just yatter, stuff more or less so, more or less not so; and thirdly, a residuum (small) of phrases that a good advocate could defend, claiming that they reveal or cover something of value.

[1] Not that my constitution wd. have weathered the strain.

AND THEREFORE TENDING

As the general reader cannot be expected to dig down into this detail, I give samples of the third and first categories in the original, with section and verse numbers. Partly to show that I am not merely scribbling vague generalities:

O.K.		RUBBISH	
δυσαφαίρετον	v. 4.	ἀρχὰς ῥαδιως	iv. 7.
χρηματιστὴς βίαιος		vi. 16.	
	v. 8.	The οὐ before τὴν τοῦ	
ἥδεσθαι τῶν ψυχικῶν		σώματος	xiii. 6.
	viii. 10.		
θεωρήσει τὰ κατ' ἀρετήν			
ἀρετην = vir(tus)			

πράξεις καὶ τὰ ἔργα		The final συνετός	
	x. 11.		xiii. 20.

unless you consider it merely a remark on current verbal usage.

I don't assert that the phrases in the left hand col. prove anything. I merely mean that profundity might be in their vicinage. . . .

IF the reader wants to do his own thinking. The proper vaccine is at the start of Schopenhauer's essay on style. The paradox or something near paradox is that Aristotle shd. combine such admirable terseness of expression with such shiftiness, such general independability. This

311

admirable terseness might well prevent the unsuspicious reader from smelling the quicksands.

But is the terseness mere triteness? Are the phrases short merely from continual use in the lecture hall, not from intensive brevity?

Arry, rotted by preceding half century of mere talk, mere university blather . . . naturally the idol of, or bait for, professorial dilettantes.

BOOK II

I wd. say to any young student or to any man in later life who has suddenly acquired the leisure for study or extensive reading:

Certain books form a treasure, a basis, once read they will serve you for the rest of yr. lives. I have almost no regrets for early omissions. I count it a blessing that I had sense enough NOT to listen to certain professors or attend courses in abstractions, philosophies and the verminous economics propaganded 1901–1907. I wish I knew more greek, but I envy Cocteau *his* greek as I shd. never envy Swinburne his probably ampler acquaintance. I do not, on the whole, believe greek is as useful to a thinking man as is latin. Were I guiding a younger European I shd. say: latin, chinese ideogram, and then greek. To an oriental I wd. say English, French and Italian.

I wd. certainly say to a student: there are certain books which you can leave. If and/or when you are 50 or 60 and have nothing better to do, you can monkey with higher dilettantism. I have no hesitation in suspecting that Aristotle belongs to dilettantism. The lecturer's professional "bosse", the need to talk for an hour. . . .

No man has a right to assume, as has been done by a gt. number of XIXth century writers, that the Roman Senate, 161 a.c., the University of Paris, 1313, Georgio Gemisto, 1437, were dead wrong or that they were blindly fanatical and acting in unseemly haste or levity.

The unseemly levity has been on the part of those who condemned them without either reflection or examination of their reasons for action.

Making our divisions: Good. The Mean

Anaisthetos also cd. contain a thought.

But II. ii. 3 is mere subversive CRAP, followed by a quotation—quite admirable—from Plato. II. iii. 5, words slide about like oil on surface of pond and Arry has SAID really nothing. Again, English thought, and in less degree European, has suffered from provincialism, and the most rancid device of the cheapest politicians, the false dilemma. Pore boobs have been spoken to, as if only alternative to Aristotle was back-slip (or slide-slip or whatever) into Plato's purple.

In any case it is crapulous to continue basing curricula on material available 300 years ago, and neglecting all new knowledge. It is not as if Chinese were Fenollosa's discovery. As to the humanities, other points being equal,

AND THEREFORE TENDING

what comparison can there be between a means of communication with 400 million living beings and a dead language never spoken by a fifth of that number of people at any time.

IF the work in the dead language be superior to that in the living tongue, that alters the question.

Re Bacon. I don't think my coincidences of view are due to unconscious memory, two men at different times may observe that poodle dogs have curly hair without needing to refer to, or derive from, a preceding "authority".

Our universities have given NO thought whatever to adjusting curricula so as to include and/or prefer the best available "classics". They are in the main stuffed to the gills with parasites and bloated dullards too mikropsuxic to give this question a half hour's attention. And the intelligent faculty members are normally squelched by obese, belly-patting presidents, or effete executive officers.

My imaginary opponent may say: well, Aristotle preaches the doctrine of the mean. Kung, however, of the mean that stands fast. And without the abominable mixture of weeds and loose language. Your historical notes shd. tell you that the Nicomachean treatise (or

AND THEREFORE TENDING

notes for lectures on ethical nomenclature?) was composed during a decadence, the greeks had already collapsed. Conscious or unconscious subversivism?

Meyer Anselm had, let us say a purpose, a race (his own race) to "avenge". He used the ONLY weapons available for a tiny minority, for a lone hand against organized goy power, pomp, militarism, rhetoric, buncombe. You can't prove, and so far as I know no one has even suggested, that Arry was deliberately or consciously subversive.

Dante uses *che sanno* in his passage on Aristotle in limbo. He uses *intendendo* for the angels moving the third heaven.

Our Teutonic friend, what's his name (Vossler is it?), talks about the schwankenden Terminologie des Cavalcanti's. I believe because he hasn't examined it.

Till proof to the contrary overwhelms me, I shall hold that our mediaevals took much more care of their terms than the greeks of the decadence.

In Bk. II.:

iv. 6, is correct view,

v. 3, on not getting angry enough, is good,

v. 4, ἀρεται προαιρέσειS

vi. 2, εξιS, meritorious suggestions that can't do any harm,

vi. 9, admirable definition of perfect work of art, that "you could neither take from it nor add to it".

We remember that in the poetics there is an admirable remark about the apt use of metaphor (better in a translation I read 30 or more years ago than in the last text—greek and italian—where I went gunning recently for it). However ix. 5 offers us the prize "bull". No oirushman ever smelt a rat brewing in the air with more vigour than:

"or by steering wide of our besetting error we shall make a middle course. This is the method adopted by carpenters to straighten warped timber."

This is followed, v. 6, by a very cheap and shoddy suggestion.

Arry is here a tin-horn professor. A *Manchester Guardian* product.

BOOK III

i. 2 reinforces my remarks on terminology, Arry's in confront with the better mediaeval writers. Rackham has made a perhaps brilliant translation of KALON as nobility. It is at any rate a translation which incites the reader to think.

The contrast of *kalon* and *hedu* need not be antipodal antithesis. KALON as beauty or order might be an antithesis of *hedu* of certain kinds.

BUT no one can contemplate the use of *hedu* in Aristotle's whole work, or any extensive fragment thereof, without feeling the general slither and slipperiness of the terms used. They OUGHT to be technical terms, stable terms. YUNG

AND THEREFORE TENDING

Both Kung and Dante have a much firmer hold on the real, and a much deeper *intendimento*.

A REAL book is one whose words grow ever more luminous as one's own experience increases or as one is led or edged over into considering them with greater attention.

When first read, the phrase, "*maestro di color che sanno*" seems a general and generous compliment. The beauty of the twilit scene takes full possession of the reader. Limbo is divested of its defects. Only today do I stop to take count of the *sanno* as the mot juste, a graded and measured word, not merely two handy syllables fitting the metre, conveniently rhyming with fanno and stanno (which it precedes).

In an America befouled with snoopers and an England more recently dabbling in secret-police methods almost always for vile reason, clean men have become a little too hard on heresy hunters, and this, because they have confused two different kinds of people. Erhlich, Semmelweis and DeKruif's men against death sought for physical heresies, for the almost invisible and, with high power microscopes, spirochete or hidden evil. Thus the true theologians sought and fought against the roots and beginnings of error. Their state of mind was aped by the ignorant, who applied excessive penalties NOT to the baccili of error but to minor symptoms and superficial or irrelevant acts or views.

This latter debased heresy hunting, as every other form of chasing the red herring, has been consciously and unconsciously encouraged by scoundrels.

AND THEREFORE TENDING

III. i. 11 (3) a sentence of considerable elevation re folly of blaming external things.

i. 13 final clause, good sense. Thing different and therefore better use a DIFFERENT word when one mentions it.

The "danger" of Aristotle arises partly from his not putting certain statements in the purely lexicographical form. The "danger" for the reader, or class, being largely that of losing time in useless discussion. For example iii. 2. Nobody deliberates about things eternal, such as the order of the universe.

IF this is put as statement about the use of the verb (BOULUETAI), it does not lead to useless yatter.

Lorenzo Valla wd. have written. Whatever mental process we indulge in re the eternal etc. we do not use the verb BOULEUOMAI in such cases. We do not . . . etc. spend time *deciding whether*, but *we observe that*.

Yet even here the quibbler might now raise questions of imaginary geometries, in considering Aristotle's geometric illustration.

Valla's method is a progress, an improvement.

Then Oh Blessed Lacedaemon!! " No Lacedaemonian deliberates about the best form of government for Scythia."

Blessed Lacedaemon! The poison of Manchester has so cursed the world that half the anglo-saxons of our time spend their lives in some such imbecility, trying to decide on the form of govt. for all other races, while themselves being eaten to death by human lice.

iii. 8 would not lead to tangential argument, IF the

greek word order were: We use the word BOULOUO in speaking of what our mind does re matters where our agency operates but does not always produce the same result.

But even the most rabidly fanatical Aristotelian can scarcely claim that Arry had completely clarified his lexicographic intentions, i.e. sorted out what is or shd. be strictly lexicographic from what he supposed to express wisdom or observations on life and nature.

Pollon d'anthropon iden OU. He is manifestly and repeatedly not an Odysseus. He is a classroom pest half the time.

iv 5. It is not for me to set myself up against Mr Rackham who knows infinitely more about greek than I do, but "good man" appears to me weak for SPOUDAIOS in this passage, where I offer "the man with gumption" as a more vigorous and valid translation. Or in the gergo or vorticist slang of 1912/14, "the serious character".

22 April anno XV. Let it stand written that somewhere about III. vii. of Aristotle's treatise I was ready to chuck up the job, as a waste of my time, and my comment likely to be a waste of the reader's. (This feeling I have had neither with the *Analects* nor the *Chi King*.)

BOOK IV

"In performing noble acts rather than in avoiding base ones." i. 7.

"not because he considers it a noble thing to do, but

because it is a necessary condition of having the means to give". i. 17.

"not on himself but on public objects". ii. 15.

"not rejoice overmuch in prosperity nor grieve overmuch in adversity". iii. 18.

"MELEIN TES ALETHEIAS MALLON E TES DOXES, rather the truth than what people think." iii. 28.

These are all good doctrine. But the newspaper leader-writer is taught to write so that the reader will find what he wants to find. These sentences *can* be excerpted. But the fourth book of the N.E. may also be accused of giving rather the portrait of the gent as seen by the superior butler than that of the gent as to himself. It is a highly civilized treatise, descriptive rather than, or at least as much as, germinal.

A preference for useless and beautiful objects is highly civilized and aesthetic. Aristotle's megalopsux is a model for Grandisons. "A lady or gent is one who never unintentionally offends" free rendering of iii. 31, final portion. Rackham uses a footnote to distinguish the megalopsux from what is now called the magnanimous. There is no denying that book IV yields copybook maxims. And you will find a pawky comment in every two or three pages. Castiglione must have read it with pleasure. One wd. not, perhaps, be grossly unfair to Arry if one called bk. IV a disquisition on manners. Useful application of which to one's juniors might conduce to professorial calm.

AND THEREFORE TENDING

BOOK V

Rackham's note on the third word in this Fifth section of the N. Ethics might almost lead one to think the whole book invalid. IF the Philosopher can't use one word for what is unjust and another for what merely contravenes some law or custom, what claim has he to be taken seriously either as thinker or writer, let alone on such a subject as JUSTICE (dikaiosune)?

Claudius Salmasius is a much more serious character, and his *De Modo Usurarum* shows real curiosity. He wants to know and to show what his terms mean, and what certain terms had meant in earlier writers. Arry was just giving a lecture?

As a matter of fact section i. shows Arry in rather favourable light. He sits up and takes notice of looseness of terms, of difference between illegal and unjust. He rather does want to distinguish between greediness, illegality etc.

DIKAIOSUNE, justice is the perfect virtue because it is the practice of perfect virtue. Office shows what a man is. It makes him part of the community, he has to use his character on others. V. i. wd. be rather a good segment of the work to use in introducing Arry to the reluctant reader. V. ii, 8/9 He dissociates

ADIKON	the unjust
PARANOMON	the illegal
ANISON	the unequal

However, before finishing that sentence we find a piece of tosh so nonsensical that we can only suppose the text has been pied. However, bk. V does register a gain over the preceding books in that we have here the concept of "the practice of virtue toward someone else". Rackham may add a touch of clarity in his translation "divisible assets of the community".

BUT the terminology is unsatisfactory. If eleutherion means free-birth in one place, and gentlemanly behaviour in another, we have not even good "pidgin", we have not even a practical business language, let alone one valid for finer distinctions of "higher thought".

It must have been meant to register exact thought, if the "lecturer" was "holding up diagrams" (mathematical). We have however a note on the usage of the term democrat, meaning "one who thought all the free-born ought to have an equal share". At least I don't see how the text can mean anything else. Principle of assignment by desert, and criterion of desert (or worthiness) being free-birth (iii. 7). There is a call to order when we reach the word aristokratoi. "The democrats make the criterion free-birth, oligarchs make it wealth, others good-birth, the aristocrats make it virtue (areten)."

Arry can not be blamed for muddles between these criteria, whatever other peccadilloes man may ascribe him.

οἱ δ' ἀριστοκρατικοὶ ἀρετήν

That is an aristocracy of character, not of inherited material position.

Nevertheless the clarity in passages on Distributive Justice is due to the translator, who has supplied capitals D. and J.

AND THEREFORE TENDING

A language having one word for proportion and another for analogy, is better for registering thought than one where *analogia* serves for both?

However, the patient greekist can sort out

DIKAIOSUNE, justice, especially dianome dikaion, Distributive Justice, and

DIORTHŌTIKON, corrective justice, il contrapasso.

A monolingual culture will never breed anything but asses or the kind of trype emitted by H. G. Wells' generation.

Up and down, long and short, I do not believe Aristotle a profound man, but one who handled at times the profundities of others, as in "exchange keeps them together". In the passage V. v. 6

μεταδόσει δὲ συμμένουσιν

on proportionate reciprocity necessary to the existence of the state. *Metadidomi* dictionaried also as the "giving a share".

"Hence the shrine to the Graces"

διὸ καὶ χαρίτων ἱερὸν

(Arry at his best.)

And he continues with great ability through V. v. 8/9/10 with most admirable emphasis, that money is BORN as a MEASURE.

He has, and let no one fail to credit him with it, come at money from the right side, as a measure. A means of ascertaining the proportionate worth of a house and a pair of shoes.

AND THEREFORE TENDING

In the hierarchy of its constituents he has got hold of the chief reason for money's existence.

Yet again it makes an infinite difference whether you translate χρεία as *demand* or USE. Here the black curse of university obfuscation descends on Rackham. The man has met somewhere a university professor of economics or some work exuded from such licery. He falls into class-room jargon, and translates χρεία as demand.

The value of a thing depends on USUS, its price may be distorted by its OPUS.

Arry has not made his paragraph fool-proof. XREIA is a wood-pile in which you can hide an indefinite number of niggers.

The viscid slither of Cambridge, the shame of the Regius foundations. The pimps' paradise of indefinite verbiage.

The idea of Money as a guarantee of future exchange is, on the contrary, clearly presented.[1]

The sentence beginning *PASXEI men oun* is taken as registering Aristotle's awareness to the wobbly nature of any monetary unit. But even Rackham's longer expository translation is much too vague to enlighten the ignorant.

---

[1] To want, to be in want OF, to need, are not identical conditions. But it wd. be quibbling to raise the point here. Aristotle has magnificently isolated a very important function of money. The guarantee or pledge of future exchange is valid BOTH for whim and necessity in the future. That is O.K. so long as the reader isn't lulled into forgetting that the statement about guarantee is INCLUSIVE of these various conditions. It makes no pretence of sorting them out. Can't expect any writer to clear up all the tangles at once.

AND THEREFORE TENDING

The careless will "assume" its comparative constancy, and will be had. As per milleniar custom they have been.

"The proper thing is to have commodity prices fixed" (Oh yeah!) and *then* money serves as a measure which makes 'em commeasurable as scarcely on sea or land in human experience, but properly Utopian. I am not arguing against it, I am merely indicating the insufficiency of our philosopher as guide.

His lucidity as to the measuring function, and his implication of money of account are both admirable.

But "their prices fixed" Rackham's rendering of PANTA TETIMESTHAI can have half a dozen different meanings. All this estimated, valued?? prices determined in Jan. and kept set? I don't think Aristotle can be invoked and saddled with the stabilization racket on the strength of *panta tetimesthai.*

Let us use his own justice on him. Not accuse him of sins of specific commission where he has merely used general terms.

There is nothing here to rule out Charlemagne's commodity denar. If Arry is to be patron of anything specific, the commodity dollar or denar is as good a great-grandchild as any.

V. x. 3 gives an admirable illustration of Aristotle in the act of registering something which has become part of occidental culture. Just as money is left in a mess, here the distinction of equity has stood. "EPIEIKES is not justice but the rectification of *legal* justice. Law always general statement, and there are cases which cannot be covered by general statement."

325

AND THEREFORE TENDING

(Query, didn't A. find this ready made?) Analogous advice might be given translators in general from x. 5, "to decide a case as the law-giver himself wd. were he present": to express a thing in your language as the author himself wd. have had he spoken it.

And yet this has exceptions. Rackham's expository version is certainly worth more than a literal one wd. have been, to any conceivable reader. (Up to now I have queried only a "do" for a "wd." in his english, ἐῶμεν back in V. vi. 5.)

The use of *mesos*, *metron* and *kanon* (V. x. 7) might be worth watching. For those interested in measures, straight rods etc.

BOOK VI

With the opening allusion to tightening the strings of the lyre, we get a further development of the idea of the just.

HOROS, the boundary, standard of measure.[1] ὅρος

The quality of the work has been rising during the Vth book, even if we allow for some of the best bits being taken from pre-existent Athenian legal terminology. As ethics, Arry is not fit to clean the boots of Confucius. With the start of the VIth book he ceases to be irritating. He has got onto his own subject and goes on quite nicely up to VI. vii. 4. One is tempted to wrangle rather with the translator over, let us say,

ἕξις μετὰ λόγου

or to suggest that the phrase about *sophia* carried over

[1] Cf. *Metaphysica* II.

AND THEREFORE TENDING

from the Gorgias. "Knowledge having a head" etc. might be rendered "hierarchy of knowledge *of things worth while*".

That wd. distinguish the *sophia* from animal prudence. At any rate a fine phrase

κεφαλεν ἔχουσα ἐπιστήμη τῶν τίμιωτάτων

with vii. 7 his remarks on prudence (PHRONESIS) bring us round to the mortar ideogram

φρόνησις τõ καθ' ἕκαστα

Along about VI. viii. 6/9 the text is very laconic. There seems to be a good deal of commentative superstructure, all quite intelligent. "Definitions are the first principles of science." Rackham, Burnet here taking arms against a sea of stupidities. Perhaps book VI that typifies the greek good sense which the western world has *not* digested.

In any case the dhirty greek perks up when he gets to art and intellectual subtilties, being a philosophy prof. this particular d. g. quotes Homer (vide Rackham's notes) inexactly. Bosse professionnelle. His dissociation of the "five" kinds of knowing is not to be sneezed at. BEGINNING with (1) teXne, skill in an art, in making things (2) knowledge of rules and invariables, such as multiplication table, acquirable by the young,

(3) phronesis or good sense in conduct due to perception of variables, (4) wisdom or the knowledge with a head and proportions, (5) what Rackham calls intuitive in a special way, the faculty that permits one to "see" that two straight lines can't enclose a surface, and that the triangle is the simplest possible polygon.

It will be seen that NO. 1 can exist without the others; 2 and 5 have a certain relation to permanents, that 5 is in a sense above 4 (the sophia) and is in another sense part of it.

The whole of the discussion from VI. iii to ix is still vivid after more than two millenia, one cannot with advantage condense it, though one can set it against R. St Victor's gradation of processes (1) the aimless flitting of the mind, (2) the systematic circling of the attention around the object, (3) contemplation, the identification of the consciousness WITH the object.

600 page parenthesis here required to discuss the implications of this confrontation (supplementary rather, I trust, than contradictory) with remarks on arabic ideas about *atasal*, union with the divine. All of which leads ultimately to the point raised on p. xxii of Rackham's introduction, which I am still reserving as conclusion to this present essay.

> chorus off stage singing:
> Gandhi, Gandhi, you're the candy
> Smack the British where its handy,
> Then come join our ho—lyband.

I wonder whether one cd. shed a little cross-light by

suggesting that *gemüthlich* cd. be translated by SUG-GNOMONIKON, but not vice versa? I mean *gemüthlich* wd. be a coloured or tinted translation of the greek term. VI. xi. 4 might be advantageously written with letters of fire, a platitude never sufficiently grasped.

ἐκ τῶν καθ᾽ ἕκαστα γάρ τά καθόλου

rules are based on particular cases.

Some books are a species of Clarkson's.[1] Any actor can go to them, as to a theatrical wardrobe, and fish out what he needs for a particular role. Naturally such books are appreciated and demanded. Usus, opus, etc.

VI. xii. 8 brings us close to the "directio voluntatis" sic: Rightness of choice of an end is secured by Virtue. *Aretes* here equalling or leading to right direction of the will. The means of implementing the choice *deinotes*. Our current phrase "terribly clever" imbedded in the greek word-form.

xii. 9 δεινότητα.

xii. 10 reading Rackham hurriedly one might say: Ah yes, here is Dante's Paradiso; forerun, the Supreme (with cap. S.) Good (with cap. G.). But isn't our able translator colouring the greek a little too Christianly, and mixing in a little too much, say Aquinas?

The "*hotidepote*" of the greek is easy to slide over. But I seem to recall a dramatist's (wasn't it) "Zeus whoever he is?" Or a touch of irony in Hermes' remarks to Calypso. The best, says Arry, won't appear save to the good (man).

[1] *Olim* London wigmakers and costumiers,

AND THEREFORE TENDING

That slips on, very nicely, over the Dantescan or mediaeval concept. But I don't think the theologian wd. have been quite content with the "whatever the deuce it may be" (I exaggerate for emphasis as query to Rackham's capitals).

I decline, say if you choose, with asperity, to believe that the human mind accomplished nothing from 300 B.C. down to 1300 anno domini. Not of course that Rackham wd. maintain the extreme thesis that it didn't. Yet it can do us no harm to measure more carefully the quantities of what was "there already" and what the less advertised centuries added.

In an age like our own we might even learn from past dangers and early calamities. The greeks, being *maqueros* (happy men) with no moral fervour, left a hole or a sense of lack, and into that hole there poured a lot of crass zeal. Note in our time the venerable Dean of C., disgusted with the utter and crapulous lack of fervour in episcopal circles, finds comfort with communists.

> Every comrade is a bit
> of concentrated hate,

says another investigator. Nothing cd. be less civil, or more hostile to any degree of polite civilization than the tribal records of the hebrews. There is not a trace of civilization from the first lies of Genesis up to the excised account of Holophernes. The revival of these barbarous texts in the time of Luther and Calvin has been an almost unmitigated curse to the occident. But Leo X. and the Hegxis ἕξις of catholicism during the Renaissance left a void into which this beastliness poured.

AND THEREFORE TENDING

I am willing to discuss the translation of ἕξις at length with Mr Rackham, and ready also to thump the pulpit as to the need of such measure of integrity in civilization as shall prevent clean and decent men from going over to blind zealots as the ONLY company where sincerity can be mentioned. I don't mean that blind zealots attain it. I mean that the thirst for it explains the "conversion" of the Roman empire to Christianity. The disgust with the fat faces of politicians, with the slithering sleekness of bishops, the general foulness of monopolists and their educational lackeys conduce to the break-up of orderly institutions, and to temporary losses to culture.[1]

You cannot get anything DONE on an amoral tradition. It will merely slide down. Arry was interested in mind, not in morals. It was in the air, it was there, the decline of the hellenic paideuma. The Homeric vigour was gone, with its sympathetic rascality, its irascible goguenard pantheon. The splintering (vide infra, p. 125) had begun.

BOOK VII

I am not attacking the conscious part of Aristotle, but the unconscious, the "everyone says", or "everyone admits", which wd. be inconceivable in the *Ta Hio*, in The steadfast Mean, or in the *Analects*.

I wd. lay it down as a principle of criticism, or a need, if criticism is to be kept awake, that gt. works and works of gt. reputation shd. be looked at from time to

---

[1] Harvard riot due to students' boredom, nothing of interest in the curriculum.

time, as from other works of equal height, or of approximately similar magnitude, not, that is, always inspected as it were from within themselves, or from the points of view of authors or works parasite on them.

Fr. Fiorentino's summary shows the pagans to advantage, because the later philosophers and/or theologians whom he discusses are mainly from them. You will find, say, a stray sentence of Plato or the platonists serving as text or root, and as such the greeks "stand out". The main ideas were there already. It is very hard to detect the value of developments and additions, even if they improve on the archetypes.

SECONDLY we might, apropos splintering, distinguish the process of lower animals which breed by scission, from the process of the schismatics. In the case of the animals, as sometimes of political groups, the detaching segment has in it all the necessary elements for life and its own operations.

But with the schismatic process, as opposed to the concept of a general KATHOLIKOS, the schismatic is a splinterer, his process is an emphasis on something fragmentary and a rejection of the totality. He does not want an organism capable of containing all faith, or the constructive urges of all. Or, at any rate, he ought to be examined with one's mind open to this possibility.

If this sound flat, let the reader pardon the defect of my expression. A difference exists between the small totality and the possibly larger fragment which has not in itself the sum of the potentials. And no good can be done by confusing them.

AND THEREFORE TENDING

We ought to note that the derogative use of the term *orthodox* is not foreign to Aristotle's thought. A *doxy* is an opinion, and he nowhere confuses it with knowledge of any kind.

The "general" church threw out Scotus Erigena several centuries after his death. We have not sufficiently investigated the matter. Erigena did not, I think, consider himself a schismatic. "Authority comes from right reason", that wd. have been *orthon logon* in greek, not *doxy*. It seems unlikely that he was heretical in this view. Was he cast out for talking nonsense on some other issue, or was it a frame-up, committed in the storm of political passion? Until we know this, we shall not know whether Bossuet and Leibniz were at loggerheads, one from stupidity and both from ignorance of the tradition (general).

YET AGAIN I don't see how one can do justice to Aristotle without some regard to chronology. The average freshman knows that Aristotle followed Plato, and that Plato came after Socrates, but I doubt if we sufficiently consider the general ambience.

Arry came not only after Plato but after Aristophanes.

Take the generally accepted dates.

Pythagoras, somewhere about 536, "fl." as they put it.

Anacreon alive 536 to 520.

Aeschylus 525/456.

Pindar about the same.

Sophokles 496/406, Euripides 480/406 and Socrates

469/399 cut short during the latter part of Sophokles' reign.

Aristophanes 444/380.

Plato circa 427/347.

Aristotle 384/322.

An era barren of poetry and letters. The epic was over, the tragedians dead, Aristophanes died when Arry was four. Theocritus and Callimachus born over a decade after A.'s death.

Book VII is not so incisive as VI tho' Pope cd. have made good couplets from "Their using the language of knowledge is no proof that they possess it", "students who have just begun a subject reel off its formulae".

In fact the first part of book VII is a bore, the interest or live thought starting at section v. with Rackham's rendering of πηρώσεις as arrested development.

I mean that the *thought* is Rackham's not Aristotle's, and that nothing in the dictionary or the text compelled R. to write something at this point (v. 1). The idea: Vice due to arrested development, is a live idea. It needs rather more attention than the reader will find given it here in the greek.

On the other hand the translator goes non-conformist when he gets to Aphrodite's girdle. Homer did not suffer from the influence of Baxter and Calvin. Of course, very hard for professors in protestant countries when they are given pagan texts, especially as honesty runs counter to so much in protestant teaching.

VII. vi. 6 as for animals being aberrations from nature,

like men who are insane. It wd. be kinder to Arry to attribute this egxistimation to some muzzy copyist. It is below Arry's worst.

BOOK VIII

x. 2. Might be noted by anyone doing a thesis on kingship etc.

x. 3. Aristocracy passes into oligarchy owing to badness of rulers who do not DISTRIBUTE what the state has to offer, etc.

xiv. 3. Citizen who contributes nowt of value to the common stock is not held in honour . . . man cannot expect to make money out of the community and receive honour as well.

BOOK IX

contains (vii. 4) "we exist in activity".

It is much easier to "sit pretty", keep one's mouth shut or speak of an author as a whole or apply general statements to a whole book, than to risk picking out the good and the bad, the brilliant and the dull—which latter IS the critic's job, especially in an age when the plenum of books and knowledge is increasing. There is more to choose FROM, and the best 100 books or the best 100,000 or million pages DOES not remain the same 100,000 or million from one age or decade to another.

I think if a man started his Aristotle with part of Bk. V and all Bk. VI of the Nichomachean notes he wd. be more curious about the rest of this author than if he ploughs on through VII, VIII, and IX.

AND THEREFORE TENDING

BOOK X

i. 2, "others because they think it to be in the interests of morality to make out that pleasure is bad."

i. 3, "involve the truth in their own discredit."

ii. There is nothing here to prevent one thinking Eudoxus considerably more profound than Arry. A nice chance for a thesis on correspondence between the thought which comes out in the Paradiso, and Eudoxus' gravitation.

iii. 4 and 5. I wd. respectfully suggest that Mr Rackham could help the readers of his third edtn. by an ample note on these paragraphs, at least to prevent 'em thinking that in speaking of kinesis and genesis Arry is contradicting what he has said earlier of egXis and of "existing in activity".

It is R's use of the term "process" that might induce this unjust view. I don't think Arry is down to bedrock, but he is at least using words different from those which he has used elsewhere in a different sense. Any man who envies Rackham his job, or fails to respect the way he mostly climbs out on top of it is a fool.

iii. 6. τὴν δ ἡδονὴν ἀναπλήρωσιν " natural state, pleasure, the replenishment of it". Here we get to real thought after words which merely imply talking about thoughts.

Again I get the feeling that Arry is like a shallow, clear layer of water, now and again flowing over the deep, that is, the thought of more compact and fibrous precursors. Always able to express what he understands, but not,

336

by a long chalk, understanding all or, at times, the best that preceded him.

Like the "woodchuck" and other London critics who disliked music if too well played. 6 and 7 downright silly, just from A's lack of grasp of what some *kundiger Mensch* might have said.

iv. 6, "pleasure perfects the activity," and following along to v. 7. The reader can tyke 'is choice as to whether Arry is running on after he has ceased to have anything to say, or whether he is trying to get at something . . . tho' with the air of a dog turning round and round before he lies down.

One can't object to his trying to get a wedge between two greek words *aesthesis* and *hedonè*. As an exercise in lexicography we might demand that his advocate drag him into the open more distinctly.

Hedonè, not thought (*dianoia*) and not aesthesis. Put in that form *hedonè* is not passive feeling, but con-comitant of action. It is not kinesis, and kinesis means motion in one place and process having separate parts in another. In fact the sands of negative definition seem fairly "quick". Not a sensation but the x which you feel when in action?

O Kay, chief! sensation, enjoyment of the sensation (of action?). And then the *eudaimonia*, split off from thaumaturgic inheritance. Considered to be a certain *energeian*, Rackham calling this activity.

Several things *have* been sorted out in the course of the whole treatise, motion, taking place in time, nobody ever thought running round the block was the same as building a house. "And so what?" as impertinent li'l boys now say to their American mammas. A way of passing a warm afternoon (in Hellas and/or the buck)?

A vastly better way than with cross-words. For IF England shd. start discriminating the meaning of words, at least some of her worst lice wd. fall off, and some of her most foetid oppressions be less easy to keep riveted on the neck of the people. Usurers will never encourage this game of making clear definitions.

In X. vii. 2 Aristotle comes out with the unsympathetic word theoretike, but the pp. 2/3/4 give the key to his place in mediaeval esteem. He plugs for contemplation as the noblest form of activity. All this passage suits Dante's purpose, for the duration of the Paradiso, save for Aristotle's "self-sufficiency", autarchia which cdn't have christianly meant self-sufficiency. I think we must call it "self-rule" if it is to apply even to Dante's God. In fact the greek *is* clear and Arry distinguishes in vii. 4 between the insufficiency of the contemplative and his degree of auto-rule. "Less than any other man can he be disturbed by others."

Arry has, and quite unconcealedly and frankly, a good deal of trouble in finding a verbal manifestation that won't fit tennis playing as well as contemplation. A more concrete or ideogramically minded professor wd. have told his class that the tennis player has no autarchy at all until he can find an opponent more or less of his own class. The good musician can however play for himself. You can call it contemplation, but yr. admirers cdn't claim that you had, in so doing, attained

AND THEREFORE TENDING

a satisfactory scientific terminology. It wd. have to be theoretike PLUS.

Nothing cd. be further from my purpose than to deny the pleasures of mental activity, yet when Arry arrives at a long sentence which Mr Rackham has to rejoin with:

"it follows that it is the activity of the intellect that constitutes complete human happiness,"
he is unconvincing.

Arguing pro-Arry we admit activity of intellect has, seriously, a value and/or is taken seriously by bon-vivants. We might even admit that certain kinds of mental activity may be as near happiness as man gets. Let the Hellenists go to it over vii. 7, νοῦ ἐνέργεια σπουδῇ, ἡ τελέια δη εὐδαιμονία αὕτη ἄν εἴν ἀνθρώπoω.

Aristotle leaves a yawning chasm into which a medi-aeval or neoPlatonic or even Mesopotamian god has to be shoved. Or, at any rate, in historic process was shoved.

In vii. 9 he treads on thin sophism. The pitfall of all men who get entoiled in their own reasoning. The element of sheer assertion slips into the argument, cut off from organic reality—the tricky "therefore" or "accordingly" that does NOT glue two statements together.

One sees, here at the end of vii. 9 and with the start of viii, where Arry got his stand-in with Aquinas. A dry and inhuman heaven. Modern improvement (for their time) after Arry's death, full lighting installation and orchestra. Arry's argument wd. apply to onanism quite nicely.

AND THEREFORE TENDING

He has no more wisdom than Laforgue's little Salomé. And unless, or even if, he is showing off for his students, the minimum of wisdom when speaking either of the Gods plural or of God in the singular wd. be first to refrain from telling what one doesn't know and secondly to refrain from non sequiturs, and/or palpably uncogent argument.

In bare logic there is no more reason why a god shdn't be engaged in living and in creating, than that he shd. be supposed to pass all his time gazing at his own umbilicus, works, reflection or some part of himself. The end of viii. 7 is just talk.

The Socrates of the Dialogues used to do this kind of thing with more imagery.

The profound flippancy of a decadence, when men don't know when to stop talking and have ceased to respect the unknown! Very well! Arry teases Heraclitus for vehement assertion, but is that assertion any worse than silly logic-chopping on the same matter?

The weakness is dyed in the very contrast between two juxtaposed words, the old thaumaturgic EUDAI-MONIA and the peculiarly urban THEORIA. Arry is hung up after one age and before the swings and round-abouts of the nine heavens came into pan-European favour. He wd. have had such a good time 12 or 15 centuries later.

Astrological bee in his bonnet, nostalgia for the wide (very and inhumanly) open spaces.

ix. 4 something very like doctrine of original sin. A lot of handy quotations for the unpleasant kind of Xtn.

ix. 8 "nurture and exercise of the young shd. be regulated by law."

ix. 21 "and what kind of institutions are suited to what national characteristics." O.K.

22 "question of legislation has been left uninvestigated by previous thinkers . . . to complete as far as possible our philosophy of human affairs. . . ."
with the climax in the notes:

"Aristotle compiled or caused to be compiled descriptions of the constitutions of 158 Greek states."

55. PERGAMENA DEEST

At his best, a serious character . . . whether or no we can sign on the dotted line under an admired Aristotelian's

"it (the Ethics) applies his rigorous scientific method to a field where the application of strict scientific analysis was most of a novelty and therefore needed the most originality".

who continues

"To some degree this is true also of the Politics, which is really only Part II of the Ethics. The whole being A's science of Human Society. In Downing St, Cambridge, they are still sniffy about recognizing this as a science, particularly that special dept. of it called Economics, they can't see that this is now at the stage their Sciences were at 300 years ago."

To the Confucian or the modern the most impressive three lines yet cited are Rackham's note. "158 constitutions." Concrete particulars assembled for examination.

That stands. That points on to Constantine and Justinian. The definition of money did not advance for 2000 years, though the canonists did spade-work on the Just Price, with usura as a subsection. To Books V and VI, I have already paid tribute. The rift is clear in Rackham's own preface which I have, with persistence, held over for a conclusion.

"Hence the tendency to think of the End not as the sum of the Goods, but as one Good which is the Best. Man's welfare thus is ultimately found to consist not in the employment of all his faculties in due proportion, but only in the activity of the highest faculty, the 'theoretic' intellect."

That leads you plumb bang down to the "split man" in Mr Wyndham Lewis' *Apes*. That is the schismatic tendency. Therein is the scizophrenia in its almost invisible embryo.

Everything that is unsatisfactory in mediaeval scholasticism. Looks harmless?

Dante put Aristotle in Limbo, having, can one say, worked all the way round to the other side of the cosmos to get his limbo into proportion. Ser D. Alighieri might have swallowed the text of book X or its latin version without a murmur.

Master of those that cut apart, dissect and divide. Competent precursor of the card-index. But without the organic sense. I say this in the face of Aristotle's repeated emphases on experience, and of testing by life.

Perhaps the finest thing in this story is that he assembled the collection of state constitutions, seeing clearly that it wd. be *no use unless* someone had the experience and intelligence to know "what to make of it".

PERGAMENA DEEST

I have come to the end of my paper. I can tell the neophyte no more in the number of pages allotted me. Contract calls for a guide TO not THROUGH human culture. Everyman must get the insides or the inside of it for himself.

56. WATCH THE BEANERIES

Obviously I can not continue to analyse all Aristotle's other writings. That wd. be a different work altogether. I can give the foregoing survey of "the most Aristotelian" of them as indication of where the Western mind or one western mind had got to by, say, B.C. 330.

Set that against Kung, or make your *Gestalt*, of Kung, Homer, the middle ages, renaissance, the present, with the greek decline in its due proportion . . . and the peripheries.

Plenty of chance for a NEW Quattrocento. Plenty of chance for a gang of scholars with gumption enough to overhaul the whole congeries, measure off Greece against China, plus technical progress,

but, in no case go to sleep on lies, on subsidies, on foundations of our truly contemptible universities, of pot-bellied toadying presidents of fat beaneries. In no case swallow fat greasy words which conceal three or four indefinite middles.

In no case leave any pimp in his cathedra after he has been caught like X. in a forgery, in a deliberate misstatement of some honest man's theorem.

In no case let one's sons spend money on "education" offered by cowards who dare not answer specific questions about their own subjects. In no case tolerate hired fools who take fifteen years to admit a truth because it is safer and more immediately profitable to them to go on teaching a falsehood. I mean, in this case, Professor X.Z., oh yes, and quite naturally.

The light of the Sorbonne shone because of the practice of "defending the thesis". The modern and typical prof holds his job because of his slickness in *avoiding* the thesis, because he crawls under the buggy rug of a motheaten curriculum in sheer craven terror of known fact and active discovery. That is what the half-louse is PAID for.

"University not here for the unusual man," Prof. S. re Carl Sandburg.

"The dean does not care to answer."

"Editor has not finished reading the book."

"I keep on dipping into it." College President.

"Said it had nothing to do with real life, but that the course cd. not be altered."

England's Cambridge on a par with that back of Boston.

Dante's *Inferno*, Canto XXI, line 139. It's the last line = voice of the modern press and the bulk of the professoriate and of pedagocracy.

Section XIII

57. EPILOGUE
to balance the frontispiece

There was in London 1908 to '14 an architect named Ricards (of Lanchester & Ricards), the last pastoral mind, and a man with true sense of form, that is in three dimensions and hollow. His buildings were magnificent until finished. Their structure was the work of genius and their final encrustation the tin-horn ornament of the never sufficiently damned 1900. AND at this same time Gaudier was out of employment and wd. willingly have made architectural odds and ends.

58. TO RECAPITULATE

I believe that the *Ta Hio* is veritably the Great Learning, to be taken with the Odes

and the rest of Confucius' teaching.

I cannot state my beliefs about art more succinctly than I have done by naming particular works and makers.

I believe even the most rabid anti-platonist must concede that Plato has repeatedly stirred men to a sort of enthusiasm productive of action, and that one cannot completely discount this value as life force.

I have left my loose phrases re Aristotle in Section I, as sort of gauge, the reader can see for himself what my residuum of opinion was before examining the Ethics, and measure that by the notes set down during my examination of that particular text.

If the reader think I have not made my meaning sufficiently clear, I cd. ask him before blaming me to reconsider the following items or nuclei in my exposition, as follows:

TO RECAPITULATE

People have, I believe, complained that Michelet allowed his imagination to run away with him. But the true historian will respect either Michelet or some, to me, unknown precursor, for having noted realities in his present. Michelet does, at any rate, try to record motivations, meaning those desires characteristic of great numbers of people, the peasants want to do this, the ambition of the worker or the small shop keeper is . . . etc. Michelet saw France as something in process; as an organism that needed, or at any rate had, certain impulses and appetites to keep it going.

Reflecting on this and proceeding from one of the Nicomachean dissociations (V. iii. 7, page 322): we see today:

I. Aristocracy; believes "people shd. do what they like". This is good society. Personal codes used for themselves.

II. Oligarchy, or plutocracy or at any rate the great

348

TO RECAPITULATE

mass of the rich, organized in circles of snobbisms, the mechanism of scandal used to keep others out and, in lower divisions, "respectability" as protection. Dominant motive "don't give anyone else a handle". Official idiocy, code of the luxury-trade magazines and swank hotels.

III. Constructive element in society. Contains the small part of intelligentzia (or the real intelligentzia) interested in ideas that are going into action. That means a few writers, a few senators and ministers (say a very few), a considerable number of engineers, inventors, etc.

IV. The Credulous, Crap, the book trade, retrospective writers, "the public", anyone ass enough to swallow editorials.

V. Producers and those who are ready to, and capable of, producing. That means the workers and the well-disposed unemployed.

VI. The dregs, that is the poor who are no better than the individual members of the oligarchy or of the "public" or the credulous. Like the credulous, they tolerate the present infamies in England, France and America. They have no desire to see scoundrels flayed and put out of office. They have nothing better to offer any more than have the credulous or swillers. This sixfold division is intended to register "as is", not to propound a theory.

ADDENDA: 1952

ARISTOTLE'S "MAGNA MORALIA"

While "Kulch" was still in the press E.P. noticed that
"before pore Ari was cold in his grave" the compilers
of the so-called "Magna Moralia" had already omitted
TEXNE from the list of mental faculties given in the
Nicomachean Ethics. E.P. wished to include this ob-
servation but a member of the British firm of Faber
thought "it would do him no good at Oxford". The
mysteries of academic circles are apt to baffle normal
observers.

AS SEXTANT

I. The FOUR BOOKS (Confucius and Mencius).

II. HOMER: Odyssey: intelligence set above brute force.

III. The Greek TRAGEDIANS: rise of sense of civic responsibility.

IV. DIVINA COMMEDIA: life of the spirit.

V. FROBENIUS: Erlebte Erdteile: without which a man cannot place any book or work of art in relation to the rest.

VI. BROOKS ADAMS: Law of Civilization and Decay: most recent summary of 'where in a manner of speaking' we had got to half a century ago. Second half of Beard's introduction indicates the essential omission from Adams' thought.

VII. The English Charters, the essential parts of BLACKSTONE, that is those dealing with history and philosophy of law. The American Constitution.

As the Four Books contain answers to all problems of conduct that can arise, a man who really understands them may regard the other six components of this list as amenities rather than necessities.

This is, naturally, not a full list of books a sane man will want to enjoy. These are books without which he cannot measure the force of the others.

[*Editor's Note*—The above is a postscript to *Kulchur*, found among Mr. Pound's papers.]

INTRODUCTORY

TEXT

BOOK

E.P.

INTRODUCTORY TEXTBOOK
(In Four Chapters)

CHAPTER I

"All the perplexities, confusion, and distress in America arise, not from defects in their constitution or confederation, not from want of honour and virtue, so much as from downright ignorance of the nature of coin, credit, and circulation."

John Adams.

CHAPTER II

". . . and if the national bills issued, be bottomed (as is indispensable) on pledges of specific taxes for their redemption within certain and moderate epochs, and be of *proper denomination* for *circulation*, no interest on them would be necessary or just, because they would answer to every one of the purposes of the metallic money withdrawn and replaced by them."

Thomas Jefferson (1816, letter to Crawford).

CHAPTER III

". . . and gave to the people of this Republic THE GREATEST BLESSING THEY EVER HAD— THEIR OWN PAPER TO PAY THEIR OWN DEBTS.

Abraham Lincoln.

INTRODUCTORY TEXTBOOK

CHAPTER IV

The Congress shall have power; To coin money, regulate the value thereof and of foreign coin and to fix the standards of weights and measures."
Constitution of the United States, Article I Legislative Department, Section 8, page 5.

Done in the convention by the unanimous consent of the States, 7th September, 1787, and of the Independence of the United States the twelfth. In witness whereof we have hereunto subscribed our names.

George Washington.
President and Deputy from Virginia

Note

The abrogation of this last mentioned power derives from the ignorance mentioned in my first quotation. Of the three preceding citations, Lincoln's has become the text of Willis Overholser's recent "History of Money in the U. S.," the first citation was taken as opening text by Jerry Voorhis in his speech in the House of Representatives, June 6, 1938, and the passage from Jefferson is the nucleus of my "Jefferson and/or Mussolini."

Douglas' proposals are a sub-head under the main idea in Lincoln's sentence, Gesell's "invention" is a special case under Jefferson's general law. I have done my best to make simple summaries and clear definitions in various books and pamphlets, and recommend as *introductory* study, apart from C. H. Douglas' " Economic Democracy" and Gesell's "Natural Economic Order," Chris. Hollis' "Two Nations," McNair Wilson's "Promise to Pay," Larranaga's "Gold, Glut and Government" and M. Butchart's compendium of three centuries thought, that is an anthology of what has been said, in "Money." (Originally published by Nott.)

Rapallo, Italy.   Ezra Pound.

OR ONE WORD WILL RUIN IT ALL,

as for example:

1. The mistranslation, or rather the insertion of the word "value", where Aristotle said χρεία, demand. Money is not a measure of value. The price is caused by demand.

2. The imbecility of the XIXth century stemming from misuse of word "creates". Both Mill and Marx and dozens of other loathsome individuals contributed to the muddle. Work does not create wealth, it *contributes to the formation of* it. Nature's productivity is the root (ref/ also Del Mar: interest is due teleologically to the increase of domestic animals and plants).

3. C. H. Douglas left room for argument by saying: Marx does not face the problem of money. There could have been little reply to the clearer: does not face question of monetary issue.

DISTINGUISH

Distinguish between claims and things. (Here Santayana was on the right track with: Must be wrong, all this invisible wealth.)
Economic injustice consists in allowing claims to come into the hands of those who have contributed nothing either to production, or to getting things to those who need them.

CHRONOLOGY
for school use

ARISTOTLE (384-322 b.c.) saw that money is not a measure of value, but of demand. Price indicating the demand. XREIA.

JOHN LAW (1671-1729) erred in trying to monetize land, which cannot be picked up and delivered.

HUME (1711-1776) saw that the total supply of money in the country must gradually increase if production and commerce are to flourish.

ALEXANDER DEL MAR (1838-1928) measured the rate at which the total volume of money should have increased in the 1880s.

C. H. DOUGLAS observed that money is far more an instrument of policy than a measure of anything. This in especial regard to the issue of money.

GESELL (following Benj. Franklin) believed that money could be measured by work.

It is necessary to consider whether the work has, or has not, been done, before you decide whether it can be considered as BASIS for money, or for credit only. One cannot evaluate the proportionate value of different kinds of work until competent judges decide on its opportunity and utility toward given ends. That is to say all kinds of work are no more uniform in value than are all kinds of gold ore.

The value of a nation's money will, in the long run, depend also on what the nation spends its money FOR.

DISEASES

Falsification of history.
Falsification of current news.
IMBECILITY of the tax system: as to cost of collection; as to obvious chances of unjust assessment; as to chances for fraud in returns; considering its incitements to crime; its making crimes of numerous activities absolutely innocent in themselves; as to its clogging the circulation of goods and money.

"Heaulmière" from the opera Villon by Ezra Pound

ce que reffussent truand-ailles — à maint homme l'ay

refu-sé. Qui n'estoit à moi grandsa gesse, Pour l'a- (lilt)

-mour d'ung garçon rusé auquel jen fiz grande large-sse- à quique je feisse fi

-nesse — , par m'ame, je l'amoye bien or ne me faisoit que rudesse,

et ne m'amoyt que pour le mien Ja ne me sceut tant de trayner

fouiller aux pieds, que ne l'aymasse et meust il peidles rains tray-ner,

s'il m'eust dit que je le baissasse et que tout mes maux oubli asse —

(spoken)   (sung)
Le glouton de mal enta-ché, m'em-brassoit, j'en suis bien- plus gras

se! que mien reste-il ? Honte et peché ! Or il est mort, passé

trente ans et je re-mains vielle et chen ue — Quand je pense Helas! au bon

temps quelle fût quelle deve-nue — Quand me re-garde toute nue —

et je me voy si très chengeé — Pauvre, seiche

maigre menue — je suis presque toute enragee Qu'est deve-

(colen)

-nue ce front poly, ces cheveulx blondssourcils voultyz grand entreoille le re-

-gard joly dont pre-noye lesplussubtilz ——— Ce beau nezdroit

PP

grand ne pe-tiz — ces petites joinctes or-eilles menton fourchu cler vis trai

-tis et ces belles le -vres ver-meilles? Ces gents espauls menues,

ces bras longs et ces mains tretisses, petits tetins hanches charnues, es-

363

levés propres factisses à tenir amoureuses lysses ces larges

reins ce sadinet assis sur grosses fermes cuysses dedans son joly

jardinet ? Le front ridé, les cheveulx gris, les sourcilz cheuz, les yeulx est-

-aincts qu' faisoient regars et ris, dont maintz marchans furent attaincts,

nez courbé de beauté loingtains, oreilles pendans et mousses, su-es levis pally, mort

et destaincts menton foncé levres peau ssues. C'est d'humaine beauté

l'yssues! Les bras courts et les mains contrainctes, les es-paul-

-es tout-es bossues mammelles, quoi! toutes retraictes, telles les hanches que les tettes, du

sadinet, fy! Quant des cuysses, cuysses ne sont plus mascuy settes grisve-leés

15

364

connus saulcisses, Ainsi le bon temps regretons entre nous pauvres

veilles sottes, assises bas à croppetons tout en ung tas com

-me pelot-tes à petit feu de chen-e - vottes tost allumées et tost est

-aincte et jadis fusmes si mig-nottes! Ainsi en prend à maintz

et maintes.....

VILLON AND COMMENT*

"It will be twenty years before they will stand it," said Mr. Antheil (1922). Four years to run on that estimate!

"But it has never been done," said Herr M. "There is no public."

Author (*re* most contemporary composers): "They can not write a melody four bars long."

Tibor Serly: "*Four* bars! They can not write one of *two* bars."

Boris de Schloezer, in the interim remarking, apropos

---

* From *Townsman*, April, 1948

of Stravinsky, that melody is the most artificial thing in all music. Furthest from anything that is just there in the accidental sonorities of nature.

The particular problem, *motz el son*, did occupy the best auditors in South Europe for at least a couple of centuries (troubadours and all that, Arnaut Daniel, Sordello to Dante), and to that epoch (as for three decades I have not wearied in TELLING fat heads and lean heads), one must still go for the ABC of the subject.

My "Villon" cannot be exploited. It has not started a revolution in opera for reasons that are not the least obvious and which are by no means flattering to the l.h.b.

Whatever the demerits of the work, this much is established: I sat in the electrician's kitchen in Rapallo when the Villon was broadcast from London, and I not only knew who was singing (so far as the singers were known to me), but I could distinguish the words, and the sense of the words.

The music is to that extent a comment on, or an elucidation of, the form of the words and possibly of their meaning, or, if you like, of the emotive contents.

It does not lead to a revolution of opera because there ARE NOT THE AVAILABLE VERBAL TEXTS to go on with. The "Cavalcanti" needed a lot more extraneous work. It needed much more play written. There was not in Guido the variety of theme and drive of the Villon text, and the contrast in melodic shape had to be imported from poems of Sordello's.

VILLON AND COMMENT

When Antheil and Serly wanted a body of English verbal *materia*, it just wasn't THERE to be musick'd.

Lay aside the fact that Antheil hadn't the verbal culture necessary for a Pericles, Shakespeare's Pericles is not a libretto. You can't make opera by taking a mass of words made to be declaimed from a stage and just shoving the pitch up and down.

Verdi used Shakespeare, but he had an Italian song text made *from* it. There is simply NOT the technique extant in English to perform a similar transfusion.

> *O come sei pallida*
>   *e tacit'*   *e mor-*   *ta!*

sings.

I am not merely being captious and heaping mud on the lousy writers of British bilge, the frumpy victorian and arid preceders of the hoop skirt. When the Island was still mentionable in a society of technicians, Henry Lawes found the same paucity. Having exhausted the frail and limited gamut of British metric invention in the cantabile sector, Lawes went on to set Greek and Latin.

Were the anglo-jute musician and/or metrist a thinking animal this would before now have caused more reflections than it has.

Why did Lawes set Greek and Latin?

Why did Waller commend him?

The technique of British verse-writing is so woolly, so lacking in variety and strophic construction when it is even singably efficient, that a good musician like Lawes, interested in the relations and counter-tensions of words and melody went on to a field of greater interest.

Idem Debussy. As Mr. Atheling and I have insisted, French concert-hall songs of the 1890's were mostly all on one tune. The unending series of mist and mashed potatoes in the French metric didn't give the composer a chance. Having squshed up his lips, stuck them two inches forward, squeezed his voice through a sort of sponge in his nozzle, the singer and/or composer had exhausted the possible varieties of intoning THAT kind of verse. The café chançon was alive. Yvette was heiress of the ages, and Debussy went back to Villon and Charles D'Orleans for his song masterwork.

To whom, as to a most admirable collateral relative, though not the first founder, nor even as a necessary aid in a process, I pay my solid respects.

The Villon has been sung. It has been broadcast. It will be sung again, and that will not end it. I have always wanted it sung in a *baraque de foire*. It will take the nasal tone of tough, open-air singing.[*] It will stand the crack of the penny in the slot pyanny. It will take puppet performance.

Having done Villon and Cavalcanti (Sordello intervening), there remained "Collis O Heliconii" (half done, and no small technical problem) and the question of presenting THAT to the public recalls Mr. Cantleman's

[*] If only Ethel Merman or Pinza would!

VILLON AND COMMENT

Mate (if I mistake not the hat-rack of memory, *videlicet:* Dear Ma, this war is a fair buggar! *Vide* the "Little Review," whenever it was and I suppose, or at any rate hope in a volume of Mr. W. Lewis in reprint).

CONDENSARE

If T. W. Hulme's latest editor hasn't quoted it I should like to conserve his "All a man ever thought would go onto a half sheet of notepaper. The rest is application and elaboration."

INDEX

INDEX

INDEX

z   **373**

INDEX

INDEX

INDEX

INDEX

INDEX

INDEX

For valued help in proof correcting and in making this index, my sincere thanks to John Drummond.—E.P. 6 April anno XVI.

New Directions Paperbooks—A Partial Listing

For complete listing request free catalog from
New Directions, 80 Eighth Avenue, New York 10011

†Bilingual